Contributions to Economics

More information about this series at http://www.springer.com/series/1262

Oliver Fiala

Natural Disasters and Individual Behaviour in Developing Countries

Risk, Trust and the Demand for Microinsurance

Springer

Oliver Fiala
Faculty of Business and Economics
TU Dresden
Dresden, Germany

ISSN 1431-1933 ISSN 2197-7178 (electronic)
Contributions to Economics
ISBN 978-3-319-53903-4 ISBN 978-3-319-53904-1 (eBook)
DOI 10.1007/978-3-319-53904-1

Library of Congress Control Number: 2017935542

Printed on acid-free paper

This Springer imprint is published by Springer Nature
The registered company is Springer International Publishing AG
The registered company address is: Gewerbestrasse 11, 6330 Cham, Switzerland

For Natasha—
Best of Wives and Best of Women

Acknowledgements

I would like to thank my supervisor, Prof. Hans Wiesmeth, for his continuous support during my time at TU Dresden and the freedom he gave me to explore my own research interests. I am also grateful for the feedback and encouragement I received from Prof. Marcel Thum, which has helped to shape this publication.

Furthermore, I would like to thank my colleagues at TU Dresden for their comments during the early stages of my research and for numerous inspiring conversations through the years. Special thanks go to Dr. Dennis Häckl for initiating our Cambodian adventures and to our colleagues at the University of Battambang, without whom the field research would not have been possible.

I am grateful to the Graduate Academy of TU Dresden for their financial support in the latter stages of the writing process.

It is with heartfelt thanks that I acknowledge my entire—now larger—family, and in particular my parents for encouraging me to ask questions and for loving and supporting me through the years.

This book would not have been possible without the person I met along the path: my wife and best friend. Our discussions have sparked new ideas and her love, encouragement and support have strengthened me on my journey towards the finishing line.

London
March 2017

Oliver Fiala

Contents

Chapter 1
Introduction

In the last 45 years, the number of natural disasters has increased constantly, affecting 6.6 billion people worldwide and causing the deaths of 3.2 million (EM-DAT 2015). Climate change is likely to further escalate the frequency and intensity of extreme weather events. Developing countries are particularly vulnerable to these effects as the damage caused by natural disasters affects their development processes, with significant impacts on poor households.

Natural disasters have severe economic and social impacts causing substantial loss of human life, livelihoods, property and public infrastructure, as well as having serious long-term effects on social and human capital. Additionally, natural disasters are traumatic events and can have significant implications for individuals' perceptions and expectations. Therefore, extreme weather events may not only create structural damage, but also affects individuals' behaviour as well as the social norms and structural factors within a community. Thereby, the individual's risk propensity and level of trust are of particular interest as they impact decision-making processes, which will determine both investments in productive activities and social trust within communities.

In order to reduce vulnerability and build resilience towards disaster risks, proactive, systematic and integrated risk management instruments are needed, involving both ex ante strategies to reduce risks as well as ex post strategies to cope with their consequences. In recent years, microinsurance—insurance provided in developing countries with a focus on the poor—has emerged as one promising instrument to counter disaster risk. However, even if microinsurance appears to be an encouraging tool to protect vulnerable populations, the overall enrolment rates remain unexpectedly low.

This study intends to investigate the complex link between natural disasters, individual behaviour—particularly risk aversion and trust—and the demand for microinsurance products in the context of disaster risk management, and its importance for economic development. Firstly, the effect of exposure to natural disaster on the individual's risk preferences and levels of trust and trustworthiness will be investigated. There is a limited amount of economic research devoted to exploring

O. Fiala, *Natural Disasters and Individual Behaviour in Developing Countries*, Contributions to Economics, DOI 10.1007/978-3-319-53904-1_1

these effects. Currently, the results are widely ambiguous and there is no consensus as to how and whether natural disasters affect individuals' behaviour.

The study will go on to explore the impact of individual behaviour as well as other social, structural, economic and personal factors on the demand for microinsurance, with a specific interest in the role of natural disaster experiences. Although previous research has analysed microinsurance as a disaster risk management instrument in recent years, the role of single determinants—particularly of disaster exposure—are not clear, and this study seeks to add solid empirical evidence to this discussion.

Finally, important results and conclusions of these analyses will be discussed in the context of economic development, and implications for resilience-building against disaster risks will be highlighted. The research framework is illustrated in Fig. 1.1. As far as is known, this is the first comprehensive research connecting these two literature threads by using both elements of experimental economics in order to analyse individual behaviour as well as a choice experiment to elicit preferences for hypothetical microinsurance demand.

Cambodia is one of the most disaster-prone countries in Southeast Asia and suffers significant social and economic impacts due to frequent and severe floods and droughts. Therefore, a unique data set following an extensive survey, two behavioural experiments and a discrete choice experiment were used in rural Cambodia to investigate the link between disaster experience, individual behaviour and the hypothetical demand for microinsurance.

Chapter 2 introduces natural disasters with a particular focus on developing countries. Following a statistical overview of disasters worldwide and in Cambodia, the various and complex consequences of natural disasters as well as their impact on developing economies and poverty will be discussed. Furthermore, a brief introduction to the concept of disaster risk management will be provided.

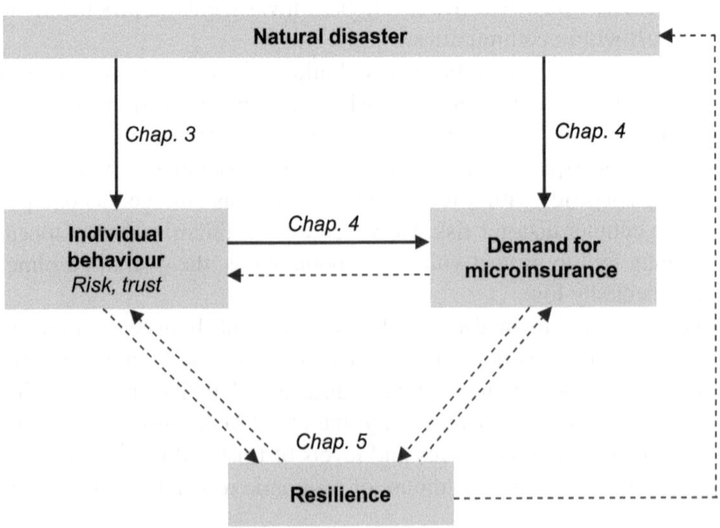

Fig. 1.1 Research framework for this study

Chapter 3 investigates the effect of disaster experiences on individual behaviour. After an introduction to possible theoretical and empirical explanations, the design of the study and the experiments conducted in Cambodia will be described. The effect of natural disasters on risk-taking propensity, trust and trustworthiness in rural Cambodia will then be considered. Chapter 4 introduces microinsurance as an instrument of disaster risk management and discusses in detail the determinants of its demand. Subsequently, the impact of natural disasters, individual behaviour and social characteristics on the demand for microinsurance in rural Cambodia will be analysed. Chapter 5 summarises the insights of the empirical analyses and discusses their implications for economic development and resilience-building. Chapter 6 provides the conclusion of the study.

Reference

EM-DAT (2015) The International Disaster Database. http://www.emdat.be/. Accessed 5 Jan 2015

Chapter 2
Natural Disasters in Developing Countries

Individuals and households are vulnerable to natural hazards, health shocks, famines, civil conflicts, crime and aggregate macroeconomic events. Rainfall, agricultural shocks and droughts are common climate-related disasters in the developing world with negative and long-lasting effects on individuals and households. These include not only the destruction of livelihoods and poverty, but also long-term impacts on human capital by affecting nutrition, education and health. Furthermore, the frequent occurrences of such disasters may lead to or sustain poverty if households are unable to recover savings and other assets during the experience of several shocks (Oviedo and Moroz 2014).

Developing countries are particularly affected as risk is a factor in daily life and a fundamental cause of underdevelopment (Cohen and Sebstad 2005; Dercon 2006; Mosley 2009). Comprehensive and innovative risk management strategies are necessary to develop social protection and break the vicious cycle of poverty and vulnerability (Mosley 2009; Gehrke 2014).

Chapter 2 sets the foundation for the following study. Therefore, the three topics of research relevant for analysis will be introduced more in detail: the occurrence of natural hazards, the economic and social impacts of natural disasters, and the concept of risk management.

Section 2.1 presents a statistical overview of natural disasters. Between 1970 and 2014, an increase in the number of natural disasters worldwide is evident, with 3.2 million killed and 6.6 billion people affected (EM-DAT 2015). Climate change is likely to increase extreme weather events, their frequency and intensity. This may result in more numerous floods and landslides, droughts and extreme temperatures. Cambodia is one of the most disaster-prone countries in East Asia and is frequently affected by severe floods and droughts.

Section 2.2 presents the various and complex consequences of natural disasters. Multiple economic and social effects will be distinguished and empirical evidence regarding short- and long-term effects on economic growth will be briefly presented. The concepts of vulnerability, exposure and resilience will be introduced and their importance for disaster impacts discussed. Based on these factors, the

O. Fiala, *Natural Disasters and Individual Behaviour in Developing Countries*,
Contributions to Economics, DOI 10.1007/978-3-319-53904-1_2

complex relationship between disaster and development will be explored: while a low level of economic development increases vulnerability towards disasters, natural disasters are likely to have long-term consequences on poverty and development.

Section 2.3 presents a brief introduction to the concept and framework of disaster risk management. Risk management tools are necessary to remove or reduce risks arising from natural disasters. The risk chain shows that the outcome of natural disasters depends on the external environment, internal conditions and risk management instruments.

Building on this introduction, the conclusion will summarise the main findings. Furthermore, based on the introduced risk management framework, the research questions for the following study will be specified and their integration into the literature will be highlighted.

2.1 Natural Disasters and the Role of Climate Change

2.1.1 Statistical Information

To understand the impact of natural disasters and to discuss possible instruments of disaster risk management, this chapter will provide a brief overview of the occurrences of extreme events worldwide, the role of climate change and the specific situation in Cambodia.

Natural hazards are naturally occurring processes or phenomena which are caused by atmospheric, geologic and hydrologic events. These can include floods, droughts, storms, earthquakes, volcanic eruptions, etc. They are harmful to humans and have the potential to cause damage. Differences in severity, scale and frequency are possible. Natural hazards can be expected, but cannot be prevented[1] (Miththapala 2008; Eder et al. 2009; United Nations and World Bank 2010).

Natural disasters are the consequences or effects of natural hazards. They occur when natural hazards cause a "serious breakdown in sustainability and disruption of economic and social progress" (Eder et al. 2009), and "a large number of deaths, displacements and damage to human well-being, as well as to ecosystem well-being" (Miththapala 2008). In addition, the IPCC (2012) highlights an immediate emergency response for human needs and external support as attributes of natural

[1]The IPCC (2012) discusses 'extreme events' and classifies these by weather or climate variables which are above (below) thresholds near the upper (lower) ends of the observed values of the variable.

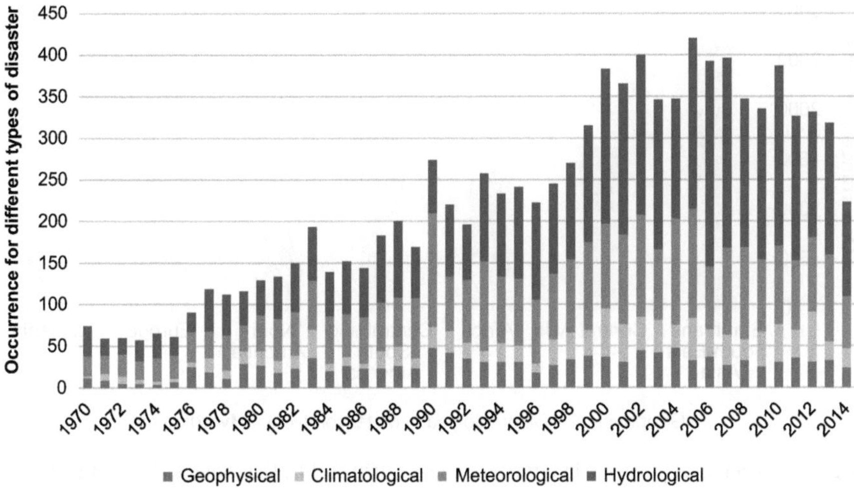

Fig. 2.1 Occurrences of different types of disaster (1970–2014). Data source: EM-DAT (2015)

disasters. In contrast to natural hazards, disasters can be prevented or the effects can be reduced by applying different measures (Miththapala 2008).[2]

Natural disaster statistics and the understanding of risk profiles are essential for efficient resource allocations (Guha-Sapir et al. 2013). There are numerous sources for statistics about the occurrence of natural disasters, although three main databases are found most frequently in the literature. The most cited is the EM-DAT database from the Center for Research on the Epidemiology of Disasters, due to its public availability.[3]

Between 1970 and 2014, an increase in the number of natural disasters is recorded as shown in Fig. 2.1. Hydrological events such as floods are the most common hazards, followed by meteorological events (predominantly storms).[4] An

[2]Different kinds of disasters can be distinguished by their cause. A common terminology was defined by, among others, Munich Re, Swiss Re, Center for Research on the Epidemiology of Disasters (CRED) and the United Nations Development Programme (UNDP) (see Banholzer et al. 2014). Geophysical (earthquake, tsunami, volcanic eruption, dry mass landslide), meteorological (hurricane, typhoon, cyclone), hydrological (flood, wet mass landslide) and climatological (drought, extreme temperatures) events are distinguished (EM-DAT 2015).

[3]The NatCat database by Munich Re and Sigma by Swiss Re are not publicly available. Although the terminology and categories are commonly defined, they have different inclusion criteria, and are therefore not strictly comparable and have their own strengths and weaknesses (United Nations and World Bank 2010).

[4]To enter a disaster into the EM-DAT database, at least one criteria must be fulfilled: ten or more people reported killed, one hundred or more people reported affected, a state of emergency declared, a call for international assistance. The database provides information about disaster type and group, country of occurrence, date; number of deaths, missing, injured (physical injuries, trauma or illness as a direct result of the disaster), homeless (house is destroyed or heavily damaged), affected (people who require immediate assistance during emergency period); estimated damage to property, crops and livestock (EM-DAT 2015).

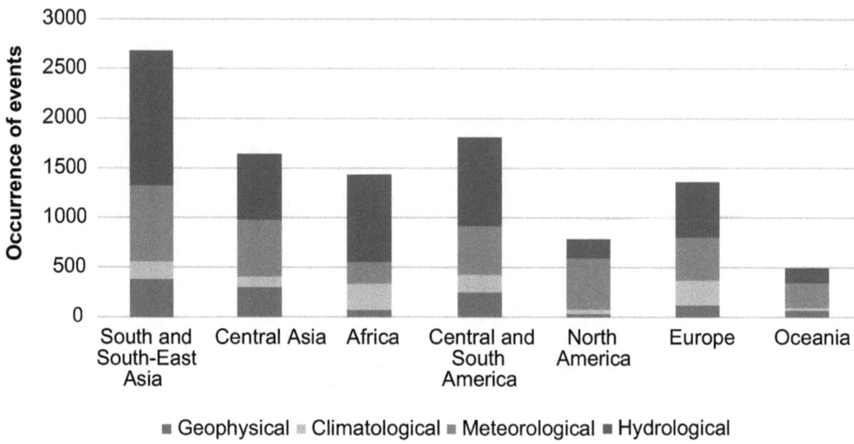

Fig. 2.2 Occurrence of events in different regions (1970–2014). Data source: EM-DAT (2015)

increasing number of disasters can be attributed to both higher exposure and vulnerability (including urbanisation, settlement patterns, etc.) and changing climate extremes, which can be partly explained by anthropogenic influences, as analysed in Sects. 2.1.2 and 2.2.3 respectively (IPCC 2012).

Figure 2.2 shows the local distribution of natural disasters and distinguishes again for the type of disaster. Asia is the region most prone to hazards. In South and Southeast Asia, 2,679 events occurred between 1970 and 2014, more than in North America, Europe and Oceania combined in the same period. Therefore, 42.4% of all events in the last 44 years happened in Asia, followed by Central and South America with 17.7% and Africa with 14.0% (EM-DAT 2015).

Between 1970 and 2014, an average of 151 million people were affected and ca. 73,000 were killed every year by natural disasters (EM-DAT 2015). Figure 2.3 illustrates the affected populations for different regions. The graph shows that Asia again has by far the highest number of affected people. The main types of disaster are climatological hazards (droughts, extreme temperatures) and hydrological disasters (floods).

Figure 2.4 illustrates, by region, the number of people killed as a direct consequence of disaster. High numbers of people are killed by geophysical events (earthquakes, tsunamis, volcanic eruptions) in Asia and Central and South America (ca. 1.3 million). Other devastating events for human lives include storms in Asia and droughts in Africa (EM-DAT 2015).

The EM-DAT database offers information about damages in US Dollars (in the year of the occurrence). Figure 2.5 shows the damages for different regions and disasters types, indicating high damages caused by storms in North America as well as geophysical events in Asia. However, other disasters, especially floods, have caused substantial damage across the world, particularly in Asia.

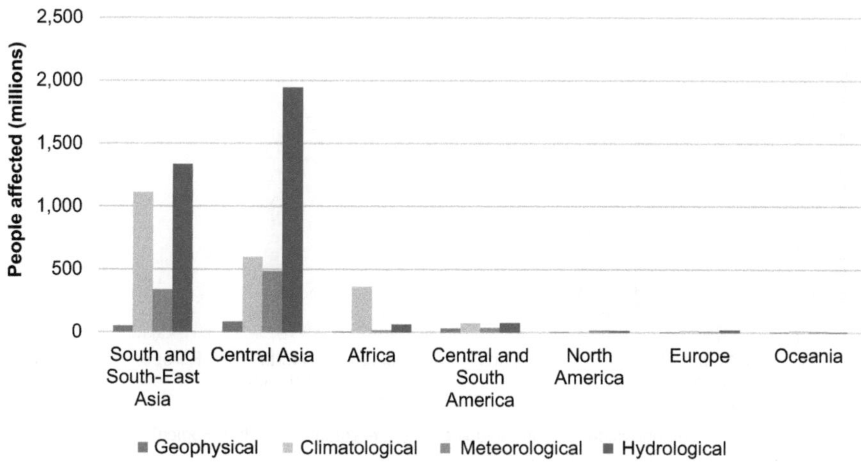

Fig. 2.3 People affected by natural disasters in different regions (1970–2014). Data source: EM-DAT (2015)

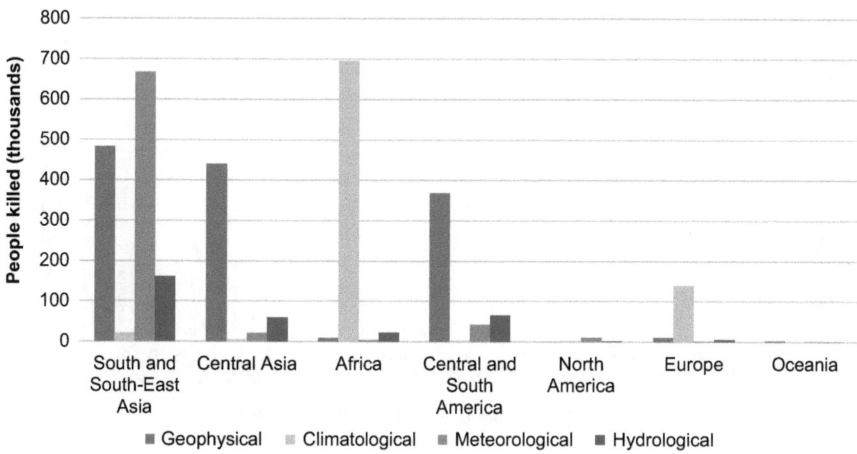

Fig. 2.4 People killed by natural disasters in different regions (1970–2014). Data source: EM-DAT (2015)

In total, ca. 3.2 million people died between 1970 and 2014 worldwide, while 6.6 billion people were affected (EM-DAT 2015). Figure 2.6 shows that deaths, numbers of affected people and damages fluctuate over time. Whilst a positive trend in the number of events is noticeable (see Fig. 2.1), there is only low statistical confidence for a positive trend over time for the numbers of people killed despite increasing population and exposure, which suggests that preventive measures have been effective (United Nations and World Bank 2010).

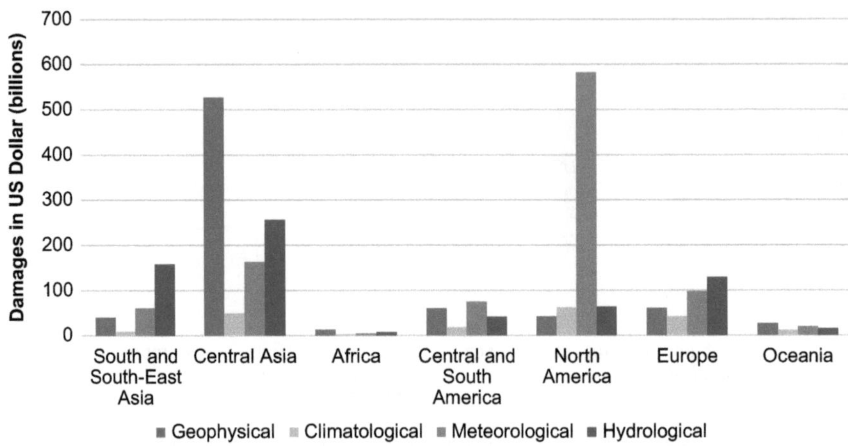

Fig. 2.5 Damages in US Dollars caused by disasters in different regions (1970–2014). Data source: EM-DAT (2015)

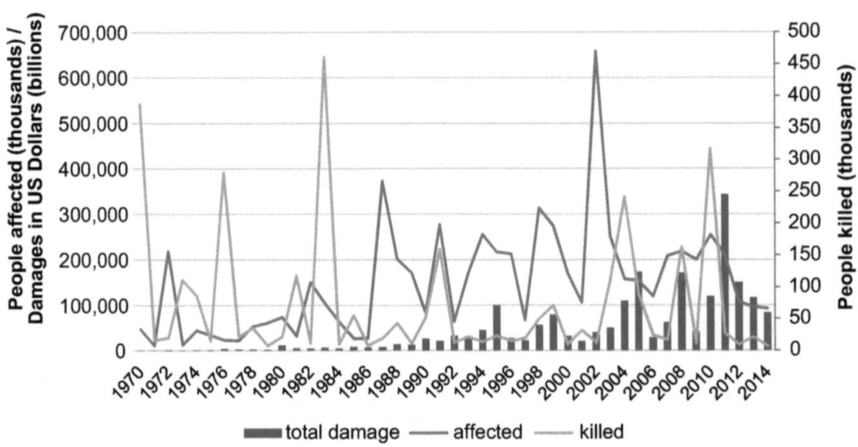

Fig. 2.6 Number of people affected, number of people killed and damages in US Dollars (1970 until 2014). Data source: EM-DAT (2015), total damages adjusted to value of US Dollars in 2014

2.1.2 Role of Climate Change

Climate change is likely to increase extreme weather events, their frequency and intensity and will worsen natural hazards in most regions of the world.[5] While

[5]Climate change describes changes in the state of the climate. Hereby the mean and/or variability of its properties change and persist for an extended period. Climate change can arise from natural processes as well as persistent anthropogenic changes. The confidence of predictions depends on many factors, including types of extremes, the region, quality of data and level of understanding of underlying processes, etc (IPCC 2012, 2014).

average changes of long-term levels in temperature, precipitation and other meteorological variables themselves have serious impacts, climate change will be felt due to changes in climate variability and express itself in weather extremes such as floods, droughts, heat waves and storms. Hereby, anthropogenic climate change will affect the location, timing, frequency, duration and intensity of extreme events (van Aalst 2006; IPCC 2012; The Royal Society 2014; Hallegatte et al. 2016).

In the literature it is seen as likely that climate change increases both the frequency and intensity of extreme precipitation events, resulting in more numerous floods and landslides (van Aalst 2006; IPCC 2012). The number of people exposed to floods could increase by between 4 and 15% in 2030 and between 12 and 29% in 2080 under a high-emission scenario (Winsemius et al. 2015). Economic losses from river floods are projected to increase by between 7 and 124% on average by 2040, depending on the applied method and the chosen region (Bouwer 2013).

The evolution of droughts depends on a complex process involving precipitation, seasonal cycles, snow packs, and evaporation rates, however medium confidence is presented that droughts will intensify during some seasons in some areas. Droughts are likely to become more common in the Mediterranean basin, Southeast Europe, North Africa, Southern Africa, Australia, South America, and Central America. Under a high-emission scenario, the number of people exposed to droughts could increase by between 9% and 17% in 2030 and between 50 and 90% in 2080 (van Aalst 2006; IPCC 2012; Winsemius et al. 2015; Hallegatte et al. 2016).

Furthermore, climate models project substantial warming in temperature extremes by the end of the century, leading to more frequent and intense heat waves in most regions of the world with significant harmful effects on ecosystem function and people's well-being (van Aalst 2006; IPCC 2012; Hallegatte et al. 2016). In addition, the mean sea level rise will have widespread consequences on coastal risk and cause, in combination with local approaches, coastal floods with disastrous consequences (IPCC 2012; Hallegatte et al. 2016). Finally, the average tropical cyclone speed is likely to increase in some areas, while the global frequency of tropical storms may decrease or remain unchanged (IPCC 2012). However, tropical storms (hurricanes, typhoons) and extratropical storms may be impacted differently (Hallegatte et al. 2016).

However, uncertainty persists around the specific magnitude of climate change and its impacts on extreme weather events. While climate models are much more reliable over long time periods and large spatial areas as well as for certain climate variables (e.g. temperature), extreme events often occur at a more local level and over shorter time scales. In addition, structural uncertainty remains around some of the underlying climate processes and the abrupt changes they cause to the global climate system (van Aalst 2006; Weitzman 2009; The Royal Society 2014).

Despite these uncertainties, many changes in climate variability and weather extremes on the regional and local levels are apparent enough to warrant attention (van Aalst 2006). Overall, climate change and its impact on extreme events highlight the adverse effects of natural hazards and disasters as well as the importance of risk and risk management. The following section highlights the significance of disaster risk in Cambodia, followed by an overview of the various and complex impacts of natural disasters.

2.1.3 Natural Disasters in Cambodia

Cambodia is one of the most disaster-prone countries in Southeast Asia, with significant social and economic impacts of hydrometeorological hazards such as floods, storms, and typhoons (World Bank 2016a). With more than 31,000 affected persons per million of the population, Cambodia has the highest rate of affected people amongst low-income member states of the Asian Development Bank (Guha-Sapir and Hoyois 2015).[6] The increasing frequency of larger extreme climate events has already resulted in more severe and frequent floods and droughts (World Bank 2016a).

The Cambodian National Committee for Disaster Management recorded 13.5 million affected people between 2000 and 2015 in the Disaster Loss Database, as well as 57,333 damaged or destroyed houses and 1975 deaths in the same period due to disasters (National Committee for Disaster Management 2016). In the same period of time, in Battambang province—the area of study for the following experiment and survey (see Chap. 3)—734,693 people were affected by disasters, 9380 houses were destroyed or damaged and 118 deaths were reported (National Committee for Disaster Management 2016). Figure 2.7 shows Cambodia as a whole and highlights Battambang province.

Figure 2.8 shows the proportion of disaster impact by type for Cambodia overall and specifically for Battambang province. Figure 2.9 presents the numbers of affected people over time for Cambodia overall and for Battambang province.

Floods are the main disaster type in Cambodia, accounting for more than 85% of the total number of victims and damages, followed by droughts and storms (National Committee for Disaster Management 2008; Guha-Sapir and Hoyois 2015). Cambodia's vast flood plains make large portions of the country naturally vulnerable to annual flooding along the Tonlé Sap Lake and Mekong River, with both beneficial and harmful effects (National Committee for Disaster Management 2008). Although Cambodia does not face flood risks of the magnitude and intensity of other Asian countries (e.g. Bangladesh), the impact of floods is severe due to a combination of exposure as well as high levels of vulnerability of rural people due to major limitations in their ability to cope (Vathana et al. 2013).

[6]Asia is particularly exposed to natural hazards. Member states of the Asian Development Bank represent 57% of the world population, but 88% of the disaster-affected. Floods accounted for more than a third of disasters in Asia between 1980 and 2012 (Guha-Sapir and Hoyois 2015).

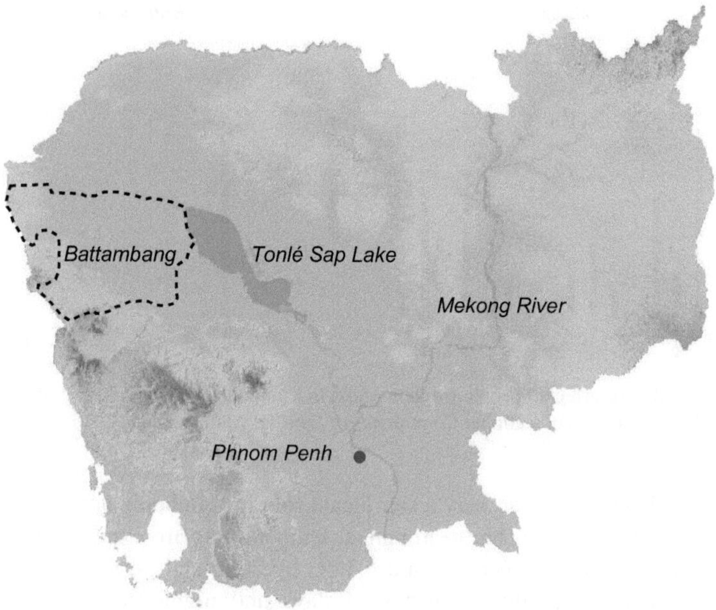

Fig. 2.7 Cambodia and Battambang province. Author's illustration, using Open Development (2016)

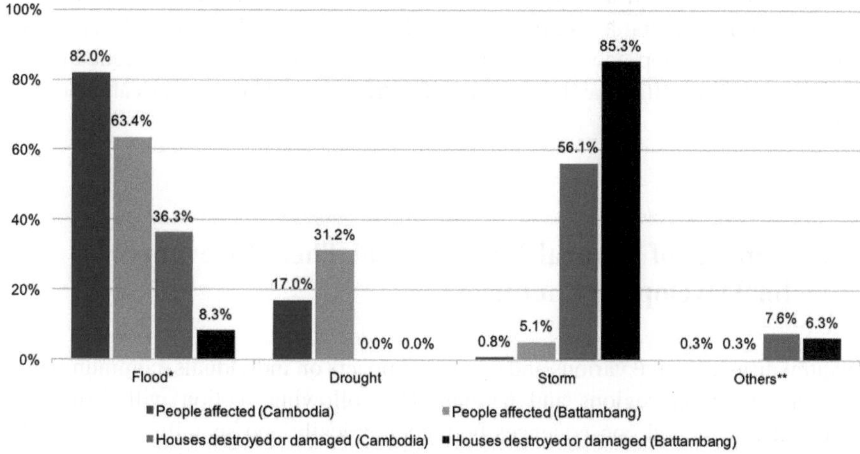

Fig. 2.8 Proportion of disaster impact by type for Cambodia and Battambang province from 2000 to 2015. Data source: National Committee for Disaster Management (2016). *Asterisks* includes river bank collapse; *Double asterisks* fire, epidemic, lightning, pest outbreak

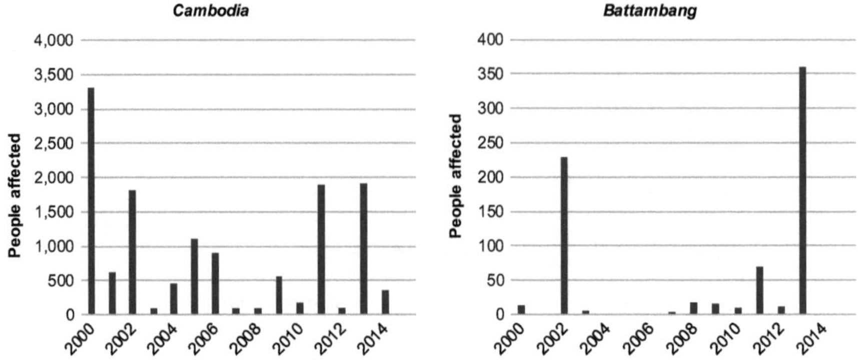

Fig. 2.9 Number of affected people (in thousands) in Cambodia and Battambang province from 2000 to 2015. Data source: National Committee for Disaster Management (2016)

Climate change will also play a significant role in Cambodia and impact future extreme weather events. The mean annual temperatures are expected to increase across Cambodia by between 1.4 and 4.3 °C by 2090 and projections indicate a substantial increase in the frequency of days and nights considered as 'hot' (World Bank 2016b). Furthermore, the direct impact of climate change may be seen in changing rainfall patterns, with increasing rainfall in the wet season and decreasing rainfall in the dry season (World Bank et al. 2013). However, due to the lack of dependable, quality long-term data series and model uncertainties, it is not possible to obtain a clear picture of climate change impact on precipitation and floods in Cambodia (Nguyen et al. 2009; World Bank 2016b). In any case, risk management approaches and climate change adaptation will be needed due to the changing magnitude and frequency of extreme weather events (Vathana et al. 2013).

2.2 Impacts of Natural Disasters and Their Relevance for Developing Countries

Natural disasters have various and complex impacts on individuals, communities as well as on larger regions and nations. The following section will distinguish different effects and consequences both economically and socially. Section 2.2.2 will present empirical evidence regarding short- and long-term effects on economic activity.

In order to investigate the diverse impacts of disasters in countries with varying levels of economic development, Sect. 2.2.3 introduces the concepts of vulnerability, exposure and resilience. Based on these concepts, the complex relationship between natural disasters and development will be analysed in more detail. Finally, the impact of natural disasters in Cambodia will be briefly presented.

Given the multiplicity of consequences, this chapter can only provide a brief overview of various dimensions. Furthermore, disaster impact on behaviour and decision-making processes will be left aside here and discussed in more detail in Chap. 3.

2.2.1 Introduction

Natural disasters can have severe economic and social impacts and can lead to substantial costs in terms of human life, property, infrastructure and others, which if avoidable could lead to large welfare gains. Even more importantly, shocks can cause significant and serious long-term impacts to human, social and physical capital[7] (Chhibber and Laajaj 2013; World Bank 2013).

Natural disaster impacts can be distinguished into direct costs (loss of human life, damage to buildings, crops, infrastructure, etc.) and indirect costs (lost output and investment, macroeconomic imbalances, lower human capital, etc.). Another distinction is into short- and long-term effects, however the following description follows the direct/indirect distinction.

Direct impacts are damages that are directly attributable to the effect of natural forces (Munich Re 2013). On the one hand, these include social impacts such as loss of human life, personal health, trauma and psychological stress (Cavallo and Noy 2010; Kousky 2012; Sharma 2015). On the other hand, significant economic impacts arise: loss of fixed assets and capital (buildings, infrastructure, property), damage to raw materials and extractable natural resources and the disruption of economic activity (Cavallo and Noy 2010; Kousky 2012; Ranger and Surminski 2013). In particular, the damage to agricultural outcome and assets (crops, livestock, farm equipment) often has a significant impact on a household's livelihood, with a particularly adverse effect on vulnerable members of a community (Haigh and Amaratunga 2010; Kousky 2012). In addition, costs of emergency response (evacuation, rescue, clean-up) can be included in direct costs (Kousky 2012). Finally, damages to the environment (water quality, soil, biodiversity, ecosystem) and other public goods (electricity supply, drinking water supply, schools, hospitals and other infrastructure) can be recorded, often with significant difficulties in

[7]Impacts (also consequences or outcomes) generally describe effects on lives, livelihoods, economies, services, infrastructures, health, ecosystems, societies, and cultures due to the interaction of extreme weather events with the vulnerability of an exposed society and system, within a specific period of time (IPCC 2014). The role of vulnerability and exposure will be discussed in Chap. 2.2.3.

estimating an economic value due to their non-market nature (Navrud and Magnussen 2013).

Indirect costs arise in the aftermath of direct costs and include a wide range of damages, from macroeconomic factors to conflicts (Munich Re 2013). In particular, this includes economic activity (notably the production of services and goods) that will not take place due to the occurrence of a disaster (Cavallo and Noy 2010). The indirect impacts may be caused by direct damages to physical infrastructure, reallocation of resources from production to reconstruction, or additional costs due to the usage of alternatives for production or distribution (Cavallo and Noy 2010; Kousky 2012). Furthermore, indirect costs include multiplier effects from both reductions in demand or increases in supply, due to destruction and recovery respectively (Kousky 2012). In addition to business interruptions, the loss of infrastructure and damages to public services can lead to utility loss of households in terms of lower quality of life or the adaptation to costly measures such as increased commuting time, individual energy supply, etc (Kousky 2012).

Furthermore, significant social costs arise indirectly from disasters. Shocks can have severe impacts on communities, ranging from short-term displacement to permanent psychosocial setbacks (Sharma 2015). In addition, significant long-term impacts on human capital (health, education) are evident. Besides adverse effects on health due to destroyed social infrastructure (hospitals, drinking water supply, etc.) and therefore problems of sanitation, natural disasters—in particular droughts—have significant impacts on the health of individuals. Evidence suggest that droughts are most harmful to children under the age of three, with long-lasting, negative effects on cognitive skills and productivity, although the effect on human capital is likely to be context specific (United Nations and World Bank 2010; Oviedo and Moroz 2014; Sharma 2015). Furthermore, there is evidence for negative effects of natural disasters on education, with significant drops in school enrolment rates following disasters (United Nations and World Bank 2010; Oviedo and Moroz 2014; Sharma 2015). Other effects include reduced agricultural output in the aftermath of a disaster due to disaster-related water scarcity, and adverse effects on economies due to disruptions in the distribution of products and in business travel (United Nations and World Bank 2010). Finally, there is evidence of a causal connection between disaster experience and conflicts, especially in Africa (World Bank 2007, 2013; United Nations and World Bank 2010; Chhibber and Laajaj 2013).

Following the overview of the vast majority of direct and indirect effects, the following section presents evidence for the macroeconomic impact of disasters, in particular on growth. The impact of natural disasters on individuals and households will be discussed in detail in Sect. 2.2.4 with respect to the roles of poverty and development.

2.2.2 *Disasters and Macroeconomics*

Natural disasters have the potential to cause macroeconomic consequences, including impacts on fiscal revenues, investment rates, levels of indebtedness and economic growth. However, the direction of this effect is not clear a priori: while severe damages decrease the aggregate output, post-disaster reconstruction increases output (Benson and Clay 2004; Collier 2005; Kousky 2012).

Various macroeconomic impacts are possible. Damage to firms could change exports and imports. A country's indebtedness could alter due to the damage to assets and income-earning opportunities—which decrease tax revenues—and government spending on emergency response. Inflation can be impacted by serious price changes resulting from a shock and foreign investment could decrease. However, the majority of the literature concentrates on the effect of natural disasters on economic growth (Otero and Martí 1995; Freeman et al. 2003; Kousky 2012; Munich Re 2013).

The following consideration of disaster impact on economic growth distinguishes between short-term effects (up to several years) and long-term effects (at least 5 years). The presented evidence provides valuable insights, particularly into long-term development. However, overall macroeconomic studies face several methodological difficulties, which is a reason that a large body of literature focuses on case studies.[8] Due to the difficulties associated with macroeconomic studies, microeconomic analyses can provide valuable insights (Benson and Clay 2004; Chhibber and Laajaj 2013).

Short-Term Impact on Economic Growth

One would expect that a disaster would reduce outputs due to both physical damage and disruptions to normal economic activities (United Nations and World Bank 2010). A small scope of older research found positive effects on gross domestic product (GDP) immediately after a disaster due to the replacement of damaged physical capital (Albala-Bertrand 1993; Otero and Martí 1995). However, most of the current research finds negative impacts of natural disaster on economic growth (Benson and Clay 2004; Raddatz 2007; Hochrainer 2009; Noy 2009; Toya and Skidmore 2012). These ambiguous effects may be explained by difficulties in identifying underlying causal effects of natural disaster production output (United Nations and World Bank 2010).

As expected, more severe events lead to greater impacts (Hochrainer 2009; Noy 2009; Kousky 2012). Although Noy and Tam (2010) show evidence for this observation in terms of lives lost and affected, costlier disasters in terms of

---

[8] Both theoretical problems as well as extreme data limitations are issues that impact actual estimations of disaster effects; even in highly developed countries, comprehensive disaster loss data is rare (Kousky 2012). Furthermore, although much attention is given to major events, the cumulative losses associated with 'smaller disasters' may be equally as significant (Chhibber and Laajaj 2013). Finally, macroeconomic shocks have indirect impacts on other—non-affected—regions and countries (food price fluctuations, etc.), which are usually not considered.

destroyed capital actually boost the economy in the short run. Economic effects are also more negative in smaller countries or in spatial areas within countries (Noy 2009; Kousky 2012). In addition, developing countries face larger output declines following a disaster than developed countries (Noy 2009). Countries with better institutions, higher per capita income, higher literacy rates as well as higher levels of trade openness and government spending are better able to withstand a disaster and to prevent further macroeconomic spill-over effects (Noy 2009). Furthermore, adverse disaster consequences also decrease with higher levels of aid and remittances (Hochrainer 2009). Finally, Cavallo et al. (2010) find negative macroeconomic impacts in cases where natural disasters were followed by a radical political revolution.

Long-Term Impact on Economic Growth

Theoretically, the effect of natural disasters on long-term consequences is not clear. Positive, negative as well as no significant impact are all possible outcomes (Benson and Clay 2004; World Bank 2007; Chhibber and Laajaj 2013).

Positive long-term effects can be explained following a Schumpeterian model of endogenous growth. The natural disaster requires capital replacement, which is likely to embody technological change that raises productivity and economic growth, compensating the negative effects of a disaster (Aghion and Howitt 1998; World Bank 2007; Chhibber and Laajaj 2013).

Negative long-term effects can be expected due to the damage of capital and human resources or reductions of productivity due to disruptions of markets and infrastructure. In particular, the disruption of education and health services explained above are likely to have negative long-term consequences. Furthermore, resources used in the aftermath of a disaster are not necessarily additional, leading to the reallocation of capital away from planned investments and therefore come with high opportunity costs. In addition, reconstruction efforts are not always well planned and organised. Finally, consecutive natural disasters create an atmosphere of uncertainty, which discourages potential future investments (Freeman et al. 2003; Benson and Clay 2004; World Bank 2007; Chhibber and Laajaj 2013).

Overall, the impact of natural disasters on long-term development is difficult to observe due to different direct and indirect effects of losses on stocks and flows as well as the multiple and complex interactions of these effects (Chhibber and Laajaj 2013). Therefore, four different scenarios are possible. Following the shock of a natural disaster, a negative impact on growth can be assumed due to immediate losses in human and physical capital and their direct and indirect effects on per capita growth.

Scenarios A and B in Fig. 2.10 show no long-term effect of the disaster on economic development, with a possible economic expansion during reconstruction in Scenario B. In Scenario C, the disaster reduces the capital stock permanently and the long-term equilibrium is therefore established at a lower level. In contrast, in Scenario D the recovery of both physical and human capital comes with technological change and therefore enhances long-term economic growth. However,

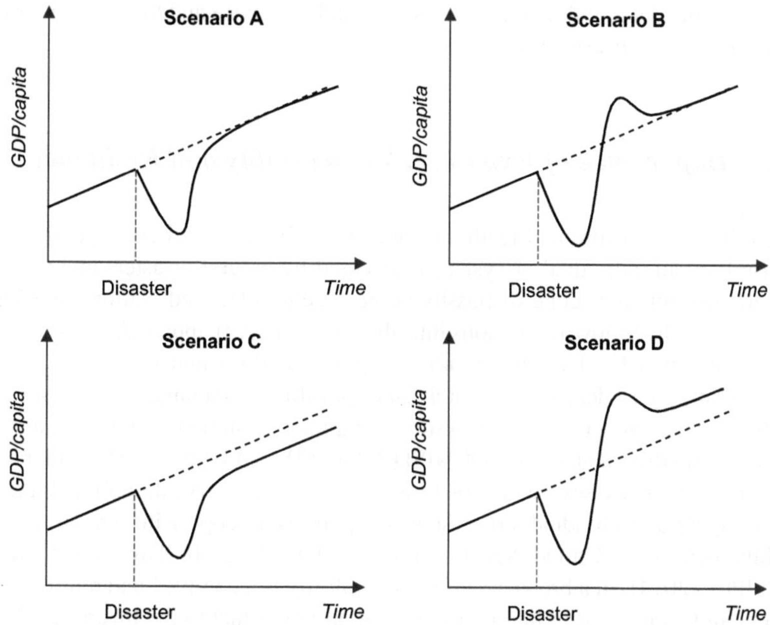

Fig. 2.10 Possible impact of natural disaster on long-term development. Own illustration following World Bank (2007) and Chhibber and Laajaj (2013)

different types of disasters can be associated with the various scenarios (World Bank 2007; Chhibber and Laajaj 2013).

There are also empirically ambiguous results of the long-term consequences of natural disasters. Albala-Bertrand (1993) finds no long-term effect of disasters on the growth rates of 26 countries from 1960 until 1976, therefore reflecting Scenarios A and B. Skidmore and Toya (2002) investigate the impact of disasters on long-run economic growth for 89 countries between 1960 and 1990 and find that the frequency of climate disasters is positively correlated with average annual growth rates as well as a positive impact of disasters on productivity. These results support Schumpeter's 'creative destruction' and therefore indicate Scenario D. An analysis by Benson (2003) for 115 countries of a period between 1960 and 1993 suggests that countries experiencing natural disasters tend to achieve lower growth rates than unaffected countries, indicating Scenario C [results reported by Benson and Clay (2004)]. Using a panel of 113 countries over 36 years, Jaramillo (2009) finds a permanent negative impact of disasters on growth rates (Scenario C).

To conclude, the effects of natural disaster on long-term development are highly ambiguous, both theoretically and empirically, and need more research. However, the role of institutions, uncertainty and systematic information as well as the types of disaster, their frequency and impact are important for a country's ability to cope with disasters (Chhibber and Laajaj 2013). The following section will introduce the different concepts of vulnerability, exposure and resilience and highlight their roles in the analysis of disaster impact.

2.2.3 Importance of Exposure, Vulnerability and Resilience

Vulnerability, exposure and resilience are regularly discussed concepts that characterise how an individual or system is affected by natural disasters and therefore how this impacts the scope of possible consequences (United Nations and World Bank 2010). The following sections introduce the different approaches and describe determinants which affect vulnerability, exposure and resilience.

Vulnerability is described as high susceptibility to damages and losses from negative shocks depending on a system's exposure, internal conditions, and risk management (Brown et al. 2006; UNISDR 2009; World Bank 2013). Vulnerability therefore comprises several characteristics (economic, social, political factors) which impact an individual's or system's capability to cope with a natural hazard (Miththapala 2008; United Nations and World Bank 2010; Toya and Skidmore 2012; IPCC 2014). In a broader sense, vulnerability is a complex and multi-sectoral concept and extends from the micro level of an individual to the macro level of an entire region (Davis 2015).

A system's vulnerability depends on its exposure to hazardous events among others (Brown et al. 2006). Exposure is the presence of people, livelihoods, ecosystems, resources, or economic, social and cultural assets in a hazard zone that are thereby subject to potential losses by an adverse shock (UNISDR 2009; United Nations and World Bank 2010; IPCC 2014). It can also be described as the external environment that determines the shock (World Bank 2013).

The third concept is resilience: the ability of an individual or system to resist, absorb and recover from the effects of an adverse shock while retaining or improving the system's functioning, and maintaining its essential structures and functions (UNISDR 2009; World Bank 2013; IPCC 2014). It is characterised by the amount of change the system can undergo whilst still maintaining control of function and structure, as well as the degree of self-organisation of which the system is capable (Brown et al. 2006). Furthermore, the ability to maintain the capacity for adaptation, learning, and transformation is an essential component (Brown et al. 2006; IPCC 2014; The Royal Society 2014). However, the definition varies according to the applied context (Haigh and Amaratunga 2010).[9]

[9]Resilience can be increased as change progresses, although steps forward are processes rather than outcomes. 'Surviving' describes most risk reduction instruments that improve the ability to cope with shocks, but may involve a lower quality of life as a result. 'Adaptation' involves changes of structures, livelihoods and lifestyles and aims to adjust to actual or expected climate effects. Finally, 'transformation' changes fundamental attributes of a natural or human system in order to increase resilience and therefore reduces the impact of large adverse shocks (IPCC 2014; The Royal Society 2014).

Bringing the different concepts together, vulnerability is a function of exposure and resilience, whereby exposure comprises the number and intensity of hazards and the population exposed to them. A higher level of exposure increases vulnerability, while resilience decreases it. Resilience comprises both instruments of preparedness and response. Therefore, disaster risk is dependent on the natural hazard as well as on exposure, vulnerability and the resilience of the system (United Nations and World Bank 2010; Chhibber and Laajaj 2013).

Determinants of Vulnerability and Exposure

Several variables serve to capture the vulnerability of a country to disasters. Various economic factors are found to be significant for a country's vulnerability. A high income per capita (as well as the land and population size of a country) increases the absolute damages of a disaster, however richer and larger countries usually have a greater capacity to absorb shocks and therefore have lower vulnerability (Cavallo and Noy 2010). Intersectoral linkages, good financial systems and trade openness also lower vulnerability by decreasing sensitivity to shocks, allowing a wider diffusion of disaster impact with fewer exchange constraints (Toya and Skidmore 2005; World Bank 2007). In contrast, inequality in a society (more unequal societies tend to have lower prevention efforts) as well as the importance of the agriculture sector (high sensitivity to natural disaster) increase the vulnerability of a country (Benson and Clay 2004; Fafchamps 2005; Sadoulet 2005; World Bank 2007; Skees 2008; Cavallo and Noy 2010). Furthermore, better institutions (more stable democratic regimes and greater security of property rights) as well as political accountability (in relation to the efficiency of allocation decisions) are generally seen as highly significant in explaining lower vulnerability (Kahn 2005; Brown et al. 2006; World Bank 2007; Raschky 2008; Cavallo and Noy 2010; Yamamura 2011). Many of these characteristics may explain the different vulnerabilities and disaster consequences which can be observed between less and more developed countries. This issue will be discussed in detail in the following section.

Vulnerability also increases with higher exposure. From 1970 to 2010, a global trend of risk-taking can be observed: while the world population grew by 87%, the population in flood plains and cyclone-prone coastlines increased by 114 and 192% respectively (Hallegatte et al. 2016). Risk areas may be more attractive in terms of economic opportunities or public services and agglomeration externalities attract people to cities, even if they are more exposed (Botzen and van den Bergh 2008; Hallegatte et al. 2016).

In general, measures to reduce vulnerability include mitigation and prevention (reduction of a hazard's likelihood and damage respectively), as well as preparedness and relief. Selected measures will be discussed later in the context of disaster risk management.

Vulnerability to natural disasters is likely to increase in the future due to climate change. The modification of meteorological and environmental variables (temperatures, precipitation, sea levels, etc.) is likely to increase the frequency and intensity of natural hazards (see Sect. 2.1). At the same time, social and economic vulnerability to disaster has been increasing (IPCC 2012; Hallegatte 2013). Larger impacts from extreme weather events can therefore be expected in the future, although the scale and speed of the changes are highly uncertain (Neumayer and Barthel 2011; IPCC 2012; Surminski 2012; Hallegatte 2013; The Royal Society 2014). Disaster will increase impacts especially in climate-related sectors such as water, forestry, health, agriculture, food security and tourism, and will influence population mobility and relocation with associated social effects (IPCC 2012). Increasing resilience and reducing vulnerability is even more urgent than before in the light of climate change, and a permanent effort to mitigate and adapt to climate change and to develop an efficient disaster risk management system is essential.

2.2.4 *Disaster, Development and Their Complex Relationship*

The following analysis will show that developing countries often have a higher vulnerability to climate risk and experience greater impacts than developed countries. However, the relationship between natural disasters and a country's level of development is highly complex. Firstly, less developed economies are more vulnerable and exposed to natural disasters and their effects. Secondly, natural disasters and their consequences impact the development of economies and households, with particular effects on the poor. The following analysis discusses the different dimensions.

Role of Development on Disaster Impacts

If aggregating growth figures and disaster damages worldwide, the world's GDP has grown about 4% per year in the last decades, while disaster losses have been growing at about 6% on average (Hallegatte 2012; Karim and Noy 2016). However, disaster losses are distributed very unequally and there is evidence that the level of a country's economic development impacts its susceptibility to natural disasters (Cavallo and Noy 2010).

Mortality due to natural disasters is frequently higher in developing countries than in more developed economies (Toya and Skidmore 2005; Surminski 2012; World Bank 2013). In contrast, highly developed countries represent 15% of the world's population exposed to four natural hazard types (earthquake, tropical cyclone, flood and drought), but account for only 1.8% of the related deaths worldwide (UNDP 2011). Low- and middle-income countries suffer 95% of natural disaster deaths worldwide (Linnerooth-Bayer et al. 2011).

A similar picture is evident for economic damages. While the value of damages is often higher in developed countries (due to higher costs of rebuilding and repairing property and infrastructure), the economic impact as damage relative to the size of the economy is often much larger for developing countries (Benson and Clay 2004; Toya and Skidmore 2005; World Bank 2006, 2013; Linnerooth-Bayer et al. 2011; Surminski 2012; Munich Re 2013).[10] The impacts are similar at the household level: while damages to assets and income in absolute terms are larger for non-poor households (because of their higher endowment), poor people lose more in relative terms (Hallegatte et al. 2016).

When distributing the direct losses on country groups, emerging economies face the highest average costs in relation to GDP; however, for major catastrophes (highest 10% of losses per year) the economic burden falls again on developing countries (Munich Re 2013).[11] In addition, households and firms are more affected in developing countries because of their low insurance cover (1% of losses) in comparison to developed countries (30% of losses) (Linnerooth-Bayer et al. 2011; World Bank 2013).

The empirical evidence shows that economic development allows a country to better mitigate and manage disaster risk (Kellenberg and Mobarak 2008). However, the higher vulnerability of developing countries may be due to various reasons such as location, sensitivity of the economy to changes as well as a lack of resources to prepare for disasters and build resilience (Surminski 2012). The following section summarises the most important explanations.

Developing countries tend to have a higher exposure to natural disasters due to their location in hot tropical and sub-tropical regions, the role of climate change as well as high urbanisation rates in exposed river and coastal regions (Surminski 2012; Munich Re 2013; World Bank 2013). Poor people are particularly exposed to higher temperatures, with an even stronger effect in countries with climates that are already hot; mixed results are found for the disproportionate effect of river floods on the poor (Hallegatte et al. 2016). Poor households in developing countries often find better opportunities for employment and livelihoods in already densely populated urban areas, although these locations are associated with higher risk exposure (Kellenberg and Mobarak 2008; Hallegatte et al. 2016). While the basic factors apply to both richer and poorer households within a country, the availability and affordability of land often pushes poorer households to settle in riskier areas (Hallegatte et al. 2016).

Households living in high-risk areas in developing countries often have a lack of institutional and economic support to face unexpected shocks (with significant long-term effects on productivity and poverty) and have to rely repeatedly on external aid and informal networks (Wahlstrom 2013). Poor people have a less diversified portfolio, with a large percentage of their assets in material form and less

[10]Even if the national impact is relatively small, the local effects of a natural disaster may be severe (World Bank 2006).

[11]A theoretical and empirical analysis by Schumacher and Strobl (2011) finds a non-linear relationship between economic losses and the level of economic development, which crucially depends on the specific hazard. While countries facing low or intermediate hazards have a bell-shaped relationship between losses and wealth, countries with high hazards have a u-shaped relationship (Schumacher and Strobl 2011). Furthermore, there is evidence that developing countries suffer more from frequent and low-cost disasters, while developed countries are more affected by rare but high-cost events (Hallegatte 2012).

access to financial institutions to better protect savings from the effects of natural disasters (Hallegatte et al. 2016).

Several factors of the economic system can explain different levels of vulnerability towards natural disasters. Developing countries are particularly characterised by a high dependence on agriculture and are therefore more sensitive to changes in weather and climate (Surminski 2012; Chantarat et al. 2013; Chhibber and Laajaj 2013; Hallegatte et al. 2016). Additionally, sectoral linkages, the quality of the financial system and trade openness impact the resilience of a country (Toya and Skidmore 2005; Chhibber and Laajaj 2013).[12]

While in developed countries, losses from disasters are typically funded by a combination of private risk-financing instrument and public spending, funding the aftermath of a disaster in developing economies often creates long-term costs. Higher expenditures for relief and reconstruction with low tax ratios and the reallocation of expenditures, reduce or divert funds from planned investments in the future. Furthermore, international aid after disasters is often not additional and various donors increase management efforts to follow specific donor conditions (Ghesquiere and Mahul 2007; Chhibber and Laajaj 2013).

A lack of economic and institutional capacity for prevention efforts can often be found as significant factors in explaining the different impact of disasters on developed and developing countries (Gurenko 2004; Cavallo and Noy 2010; World Bank 2013; Brata et al. 2014; Said et al. 2015). Political instability, a lack of willingness to prioritise preparedness, a lack of transparency (in reporting relevant expenditures, post-disaster reallocation), as well as the low enforcement of building codes, land-using rules and other mitigation rules are key obstacles to higher resilience (Benson and Clay 2004; Toya and Skidmore 2005; Cavallo and Noy 2010; Chhibber and Laajaj 2013; World Bank 2013; Cameron and Shah 2015).[13]

Socioeconomic implications of disasters are more severe in rural areas and less developed districts as well as urban poor settlements and coastal areas, due to their lower capacity to cope and recover. In particular, these areas are often characterised by low income and saving rates and very limited access to safety nets (insurances, public health facilities, etc.) (Dercon 2005a; Heltberg et al. 2015; Sharma 2015).

In addition, a lack of know-how and resources to understand climate change and invest in research as well as missing technologies to cope with climate effects increases the vulnerability of developing economies. Furthermore, more advanced elements of risk-sharing at both the government level (disaster-assistance

[12]In contrast to developed economies, developing countries often have smaller multiplier effects due to weak intersectoral linkages, poor infrastructure and a generally less integrated economy (Benson and Clay 2004).

[13]Emerging economies are particularly impacted by natural disasters due to an already substantial capital base in combination with a relatively highly interconnected economy on the one hand, and a lack of economic and institutional resources in order to enforce safety regulations, invest in preparedness and increase resilience on the other (Munich Re 2013).

programmes) as well as at the individual level (insurances) are needed in order to transfer financial risk (World Bank 2007).

Finally, the non-linear relationship between development and disaster damages can be explained by a change in behavioural choices and different risk preferences. While higher levels of production may carry greater disaster risk as a by-product, households have the choice to reduce consumption in order to mitigate this additional risk. However, due to the high marginal utility of consumption for low levels of income, poor households may be willing to favour consumption instead of mitigating the risk. This higher risk-taking behaviour may explain more risk exposed location decisions found in developing countries. This observation appears to be stronger for floods, landslides and storms than for extreme temperatures or earthquakes (Banerjee 2005; Kellenberg and Mobarak 2008; Cavallo and Noy 2010).

Impact of Disasters on Development and Poverty

The previous section has shown evidence that the level of development impacts the capability to build resilience and that less developed countries are therefore more vulnerable to the consequences of natural disasters. However, more recent literature investigates the inverse impact of disasters on development, and poverty in particular. The experience of a natural disaster—as well as the pure risk of it—is likely to have significant effects on poverty and can set back development efforts by years (Sadoulet 2005; Surminski 2012; Clarke and Reid 2013; Ranger and Surminski 2013; World Bank 2013; Oviedo and Moroz 2014; Gehrke 2014; Hallegatte et al. 2016; Karim and Noy 2016).[14]

Disasters affect poor and more vulnerable individuals disproportionately due to their lower resilience, described above, as well as their limited access to coping mechanisms such as savings, insurance, social safety nets, etc (Clarke and Reid 2013; Hallegatte et al. 2016). Even short periods spent in poverty may have long term consequences for households, depending on the chosen coping mechanisms and their long-run effects (Clarke and Reid 2013; Ranger and Surminski 2013).

Households without access to savings or insurance mechanisms often limit consumption, mainly food, as a response to shocks, with unequal effects on household members (Sadoulet 2005; World Bank 2013; Carter et al. 2014; Heltberg et al. 2015; Karim and Noy 2016). The impacts of natural disasters are particularly costly for children, as malnutrition due to lower consumption can cause irreversible long-term consequences on human capital (Hazell et al. 2010; Chhibber and Laajaj 2013; World Bank 2013; Hallegatte et al. 2016). Furthermore, in exchange for having an additional workforce after the experience of a disaster, households sacrifice investments in education, reducing long-term prospects for escaping poverty (Ranger and Surminski 2013; World Bank 2013; Hallegatte et al. 2016).

[14]Household studies in India and Bangladesh show that natural disasters and the loss of natural assets are named as main reasons for households falling into poverty. Households which were affected by droughts in the past are 15 times more likely to fall into poverty (Sen 2003; Krishna 2006; Hallegatte et al. 2016).

Investments may also be diverted away from new technology and equipment, and psychological experiences (shock-induced stress) can increase domestic abuse with significant long-lasting physical and psychological effects on identity and behaviour (Ranger and Surminski 2013; World Bank 2013). Finally, natural disasters impact households indirectly through production-related price shocks, health issues following the destruction of sanitary infrastructure, and decreased employment after productive capital is destroyed. All factors have again long-term consequences on asset accumulation, productivity and human capital (Hallegatte et al. 2016).

Ex Ante Impact of Natural Disaster In addition to the substantial ex post impacts of natural disasters, disaster risk has also ex ante impacts (Oviedo and Moroz 2014). Household choices on trade-offs involving risks depend on the ability to cope with possible negative effects (Hallegatte et al. 2016). With limited coping strategies, the anticipation of shocks leads to an engagement of (particularly poor) households in low-risk, low-return strategies in order to decrease income variability (Skees 2008; Mosley 2009; Oviedo and Moroz 2014; Hallegatte et al. 2016; Karim and Noy 2016). Therefore the expectation of a loss in combination with the anticipation of limited coping strategies leads to an adjustment of individual behaviour, which is rational in order to reduce exposure and therefore vulnerability towards shocks (Dercon 2005b; Carter et al. 2014). Broad empirical evidence can be found in various developing countries (Elbers et al. 2007; Dercon 2008; Jacobsen 2009; Dercon and Christiaensen 2011; Mobarak and Rosenzweig 2012; Cole et al. 2013; Awel and Azomahou 2014; Bandyopadhyay and Skoufias 2015).

Thereby, ex ante impacts are highly significant and can be as important as the actual (ex post) consequences of a disaster (Oviedo and Moroz 2014; Hallegatte et al. 2016). Studies focused on agricultural outcomes show significantly higher outputs and consumption for households which sow less low-risk, low-return plants (Dercon 2008; Dercon and Christiaensen 2011). Furthermore, economy-wide ex ante impacts are evident; in a simulation-based model for Zimbabwe, almost half of the income reduction due to droughts could be explained by ex ante impacts from increased weather risk (Elbers et al. 2007). Finally, households consider their vulnerability to natural disasters in decision-making processes in other domains, whereby higher background risk due to floods or other hazards may contribute to less risky decisions, e.g. in the decision-making processes for innovation or entrepreneurship (Gollier and Pratt 1996; Hallegatte et al. 2016).

The Existence of Poverty Traps On the household and country levels, there is some evidence that adverse shocks such as natural disasters can lead to poverty traps: vulnerability and high exposure to disasters increase the negative effects of these, which harm development and contribute to higher vulnerability and increased exposure to future events (Carter et al. 2007; Chhibber and Laajaj 2013; World Bank 2013; Oviedo and Moroz 2014). Poverty traps can result from both ex post and ex ante impacts (Oviedo and Moroz 2014). Although one disaster may not necessarily create long-term consequences, successive disasters prevent households or countries from capital accumulation and investment and result in high instability with associated long-term effects (Chhibber and Laajaj 2013;

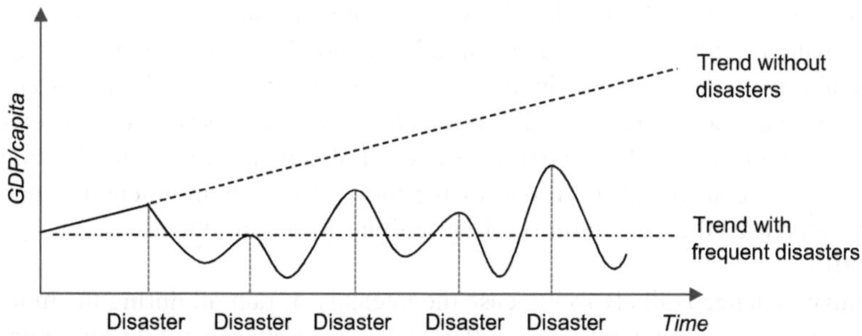

Fig. 2.11 Successive disasters and their possible long-term impact on income. Own illustration after Chhibber and Laajaj (2013)

Oviedo and Moroz 2014). To overcome this situation, the development of households and countries must be accompanied by increased resilience and reduced vulnerability (Chhibber and Laajaj 2013). Figure 2.11 illustrates the effects.

The empirical evidence for poverty traps is mixed (Oviedo and Moroz 2014; Hallegatte et al. 2016). While some studies show the existence of such vicious circles after the experience of shocks (Carter et al. 2007; Elbers et al. 2007; Dercon 2008; Dercon and Christiaensen 2011), other studies cannot find such evidence. However, this research does find that poorer households recover more slowly from the adverse effects of shocks than wealthier ones (Oviedo and Moroz 2014).

2.2.5 Impacts of Natural Disasters in Cambodia

Vulnerability

Cambodia is highly vulnerable to climate events due to a combination of seasonal occurrences of floods and droughts on the one hand and high poverty levels and dependency on agriculture on the other (Nguyen et al. 2009; World Bank 2016b).[15]

Due to its unique hydrological regime with vast flood plains, Cambodia is vulnerable to natural disasters in general and floods in particular, along the Tonlé Sap and Mekong rivers (National Committee for Disaster Management 2008;

[15]Following the 'INFORM' model, Cambodia is classified as highly vulnerable, taking into account vulnerability (physical and socio-economic), exposure and coping capacity (PreventionWeb 2016). Investigating sovereign credit risk, Standard & Poor's (2014) assign Cambodia as the country with the highest vulnerability to climate change. To capture various vulnerability factors, the ranking takes into account the share of the population living in coastal areas (exposure), the importance of agriculture (sensitivity) and an independent vulnerability index capturing the ability to cope with climate change (adaptive capacity) (Standard & Poor's 2014).

Vathana et al. 2013).[16] Of 2.8 million documented houses, approximately 55% were found in areas that could potentially be flooded (Mochizuki et al. 2015). Vulnerability to droughts has increased in recent years due to the occurrence of consecutive disasters without opportunities for recovery in between (Nguyen et al. 2009). Furthermore, land degradation as a result of human activity, floods, droughts and others, is considered to be one of the most severe environmental issues and further increases the vulnerability of agriculture (General Directorate of Agriculture 2013).

Climate change is likely to increase the intensity of rainfall during the monsoon seasons and may significantly impact flood response management. Furthermore, the rise in sea levels may threaten low-lying areas and a projected increase in temperatures is likely to exacerbate already common occurrences of drought (World Bank 2016b).

Economically, a high dependency on agriculture and other ecosystem-dependent livelihoods make the country especially vulnerable, in particular the rural poor, who often rely on subsistence agriculture (Vathana et al. 2013).[17] The country's vulnerability is increased by low productivity and a lack of diversification of income activities; rice cultivation accounts for 90% of the total cultivated area and 80% of agricultural labour, however the yields remain low as compared to neighbouring countries due to the limited use of improved seeds, fertiliser and water management (Vathana et al. 2013). In total, the weather and climate-dependent economic sector contributes to 65% of the GDP (World Bank et al. 2013). Furthermore, a weak adaptive capacity due to poor infrastructure, limited institutions and high poverty levels—reflecting the impact of 30 years of war, social and political instability—exacerbate the country's vulnerability (General Directorate of Agriculture 2013; World Bank 2016b).

Impacts of Natural Disasters

Previous disasters such as floods and droughts have increasingly been affecting rural livelihoods and have been found to be a main driver of poverty and food insecurity (Nguyen et al. 2009; World Bank 2016b). The economic damage in the last 10 years has been evaluated at USD214 million, with reduced opportunities to recover in the short run due to consecutive annual disasters (World Bank 2016a).

More specifically, natural disasters have potential direct impacts on the economic and social sectors (World Bank et al. 2013). Economically, the agriculture sector is particular affected through loss of income, destruction of livelihoods, disruption of business, damaged irrigation systems, dams and other agricultural infrastructure (Nguyen et al. 2009; World Bank et al. 2013). Furthermore, direct

[16]However, floods have—until they become excessive—a beneficial impact on certain agricultural-based livelihoods (improved fertility for agriculture, ground and surface water recharge, ecological benefits for fisheries), and these are important factors for the livelihoods of hundreds of communities (National Committee for Disaster Management 2008).

[17]However, risks are not limited to farming cultivators; landless labourers are particularly vulnerable to income fluctuations (Kreimer and Arnold 2000).

impacts on the transportation, communication, energy and tourism sectors are possible (World Bank et al. 2013). Socially, floods and droughts impact location decisions and resettlements as well as water quality and sanitation. They can lead to significant, and in some case long-term, consequences for health and education (Nguyen et al. 2009; World Bank et al. 2013).

ACAPS (2016) investigated the effects of the 2011 flood in Cambodia, which destroyed over three million hectares of cropland and damaged 13% of the rice harvest, resulting in food shortages and high rice prices. Furthermore, the flood prolonged the dengue fever season and increased the cases of other flood-associated health risks. Finally, education opportunities were significantly limited, affecting 455,000 children: extensive damage to school infrastructure resulted in children missing weeks and months of school (ACAPS 2016).

In conclusion, Cambodia is highly vulnerable to the consequences of floods and other disasters as well as to the impacts of climate change, with reductions in crop yields, decreased water availability and implications for health and education (National Committee for Disaster Management 2008; World Bank et al. 2013). The impact of natural disasters is likely to increase due to climate change and fragile ecosystems and will consequently cause rising poverty and the malnutrition of children (World Bank et al. 2013; Mochizuki et al. 2015). In order to reduce vulnerability and increase resilience, particularly in the agricultural sector, farming practices and crop diversification must be improved, accompanied by better knowledge and access to weather information for farmers and the restoration of flood protection infrastructures (National Committee for Disaster Management 2008).

2.3 Disaster Risk Management

In order to deal with high risk situations, households, communities, governments and other organisations adopt ex ante strategies to reduce risk exposure, and ex post mechanisms to cope with the impacts of risks—both come at a high cost. The following section introduces the concept of disaster risk management and presents a framework including the significant factors of as well as main obstacles towards risk management.

Risk management is described as a process which involves the preparation for risks (ex ante) and coping with their consequences (ex post) (World Bank 2013). Similarly, the IPCC (2012) describes disaster risk management as a complex combination of different processes which focus on the design, implementation and evaluation of strategies, policies and measures; these enable the understanding of disaster risk, foster risk reduction and promote disaster preparedness, response and recovery practices. It is an essential tool for development, especially in developing counties, to build resilience and manage risks in a pro-active, systematic and integrated way. Successful disaster risk management highlights the importance of ex ante planning and preparation in a context of uncertainty and shifts resources from unplanned, ad hoc responses to forward-looking preparation at various levels of society (IPCC 2012; World Bank 2013).

Disaster risk management, as well as adaptation to climate change,[18] concentrate on increasing resilience, reducing vulnerability and exposure to the negative impacts of climate extremes and natural disasters (IPCC 2012). However, both concepts have been developed independently in the relevant research and employ different interpretations of concepts, strategies, methods, vocabularies and frameworks (Thomalla et al. 2006; IPCC 2012). While disaster risk management focuses on both climate and geophysical hazards, climate change adaptation comprises climate hazards as well as non-disaster aspects, including positive benefits from climate change (Davis 2015). The intersection between the two concepts lie in climate hazards and their impacts. Therefore, both disaster risk management and climate adaptation are aimed at reducing exposure and vulnerability to climate-related risks and enhancing resilience to their adverse impacts (IPCC 2012; Davis 2015; Linnerooth-Bayer and Hochrainer-Stigler 2015).[19]

2.3.1 Risk Management Framework

The impact of shocks on an individual or system is determined by various factors, namely the external environment, internal conditions and risk management approaches. In order to illustrate these interactions, the World Development Report 2014 presents the concept of a risk chain, shown in Fig. 2.12[20] (World Bank 2013).

The external environment determines the individual's exposure to risk. The individual's vulnerability depends on their exposure, internal conditions and risk management. Although the idea of a risk chain implies a linear connection, there are indeed several feedback effects in which outcomes and risk management impact future shocks (World Bank 2013).

Following the World Development Report 2014, risk management includes four components: knowledge, protection, insurance and coping. While the first three can be taken in advance (preparation), the latter takes place once a shock has occurred.

[18]Adaptation can be described as the process of adjustment to expected or actual effects due to climate change, in order to moderate their adverse impacts. The importance of adaptation is growing due to the absence of satisfying mitigation efforts and the fact that even with significant mitigation efforts, severe climate-related impacts will occur (de Muirieta et al. 2014). However, it should be emphasised that adaptation and mitigation can complement each other in reducing risks (Bräuninger et al. 2011; IPCC 2012).

[19]For the sole consideration of climate hazards, as in this study, a further distinction between the concepts is not expedient. However, the majority of research in this field is attached to the discussion of disaster risk management. Therefore, this study will concentrate on disaster risk management.

[20]The idea of a risk chain follows three parts: risk, risk management options and outcome (Alwang et al. 2001).

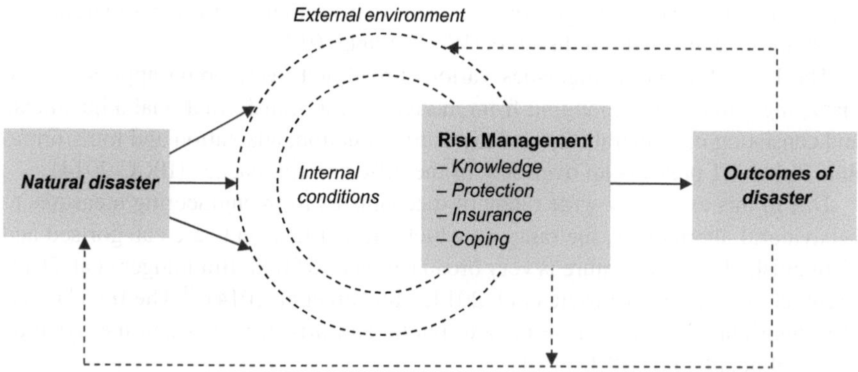

Fig. 2.12 Risk chain: the outcome of natural disasters dependent on external environment, internal conditions and risk management. Illustration follows World Development Report 2014 (World Bank 2013)

While a risk management approach is often seen as strong when it includes all four components, the specific composition of knowledge, protection, insurance and coping is context-dependent (World Bank 2013).

Knowledge involves both the assessment of information about possible events and their likelihoods and judgement regarding one's own exposure to adverse events and possible outcomes. Knowledge is therefore the basis for decision-making processes. Protection includes actions of the individual or system to lower either the probability or the dimensions of a disaster. Insurance includes instruments that transfer resources over time or across people, from good to bad states of nature. Both a complementary and substitutive relationship between insurance and protection is possible. Finally, coping comprises all actions that take place once a shock has occurred, such as recovery and rebuilding. However, significant investments in preparation, and thus lower vulnerability, reduce costs for coping mechanisms (World Bank 2013).

2.3.2 Approaches of Disaster Risk Management

Individual risk management approaches include the acquisition and sharing of knowledge about risk (weather risk, better agricultural technologies, etc.) and the accumulation of financial and physical assets (savings, access to credits, accumulation of livestock and jewellery, etc.) in order to invest in prevention and insurance. Furthermore, individuals can invest in human capital to increase protection due to education, better nutrition, sanitation, preventive health care and others. Other individual risk management instruments include the diversification of income sources in different sectors (farming, services, etc.) and locations (rural, urban) as well as the creation of informal insurance systems through family formation, fertility and marriage. Finally, the application of low-risk, low-return strategies (as discussed above) or migration are used as instruments in order to strengthen preparation against natural disasters (World Bank 2013).

The IPCC (2014) distinguishes various broad and overlapping approaches for managing climate risks, ranging from incremental to transformational adjustments and consisting of vulnerability and exposure reduction, adaptation and transformation. Table 2.1 presents an overview of the different approaches (IPCC 2014).

Due to this extremely wide range of mechanisms from engineering measures to behavioural alternatives, the range in which these instruments are categorised and distinguished in the literature is very broad (Francisco 2008; Bräuninger et al. 2011; Carter et al. 2014; de Muirieta et al. 2014; Mitchell et al. 2014).[21] The IPCC report also highlights the importance of both public and private actors and the dynamic nature of adaptation (IPCC 2014).

If preparation is lacking, natural disasters and other large shocks can force poor people in particular to use costly coping instruments and therefore reduce their ability to escape poverty (World Bank 2013). However, to implement cost-efficient risk management instruments, cost-benefit analyses are needed to assess their impact on risk prevention. Preventive instruments of disaster risk management are found to generate considerable returns (Mechler and Islam 2013). However, certain conditions have to be met in order to use cost-benefit analyses as an useful evaluation tool, including considering complexities of estimating risk (Kull et al. 2013; Foudi and Oses-Eraso 2014).

2.3.3 *Obstacles to Risk Management*

Several obstacles to disaster risk management arise on the individual and systemic levels. The following section presents only a brief overview, while the specific factors will be discussed in more detail in the upcoming chapters.

Lack of resources due to large up-front costs and limited access to financial instruments are of particular importance for risk management in developing countries. Furthermore, the lack of information and cognitive failures may impact decision-making processes due to the non-availability of relevant information or

[21]For example, a distinction is made between market-based instruments, public-private partnerships, financial instruments and risk-financing instruments (the latter concentrating on a pre-arranged risk-sharing mechanism, while financial instruments increase the accessibility of loans for adaptation activities) (Bräuninger et al. 2011). Adaptation measures can also be classified as reactive (undertaken as a response) and anticipatory (undertaken before the impact) (Francisco 2008). Similarly, adaptation policies can be classified by the nature of the agents involved (public versus private), by the spatial scope (localised versus widespread) or the temporal scope (short- versus long-term) (de Muirieta et al. 2014). Policy options can also be distinguished by the reduction of risk (reduced vulnerability, hazards and exposure, and pooled, transferred and shared risks), as well as the management of residual risk and uncertainties (preparation and response, increased capacity to cope) (Mitchell et al. 2014). Similarly, Carter et al. (2014) group risk avoidance, risk reduction, risk retention and risk transfer.

Table 2.1 Approaches for managing climate risks

Category	Examples	Overlapping approaches
Human development	Access to education, health care, energy, etc.	Vulnerability and exposure reduction
Poverty alleviation	Disaster risk reduction, social safety nets, social protection, etc.	
Livelihood security	Diversification of income, assets and livelihood	
Disaster risk management	Early warning systems, hazard mapping, shelters, building codes, storm and water management	
Ecosystem management	Maintaining wetlands and urban green spaces, coastal afforestation, etc.	
Spatial or land-use planning	Provision of adequate housing, infrastructure and services, managing development in high risk areas, etc.	
Structural/ Physical	Engineered options (sea walls, flood levees, shelters, etc.)	
	Technological options (new crop varieties and technologies, water-saving technologies, etc.)	
	Ecosystem-based options (ecological restoration, reforestation, etc.)	
	Services (social safety nets and social protection, essential public health systems, emergency medical services)	Adaptation
Institutional	Economic options (financial incentives, insurance, catastrophe bonds, etc.)	
	Laws and regulations (land zoning laws, building standards, defined property rights, etc.)	
	National policies and programmes (adaptation plans, economic diversification, disaster planning and preparedness, etc.)	
Social	Educational programmes (awareness raising, gender equity in education and others)	
	Informational options (hazard and vulnerability mapping, early warning and response systems, etc.)	Transformation
	Behavioural options (household preparation, education planning, migration, reliance on social networks)	
Spheres of change	Practice (social and technical innovations, behavioural shifts)	
	Politics (political, social, cultural and ecological decisions, sustainable development)	
	Personal beliefs, values and assumptions	

Table follows IPCC (2014, fig. SPM.1)

the lack of ability to understand such information. Finally, behavioural failures may arise, preventing individuals from actions and from risk preparation even in the presence of existing information exists (World Bank 2013).

Beyond the control of individuals, missing markets and the lack of public goods are important factors which hinder effective risk management instruments. Credit and insurance markets are often weakly developed in developing countries and particularly poor households have limited access to them. Similarly, the availability of public goods—such as political and economic stability, law and order, basic infrastructure—is not always guaranteed. Furthermore, government failures, social and economic externalities as well as deep uncertainty can be important obstacles to effective disaster risk management (World Bank 2013).

2.4 Conclusion

The following conclusion summarises key information and concepts presented in Chap. 2. Then the research question for the following empirical analysis will be specified.

2.4.1 Summary

The number of natural disasters has increased in the last half-century, with hydrological events such as floods as most common hazards. South and Southeast Asia are the regions most prone to hazards, mainly hydrological and meteorological events (storms, floods, landslides, etc.). During the last 45 years, 6.6 billion people worldwide were affected by natural disasters, while 3.2 million died. In the future, climate change is likely to increase extreme weather events, their frequency and intensity. The effects will be keenly felt due to changes in climate variability, resulting in more numerous floods and landslides with significantly higher numbers of people exposed and greater economic losses. Cambodia is hereby one of the most disaster-prone countries in East Asia with significant social and economic impacts due to frequent and severe floods and droughts (IPCC 2012; EM-DAT 2015; Hallegatte et al. 2016).

Natural disasters can lead to severe economic and social impacts with substantial costs in terms of human life, livelihoods and property as well as public infrastructure of various kinds. Furthermore, shocks cause significant long-term impacts to human, social and physical capital due to malnutrition, health issues and lower participation in education schemes. Thus, disasters have the potential to cause macroeconomic consequences, including impacts on fiscal revenues, investment rates and indebtedness. Most macroeconomic research focuses on economic growth. While most current research finds negative impacts of disasters on growth in the short-term, the long-term effects are highly ambiguous. Finally, disaster exposure has significant impacts on individual perceptions and decision-making processes as discussed in Chap. 3 (World Bank 2007, 2013; Kousky 2012; Chhibber and Laajaj 2013; Oviedo and Moroz 2014).

The previous chapter has also introduced the concepts of vulnerability, exposure and resilience and highlighted the importance of these in determining economic and social impacts. Various factors influence the vulnerability of a country, including interconnections within its economy, equality in society, importance of the agriculture sector and the quality of institutions. However, resilience particularly depends on the country's income and its level of development (World Bank 2007; Cavallo and Noy 2010; IPCC 2014).

The relationship between natural disasters and level of a country's development is highly complex. On the one hand, less developed economies are more vulnerable and exposed to natural disasters and their effects. Although the value of damages is often higher in developed countries, the damage relative to the size of the economy is usually larger for developing countries. The case remains similar on the household level where poor households tend to lose more in relative terms. On the other hand, natural disasters and their consequences impact the development of economies and households due to effects on human, social and physical capital. These effects have particular significance for poor households. There is also some evidence of a substantial ex ante impact of risk due to investments in low-risk, low return strategies that decrease vulnerability. Finally, the combination of frequent disasters and high vulnerability may lead to so-called poverty traps, where the experience of disasters increases vulnerability and harms development, contributing to a higher vulnerability to future events in return (Benson and Clay 2004; World Bank 2013; Oviedo and Moroz 2014; Hallegatte et al. 2016).

To deal with high risks such as natural disasters, both ex ante strategies to reduce risks as well as ex post strategies to cope with their consequences must be adopted. The process of development and implementation of such strategies has been discussed as disaster risk management.

2.4.2 Specification of Research Questions

The presentation of the three issues—natural hazards, impact and risk management—has been introduced briefly into the main research questions and developments within the area of natural disaster, development and risk management. However, the topic is extremely complex and cannot be analysed in its entirety within this study.

The following theoretical and empirical analysis concentrates on two specific connections within the framework of the risk chain presented above. Firstly, the impact of natural disasters on the individual's risk-taking propensity and level of trust, both variables of high importance for decision-making processes. Both factors are of particular interest for disaster risk management in developing countries due to the significant role of uncertainty and the reliance on social communities to build

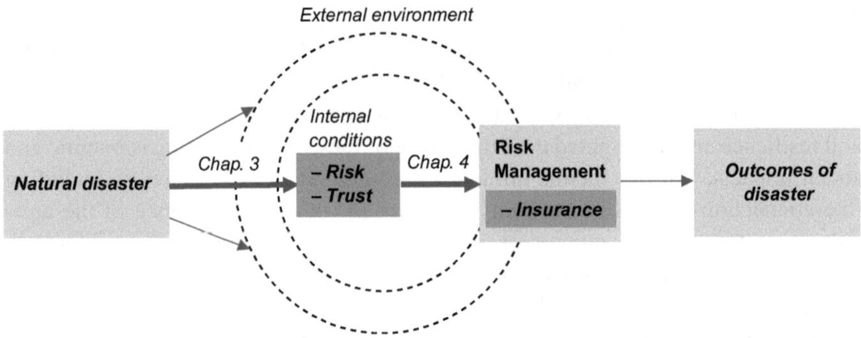

Fig. 2.13 Research questions within the risk chain framework. Illustration follows World Development Report 2014 (World Bank 2013). For greater clarity, the feedback *arrows* are omitted

resilience towards natural disasters. Chapter 3 presents the theoretical discussions as well as the empirical evidence regarding the impact of disaster experience on risk and trust in rural Cambodia.

Secondly, the impact of disaster experience as well as risk and trust on the demand for insurance products is analysed within this study. This is placed in the context of microinsurance, a promising disaster risk management instrument which has been emerged in recent years against natural hazards in developing countries. Although being an encouraging tool to protect vulnerable populations, the overall enrolment rates remain low. The related literature found several important determinants of microinsurance demand, including risk exposure, risk behaviour and trust. An extensive discussion of microinsurance, its various determinants as well as the results of an empirical investigation in rural Cambodia are presented in Chap. 4. Figure 2.13 illustrates the two main research questions in the context of the risk chain.

References

van Aalst MK (2006) The impacts of climate change on the risk of natural disasters. Disasters 30:5–18

ACAPS (2016) Disaster needs analysis: Cambodia—flooding. Glob Emerg Overv. http://geo.acaps.org/docs/438. Accessed 27 Jan 2016

Aghion P, Howitt PW (1998) Endogenous growth theory. MIT Press, Cambridge, MA

Albala-Bertrand JM (1993) Political economy of large natural disasters: with special reference to developing countries. Oxford University Press, Oxford

Alwang J, Siegel PB, Jørgensen SL, Tech V (2001) Vulnerability: a view from different disciplines. The World Bank Social Protection Discussion Paper Series 0115, Washington, DC

Awel YM, Azomahou TT (2014) Productivity and welfare effects of weather index insurance: quasi-experimental evidence. Maastricht

Bandyopadhyay S, Skoufias E (2015) Rainfall variability, occupational choice, and welfare in rural Bangladesh. Rev Econ Househ 13:589–634

Banerjee AV (2005) The two poverties. In: Dercon S (ed) Insurance against poverty. UNU-WIDER Studies in Development Economics/Oxford University Press, Oxford, pp 59–75
Banholzer S, Kossin J, Donner S (2014) Reducing disaster: early warning systems for climate change. Springer, Dordrecht
Benson C (2003) The economy-wide impact of natural disasters in developing countries. University of London, London
Benson C, Clay EJ (2004) Understanding the economic and financial impacts of natural disasters. The World Bank, Washington, DC
Botzen WJW, van den Bergh JCJM (2008) Insurance against climate change and flooding in the Netherlands: present, future, and comparison with other countries. Risk Anal 28:413–426
Bouwer LM (2013) Projections of future extreme weather losses under changes in climate and exposure. Risk Anal 33:915–930
Brata AG, Rietveld P, de Groot HLF et al (2014) Living with the Merapi Volcano: risks and disaster microinsurance. ANU Working Papers in Trade and Development 13, Canberra
Bräuninger M, Butzengeiger-Geyer S, Dlugolecki A et al (2011) Application of economic instruments for adaptation to climate change. HWWI, Hamburg
Brown O, Crawford A, Hammill A (2006) Natural disasters and resource rights: building resilience, rebuilding lives. International Institute for Sustainable Development, Winnipeg
Cameron L, Shah M (2015) Risk-taking behavior in the wake of natural disasters. Hum Resour 50:484–515
Carter MR, Little PD, Mogues T, Negatu W (2007) Poverty traps and natural disasters in Ethiopia and Honduras. World Dev 35:835–856
Carter M, De Janvry A, Sadoulet E, Sarris A (2014) Index-based weather insurance for developing countries: a review of evidence and a set of propositions for up-scaling. FERDI, AFD, Paris
Cavallo E, Noy I (2010) The economics of natural disasters—a survey. IDB Working Paper Series 124, Washington, DC
Cavallo E, Galiani S, Noy I, Pantano J (2010) Catastrophic natural disasters and economic growth. IDB Working Paper Series 183, Washington, DC
Chantarat S, Pannangpetch K, Puttanapong N et al (2013) Index-based risk financing and development of natural disaster insurance programs in developing Asian countries. ERIA Discussion Paper Series 9, Jakarta
Chhibber A, Laajaj R (2013) The interlinkages between natural disasters and economic development. In: Guha-Sapir D, Santos I (eds) The economic impacts of natural disasters. Oxford University Press, New York, pp 28–56
Clarke D, Reid R (2013) Disasters and their impact on poverty. In: Mitchell T, Jones L, Comba E, Lovell E (eds) Disaster risk management in post-2015 development goals. Overseas Development Institute, London, pp 33–40
Cohen M, Sebstad J (2005) Reducing vulnerability: the demand for microinsurance. J Int Dev 17:397–474. doi:10.1002/jid.1193
Cole S, Giné X, Tobacman J et al (2013) Barriers to household risk management: evidence from India. Am Econ J Appl Econ 5:104–135
Collier P (2005) The macroeconomic repercussions of agricultural shocks and their implications for insurance. In: Dercon S (ed) Insurance against poverty. UNU-WIDER Studies in Development Economics/Oxford University Press, Oxford, pp 137–154
Davis I (2015) The vulnerability challenge. In: Davis I (ed) Disaster risk management in Asia and the Pacific. Routledge, New York, pp 65–108
Dercon S (2005a) Risk, insurance, and poverty: a review. In: Dercon S (ed) Insurance against poverty. UNU-WIDER Studies in Development Economics/Oxford University Press, Oxford, pp 9–37
Dercon S (2005b) Overview. In: Dercon S (ed) Insurance against poverty. UNU-WIDER Studies in Development Economics/Oxford University Press, Oxford, pp 1–8

Dercon S (2006) Vulnerability: a micro perspective. In: Bourguignon F, Pleskovic B, van der Gaag J (eds) Securing development in an unstable world. World Bank Publications, Washington, DC, pp 117–145

Dercon S (2008) Fate and fear: risk and its consequences in Africa. J Afr Econ 17:97–127. doi:10.1093/jae/ejn019

Dercon S, Christiaensen L (2011) Consumption risk, technology adoption and poverty traps: evidence from Ethiopia. J Dev Econ 96:159–173

Eder W, Takara K, Wan F (2009) International cooperation initiatives. In: Sassa K, Canuti P (eds) Landslides—disaster risk reduction. Springer, Berlin, Heidelberg, pp 517–530

Elbers C, Gunning JW, Kinsey B (2007) Growth and risk: methodology and micro evidence. World Bank Econ Rev 21:1–20

EM-DAT (2015) The International Disaster Database. http://www.emdat.be/. Accessed 5 Jan 2015

Fafchamps M (2005) Inequality and risk. In: Dercon S (ed) Insurance against poverty. UNU-WIDER Studies in Development Economics/Oxford University Press, Oxford, pp 76–106

Foudi S, Oses-Eraso N (2014) Flood risk management. In: Markandya A, Galarraga I, de Murieta ES (eds) Routledge handbook of the economics of climate change adaptation. Routledge, London, pp 317–334

Francisco HA (2008) Adaptation to climate change—needs and opportunities in Southeast Asia. ASEAN Econ Bull 25:7–19

Freeman PK, Keen M, Mani M (2003) Dealing with increased risk of natural disasters—challenges and options. IMF Working Paper WP/03/197, Washington, DC

Gehrke E (2014) The insurability framework applied to agricultural microinsurance: what do we know, what can we learn? Geneva Pap Risk Insur Issues Pract 39:264–279

General Directorate of Agriculture (2013) Plan of action for disaster risk reduction in agriculture 2014-2018. Kingdom of Cambodia, Ministry of Agriculture, Forestry, and Fisheries, Phnom Penh

Ghesquiere F, Mahul O (2007) Sovereign natural disaster insurance for developing countries: a paradigm shift in catastrophe risk financing. The World Bank Policy Research Working Paper 4345, Washington, DC

Gollier C, Pratt JW (1996) Risk vulnerability and the tempering effect of background risk. Econometrica 64:1109–1123

Guha-Sapir D, Hoyois P (2015) Trends and patterns in disasters and their impact in the Asia-Pacific members of the Asian Development Bank. In: Davis I (ed) Disaster risk management in Asia and the Pacific. Routledge, New York, pp 35–64

Guha-Sapir D, D'Aoust O, Vos F, Hoyois P (2013) The frequency and impact of natural disasters. In: Guha-Sapir D, Santos I (eds) The economic impacts of natural disasters. Oxford University Press, New York, pp 7–27

Gurenko E (2004) Introduction. In: Gurenko E (ed) Catastrophe risk and reinsurance: a country risk management perspective. Risk Books, London, pp 3–16

Haigh R, Amaratunga D (2010) An integrative review of the built environment discipline's role in the development of society's resilience to disasters. Int J Disaster Resil Built Environ 1:11–24

Hallegatte S (2012) An exploration of the link between development, economic growth, and natural risk. The World Bank Policy Research Working Paper 6216, Washington, DC

Hallegatte S (2013) Challenges ahead: risk management and cost-benefit analysis in a changing climate. In: Guha-Sapir D, Santos I (eds) The economic impacts of natural disasters. Oxford University Press, New York, pp 107–127

Hallegatte S, Bangalore M, Bonzanigo L et al (2016) Shock waves: managing the impacts of climate change on poverty. The World Bank, Washington, DC

Hazell P, Anderson J, Balzer N et al (2010) The potential for scale and sustainability in weather Index Insurance for agriculture and rural livelihoods. World Food Programme, Rome

Heltberg R, Oviedo AM, Talukdar F (2015) What do household surveys really tell us about risk, shocks, and risk management in the developing world? J Dev Stud 51:209–225

Hochrainer S (2009) Assessing the macroeconomic impacts of natural disasters: are there any? The World Bank Policy Research Working Paper 4968, Washington, DC

IPCC (2012) Managing the risks of extreme events and disasters to advance climate change adaptation. In: A special report of working groups I and II of the Intergovernmental Panel on Climate Change. Cambridge University Press, Cambridge, New York

IPCC (2014) Climate change 2014: impacts, adaptation, and vulnerability. Part A: global and sectoral aspects. In: Contribution of working group II to the fifth assessment report of the Intergovernmental Panel on Climate Change. Cambridge University Press, Cambridge, New York

Jacobsen G (2009) Health and death risk and income decisions: evidence from microfinance. J Dev Stud 45:934–946

Jaramillo CR (2009) Do natural disasters have long-term effects on growth? Universidad de los Andes, Documentos CEDE 24, Bogotá

Kahn ME (2005) The death toll from natural disasters: the role of income, geography, and institutions. Rev Econ Stat 87:271–284

Karim A, Noy I (2016) Poverty and natural disasters – a qualitative survey of the empirical literature. Singapore Econ Rev 61:1640001

Kellenberg DK, Mobarak AM (2008) Does rising income increase or decrease damage risk from natural disasters? J Urban Econ 63:788–802

Kousky C (2012) Informing climate adaptation: a review of the economic costs of natural disasters, their determinants, and risk reduction options. Resources for the Future Discussion Paper 12-28, Washington, DC

Kreimer A, Arnold M (2000) Managing disaster risk in emerging economies. The World Bank, Washington, DC

Krishna A (2006) Pathways out of and into poverty in 36 villages of Andhra Pradesh, India. World Dev 34:271–288

Kull D, Mechler R, Hochrainer-Stigler S (2013) Probabilistic cost-benefit analysis of disaster risk management in a development context. Disasters 37:374–400

Linnerooth-Bayer J, Hochrainer-Stigler S (2015) Financial instruments for disaster risk management and climate change adaptation. Clim Change 133:85–100

Linnerooth-Bayer J, Mechler R, Hochrainer-Stigler S (2011) Insurance against losses from natural disasters in developing countries. Evidence, gaps and the way forward. J Integr Disaster Risk Manag 1:59–81

Mechler R, Islam KMN (2013) Cost-benefit analysis of disaster risk management and climate adaptation: the case of Bangladesh. In: Guha-Sapir D, Santos I (eds) The economic impacts of natural disasters. Oxford University Press, New York, pp 80–106

Mitchell T, Mechler R, Peters K (2014) Disaster risk management and adaptation to extreme events. In: Markandya A, Galarraga I, de Murieta ES (eds) Routledge Handbook of the economics of climate change adaptation. Routledge, London, pp 417–436

Miththapala S (2008) Integrating environmental safeguards into disaster management: a field manual. International Union for Conservation of Nature and Natural Resources, Colombo

Mobarak AM, Rosenzweig M (2012) Selling formal insurance to the informally insured. Economic Growth Center Discussion Paper 1007, New Haven

Mochizuki J, Vitoontus S, Wickramarachchi B et al (2015) Operationalizing iterative risk management under limited information: fiscal and economic risks due to natural disasters in Cambodia. Int J Disaster Risk Sci 6:321–334

Mosley P (2009) Assessing the success of microinsurance programmes in meeting the insurance needs of the poor. UN/DESA Working Paper 84, New York

de Muirieta ES, Markandya I, Galarraga A (2014) Introduction to the economics of adaptation to climate change. In: Markandya A, Galarraga I, de Murieta ES (eds) Routledge handbook of the economics of climate change adaptation. Routledge, London, pp 3–26

Munich Re (2013) Economic consequences of natural catastrophes: emerging and developing economies particularly affected—insurance cover is essential. Munich Re Economic Research Position Paper, Munich

National Committee for Disaster Management (2008) Strategic national action plan for disaster risk reduction 2008-2013. Kingdom of Cambodia, Ministry of Planning, Phnom Penh

National Committee for Disaster Management (2016) Disaster Loss Database (CamDi). http://camdi.ncdm.gov.kh/. Accessed 27 Jan 2016

Navrud S, Magnussen K (2013) Valuing the impacts of natural disasters and the economic benefits of preventing them. In: Guha-Sapir D, Santos I (eds) The economic impacts of natural disasters. Oxford University Press, New York, pp 57–79

Neumayer E, Barthel F (2011) Normalizing economic loss from natural disasters: a global analysis. Glob Environ Chang 21:13–24

Nguyen H, Prabhakar SVRK, Shaw R (2009) Adaptive drought risk reduction in Cambodia: reality, perceptions and strategies. Environ Hazards 8:245–262

Noy I (2009) The macroeconomic consequences of disasters. J Dev Econ 88:221–231

Noy I, Tam BV (2010) The economics of natural disasters in a developing country: the case of Vietnam. J Asian Econ 21:345–354

Open Development (2016) Open development mapping kit. http://www.opendevelopmentcambodia.net/maps/. Accessed 29 Apr 2016

Otero RC, Martí RZ (1995) The impacts of natural disasters on developing economies: implications for the international development and disaster community. In: Munasinghe M, Clarke C (eds) Disaster prevention for sustainable development: economic and policy issues. World Bank, Yokohama

Oviedo AM, Moroz H (2014) A review of the ex post and ex ante impacts of risk. The World Bank, Background Paper for the World Development Report 2014, Washington, DC

PreventionWeb (2016) Cambodia—disaster & risk profile. http://www.preventionweb.net/countries/khm/data/. Accessed 27 Jan 2016

Raddatz C (2007) Are external shocks responsible for the instability of output in low-income countries? J Dev Econ 84:155–187

Ranger N, Surminski S (2013) Disasters and their economic impacts. In: Mitchell T, Jones L, Comba E, Lovell E (eds) Disaster risk management in post-2015 development goals. Overseas Development Institute, London, pp 7–24

Raschky PA (2008) Institutions and the losses from natural disasters. Nat Hazards Earth Syst Sci 8:627–634

Sadoulet L (2005) Learning from visa? Incoporating insurance provision in microfinance contracts. In: Dercon S (ed) Insurance against poverty. UNU-WIDER Studies in Development Economics/Oxford University Press, Oxford, pp 387–421

Said F, Afzal U, Turner G (2015) Risk taking and risk learning after a rare event: evidence from a field experiment in Pakistan. J Econ Behav Organ 118:167–183

Schumacher I, Strobl E (2011) Economic development and losses due to natural disasters: the role of hazard exposure. Ecol Econ 72:97–105

Sen B (2003) Drivers of escape and descent: changing household fortunes in rural Bangladesh. World Dev 31:513–534

Sharma A (2015) The social and economic challenge. In: Davis I (ed) Disaster risk management in Asia and the Pacific. Routledge, New York, pp 109–134

Skees JR (2008) Innovations in Index Insurance for the poor in lower income countries. Agric Resour Econ Rev 1:1–15

Skidmore M, Toya H (2002) Do natural disasters promote long-run growth? Econ Inq 40:664–687

Standard & Poor's (2014) Climate change is a global mega-trend for sovereign risk. Glob Credit Portal. https://www.globalcreditportal.com/ratingsdirect/renderArticle.do?articleId=1318252&SctArtId=236925&from=CM&nsl_code=LIME&sourceObjectId=8606813&sourceRevId=1&fee_ind=N&exp_date=20240514-20:34:43. Accessed 28 Jan 2016

Surminski S (2012) Climate change and extreme weather events in developing countries. In: Future risk: climate change and energy security—global challenges and implications. Chartered Insurance Institute, London, pp 23–30

The Royal Society (2014) Resilience to extreme weather. The Royal Society, London

Thomalla F, Downing T, Spanger-Siegfried E et al (2006) Reducing hazard vulnerability: towards a common approach between disaster risk reduction and climate adaptation. Disasters 30:39–48

Toya H, Skidmore M (2005) Economic development and the impacts of natural disasters. University of Wisconsin Working Paper 05-04, Whitewater

Toya H, Skidmore M (2012) Do natural disasters enhance societal trust? CESifo Working Paper 3905, Munich

UNDP (2011) Reducing disaster risk—a challenge for development. United Nations Development Programme, New York

UNISDR (2009) Terminology on DRR. http://www.unisdr.org/we/inform/terminology. Accessed 14 Jan 2015

United Nations, World Bank (2010) Natural hazards, unnatural disasters—the economics of effective prevention. United Nations, World Bank, New York, Washington, DC

Vathana S, Oum S, Kan P, Chervier C (2013) Impact of disasters and role of social protection in natural disaster risk management in Cambodia. ERIA Discussion Paper 2013-10, Jakarta

Wahlstrom M (2013) Foreword. In: Guha-Sapir D, Santos I (eds) The economic impacts of natural disasters. Oxford University Press, New York, pp vii–viii

Weitzman ML (2009) On modelling and interpretating the economics of catastropic climate change. Rev Econ Stat 91:1–19

Winsemius HC, Jongman B, Veldkamp TIE et al (2015) Disaster risk, climate change, and poverty: assessing the global exposure of poor people to floods and droughts. The World Bank Policy Research Working Paper 7480, Washington, DC

World Bank (2006) Hazards of nature, risks to development—an IEG evaluation of World Bank assistance for natural disasters. World Bank, Washington, DC

World Bank (2007) Disasters, climate change, and economic development in sub-Saharan Africa—lessons and future directions. World Bank, Washington, DC

World Bank (2013) World development report 2014: risk and opportunity—managing risk for development. World Bank, Washington, DC

World Bank (2016a) Disaster risk management—Cambodia. Disaster Risk Manag East Asia Pacific. http://go.worldbank.org/SYXPJ6M450. Accessed 27 Jan 2016

World Bank (2016b) Climate change knowledge portal (country adaptation profile)—Cambodia. http://sdwebx.worldbank.org/climateportal/index.cfm?page=country_historical_climate&ThisRegion=Asia&ThisCCode=KHM. Accessed 27 Feb 2016

World Bank, United Nations Office for Disaster Risk Reduction, National Hydrological and Meteorological Services et al (2013) Country assessment report for Cambodia—strengthening of hydrometeorological services in Southeast Asia. World Bank, Washington, DC

Yamamura E (2011) Institution, economic development, and impact of natural disasters. MPRA Paper 32069, Munich

Chapter 3
Experiencing Natural Disasters: How This Influences Risk Aversion and Trust

As demonstrated in the previous chapter, natural disasters have enormous economic and social impacts, leading to substantial costs in human life, property, infrastructure and others, with significant and serious long-term effects on social and human capital. In addition, natural disasters are traumatic events and it is therefore a reasonable assumption that the experience or observation of such an event and its post-disaster circumstances also have significant implications on individual behaviour and on social norms within a community. This impact and its influence on decision-making processes are of importance for this analysis. Although several dimensions are possible, the following theoretical and empirical research concentrates on the individual's risk propensity as well as levels of trust and trustworthiness.

Both risk-taking propensity and levels of trust are important factors in economic decision-making processes. Therefore natural disasters and their consequences (negative shock to wealth and income, increase in perceived likelihood of future events, strong emotions evoked by disasters, experience of help within communities) do not only create structural damage, but also affect risk behaviour, trust and trustworthiness and their impacts on investments in productive activities and social trust within communities (Cassar et al. 2012; Fleming et al. 2014). Additionally, in order to build resilience towards natural disasters, both risk and trust are of interest for disaster risk management in general and for the demand for microinsurance in particular, due to the significant role of uncertainty and the reliance on social communities.

Section 3.1 provides definition and highlights the importance of individual behaviour in economic decisions. Section 3.2 presents the theoretical background and existing empirical results in the literature which builds the foundation for the development of the research hypotheses. In Sect. 3.3, a detailed description of the underlying experiment and questionnaire, its methodology and the study area are presented. Sections 3.4 and 3.5 exhibit the results of the empirical research regarding risk and trust respectively and show statistical evidence for the proposed hypotheses.

O. Fiala, *Natural Disasters and Individual Behaviour in Developing Countries*, Contributions to Economics, DOI 10.1007/978-3-319-53904-1_3

3.1 Risk and Trust

The following section provides for both risk and trust definitions and highlights the relevance of this individual behaviour for economic development. Additionally, the interaction of risk and trust is described in a conceptual framework.

3.1.1 Risk

Definition

'Risk' as a term is variously used in literature of multiple fields, including economics, sociology, psychology, management and finance (Ahsan 2014). Sitkin and Pablo (1992) define risk as a characteristic, which determines the extent of uncertainty about the possible outcomes which will be realised. The risk-taking propensity is described as a personal characteristic measuring an individual's willingness to take risks (Das and Teng 2004).

Although often interpreted in a negative way (MacCrimmon et al. 1988; Rousseau et al. 1998; World Bank 2013), risk has both positive and negative dimensions (March and Shapira 1987; Ahsan 2014). Risk is defined as "reflecting the variation in the distribution of possible outcomes, their likelihoods, and their subjective values" (March and Shapira 1987). Risk is therefore a situation in which the possibility of various outcomes should be expected.

Following MacCrimmon et al. (1988), risky situations are characterised by lack of control, information and time. If the individual could control the situation completely, have full access to information and unlimited time to decide, the best alternative would be chosen, or the individual could wait until the uncertainty disappears (MacCrimmon et al. 1988).

The Relevance of Risk Behaviour for Economic Development

Individual risk attitudes significantly impact economic behaviour (Ingwersen 2014). Specifically, this includes decisions about investment in productive activities, e.g. education, entrepreneurship, agricultural technologies or migration (Said et al. 2014). Thereby a link between risk-taking propensity and higher investment in physical and human capital as well as wage growth is evident (Levhari and Weiss 1974; Shaw 1996; Dang 2012; Hallegatte 2012).

Also Cameron and Shah (2015) highlight the correlation with 'real life' risk-taking decisions such as opening a new business or changing jobs. These impacts are clearly significant for economic development.

In the context of natural disasters, risk is a decisive factor for both the exposure and vulnerability of households (see Chap. Chap. 2). Firstly, risk-taking behaviour may explain more exposed location decisions found in developing countries. Kellenberg and Mobarak (2008) argue that people with a low income may be willing to take on more risk, if it comes as a necessary by-product of higher income-generating activities. Therefore, a poor household may migrate into an area with higher disaster exposure in order to find better employment opportunities (Kellenberg and Mobarak 2008; Cavallo and Noy 2010).

Secondly, the risk of natural disaster—either the experience or the pure risk of it—is likely to impact production strategies as well as investments in disaster preparation with impacts on poverty and development processes. The effect of production strategies is discussed in detail in Chap. 2 as an ex ante impact of natural disaster: the anticipation of future shocks may lead to low-risk, low-return strategies, which in return increases vulnerability to future shocks. Such investment decisions have significant impacts on the development process and may be connected to investments in disaster preparation (World Bank 2013; Hallegatte et al. 2016; Karim and Noy 2016).

3.1.2 Trust and Trustworthiness

Definition

Trust can be defined as the subjective probability of one agent that another agent or group will perform a beneficial action (Gambetta 1988; Schechter 2007). It is therefore dependent on personal characteristics, which animate expectation of positive actions of another individual towards oneself (Butler and Cantrell 1984; Lewicki et al. 1998; McKnight et al. 1998; Ahsan 2014). Rousseau et al. (1998) discuss the different definitions in economics, psychology and sociology and discuss trust in a wider framework. From a broader view, trust is seen as an important component of social capital, amongst others, and can be used as a proxy for such (Toya and Skidmore 2012; Fleming et al. 2014). Trustworthiness or reciprocity are the fulfilment of expectations that somebody else has of an individual (Fleming et al. 2014).

Das and Teng (2004) distinguish different trust components: trust propensity (characteristics that make a person both ‘trusting’ and ‘trustworthy’); subjective trust (trust perception, referring to the individual’s experience of a psychological state); and behavioural trust (realising actions result from subjective trust). Hereby, subjective trust can be understood as “a belief, attitude, or expectation concerning the likelihood that the actions or outcomes of another individual, group or organization will be acceptable or will serve the actor’s interests” (Sitkin and Roth 1993). Both community characteristics and individual experiences impact people’s level of trust (Alesina and La Ferrara 2002).

The Relevance of Trust for Economic Development

Trust is important for economic transactions in many respects. Most transactions contain an element of trust and therefore trust has an impact on economic success and growth (Ahsan 2014). Trust leads to less conflict between individuals and therefore increases economic activity (Fleming et al. 2014).

Communities with a high level of trust and trustworthiness (reciprocity) are more productive due to the stock of norms, which substitutes formal institutions and helps to complete contracts (Cardenas and Carpenter 2008). Zak and Knack (2001) show in a general equilibrium growth model that high-trust societies have higher rates of investment and growth. Knack and Keefer (1997) also show a positive correlation between interpersonal trust and economic growth, while Narayan and Pritchett (1999) find increasing village incomes in rural Tanzania due to trust and social capital. Societies with higher levels of trust beyond families ties have reached higher levels of economic development and trust is also a determinant for better-functioning organisations (Fukuyama 1995).

Furthermore, positive relationships between trust and factor productivity (Bjørnskov and Méon 2010) as well as between trust and both education and quality of institutions (Bjørnskov and Méon 2013) have been found. Toya and Skidmore (2012) say that trust is highly correlated with other measures of social capital and is an important determinant of corruption and violent crime. Similar to the importance of trust, trustworthiness and reciprocity are also relevant for the welfare of communities (Karlan 2005; Fleming et al. 2014).

In the context of natural disasters, individuals' levels of trust play a crucial role for the stability and effectiveness of informal community-based risk-sharing instruments. They are also an important factor in decision-making processes towards formal insurance instruments, given a context of low financial literacy and the limited enforcement of legal rights (De Bock and Gelade 2012; Cole et al. 2013; World Bank 2013; Clarke and Grenham 2013). A further discussion of the role of trust for decisions regarding informal and formal insurance is provided in Chap. 4.

A natural disaster may create not only physical and direct economic losses: interactions with other members of the community in the aftermath of a disaster can foster trust and trustworthiness (positive social interactions, receiving support, and others) or decrease them (rivalry for limited recourses, disaster-related migration, etc.), as discussed in more detail in Sect. 3.2.2 (Cassar et al. 2012; Fleming et al. 2014). However, changing levels of trust and trustworthiness can create additional indirect economic losses (Fleming et al. 2014). Social capital is also a crucial factor after disasters due to its contribution to the creation of local safety nets, its reinforcement of institutions and its support of the effectiveness of socio-economic recovery programmes in the long term (Fleming et al. 2014).

3.1.3 Interactions Between Risk and Trust

Although different concepts, risk and trust interact with each other. Trust can be seen as an expectation about the behaviour of another agent, where the action of a trustor is risky (Sheppard and Sherman 1998; James 2002). Trust as a future expectation therefore implicitly includes a risky element, even if not explicitly mentioned (Das and Teng 2004).

As described above, trust has three dimensions, while the focus here will be on subjective trust. Hereby, subjective trust consists of two components: observable choice behaviour on the one hand and a personal state which is subject to the manifest choice behaviour on the other (Kee and Knox 1970). Therefore, subjective trust can be interpreted as one's probability of another person's expected behaviour (Das and Teng 2004).

In a risk-based view of trust, an individual's subjective trust is inversely related to perceived risk (Das and Teng 2004). Given this conceptual framework, the connection between the risk perception and risk-taking must be considered in the design of the experiment (Sect. 3.3) as well as in the interpretation of measured risk-taking and levels of trust (Sects. 3.4 and 3.5).

3.2 The Impact of Natural Disasters on Individual Behaviour

Cassar et al. (2012) mention several channels through which disastrous events could affect individual ex post behaviour: a large negative shock to wealth and income; the potential increase in the perceived likelihood of other negative events in the future; the strong emotions evoked by disasters could impact the cognitive process of decision-making; people may receive help from other members of their community, governments, international organisations, etc. and may provide help to others. These experiences have the possibility to affect an individual's attitudes and behaviours after the experience of a disaster.

Only a small amount of economic research has investigated these questions at the household level, however there is no consensus as to whether and how natural disasters affects individuals' behaviour. Hereby studies have investigated the impact of a variety of events, including floods (Nguyen et al. 2012; Page et al. 2014; Ahsan 2014; Cameron and Shah 2015; Said et al. 2015), tsunamis (Cassar et al. 2012; Ingwersen 2014), hurricanes (Eckel et al. 2009; Castillo and Carter 2011) and earthquakes (Li et al. 2011; Fleming et al. 2014). As far as is known, only Ahsan (2014) and Cassar et al. (2012) have a comprehensive view of risk behaviour and trust in the context of natural disasters; the other research investigates only either risk or trust.

The following section presents both the theoretical background and the empirical evidence for the impact of disaster exposure on risk behaviour, trust and trustworthiness. The literature review is the basis both for the design of the experiment (Sect. 3.3) and for the interpretation of the empirical findings on risk and trust in rural Cambodia (Sects. 3.4 and 3.5).

3.2.1 The Impact of Disaster Exposure on Risk Behaviour

Theoretical Background

Different channels can be described through which an experience of a natural disaster could affect an individual's risk-taking propensity (Cassar et al. 2012; Dang 2012). The segregation of the different effects can be challenging due to their partial interaction. In the following section, four effects will be distinguished:

- Income effect: Due to disasters, large negative shocks on income and wealth occur, which may change risk-taking behaviour.
- Update of information: In a world of limited information, disasters are likely to provide new information about the frequency and impact of natural disasters. Therefore, the experience of such an event can be interpreted as an update of information, which will affect the risk-taking propensity of an individual.
- Perception of risks: Psychological factors play an important role in how individuals perceive risk, whereby the perceived risk does not necessarily have to be aligned with the actual risk. The experience of natural disaster may change the perception of risk and therefore has impacts on risk-taking behaviour.
- Emotions: Psychological literature shows that emotions play an important role in individual decision-making. Disasters create fears and worries and could lead to emotional responses, with an associated impact on the individual's risk behaviour.

Whilst the classical economic theory assumes that individual preferences are fixed and only constraints are changing (knowledge of potential outcomes and respective probabilities), there is a large psychological and behavioural literature investigating behavioural learning and the dynamic nature of risk preferences. Personal experiences impact risk preferences; particularly emotions—as a result of exogenous factors or previous decisions—but the cultural and political environments also play a role. Furthermore, individuals may prefer simple behavioural rules to complicated rational decision-making processes, and do not make decisions in isolation but in groups (van den Berg et al. 2009; Malmendier and Nagel 2011; Dang 2012; World Bank 2013; Dillenberger and Rozen 2015; Said et al. 2015).

Nguyen et al. (2012) highlight that decision-making under risk involves a different mechanism. On the one hand, there is a cognitive approach, which involves the possibilities and possible outcomes of an event. On the other hand, emotions are an important part of decision-making and allow for a faster, more automatic and intuitive decision (Nguyen et al. 2012). In the following section, both expected utility theory and prospect theory will be introduced as theoretical frameworks. Hereafter, the various effects of disasters on individual risk behaviour introduced above (income effect, update of information, perception of risks, emotions) will be outlined and linked to explaining theories.

Expected Utility Theory Much focus in theoretical and empirical research has been on the expected utility theory when investigating decisions under risk and uncertainty. The theory is based on the individual attempt to maximise expected utility when making choices between various risky options, whereby the utilities of the individual outcomes are weighted by their probability. An individual's attitude towards risk is implicitly defined by the shape of the utility function. While the risk-seeking or risk-neutral behaviour of an individual is represented by a convex or linear expected utility function respectively, a risk-averse individual faces a concave function (as shown in Fig. 3.1). Although the theory is an attractive normative model of rational choice, its prediction has often been shown to be inconsistent with observed behaviour (Kahneman and Tversky 1979; Schoemaker 1982; Levy 1992; Tamura 2005).

Prospect Theory Kahneman and Tversky (1979) have laid the foundation for the prospect theory as an alternative model to explain empirical anomalies in the expected utility theory. The theory was developed further by Tversky and Kahneman (1992) and Schmidt et al. (2008). Prospect theory is based on five main ideas: reference dependency, declining sensitivity, loss aversion, non-linear weighting of probabilities, and framing effects.

Rather than assessing wealth absolutely, individuals think in terms of gains and losses of wealth in relation to a reference point. A significant result of the prospect theory is the observation that individuals treat gains differently to losses, with a tendency to show risk-averse behaviour with respect to gains and risk-seeking behaviour with respect to losses. Therefore, the utility function is concave in the domain of gains and convex in the domain of losses (declining sensitivity). Furthermore, it is observed that individuals value a loss of a certain amount higher than a gain of the same amount (losses loom larger than gains), described as loss aversion. Moreover, individuals value each outcome in an uncertain situation by

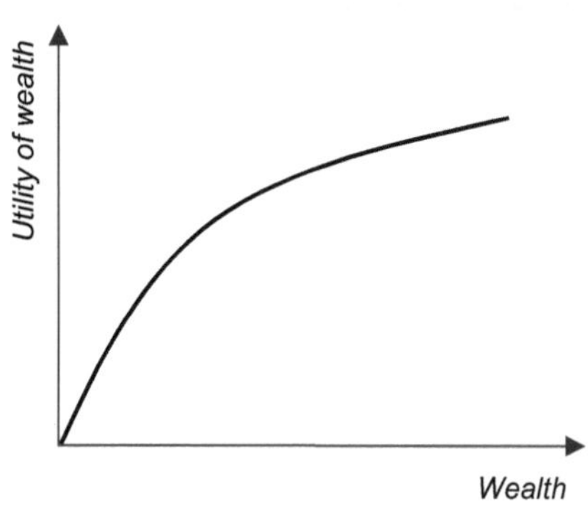

Fig. 3.1 Expected utility function (risk-averse individual)

a decision weight, whereby they overweight small probabilities and underweight large ones. Finally, the way a problem is framed plays a crucial role due to the significance of the reference point. Therefore a value function is defined, which is: deviating from the reference point, in general concave for gains and convex for losses, and steeper for losses than for gains (see Fig. 3.2) (Kahneman and Tversky 1979; Levy 1992; Dhami and Al-Nowaihi 2007).

The prospect theory distinguishes two phases of decision-making. In the first, the editing phase, a preliminary analysis of the choice problem is conducted, which includes the identification of available options, possible outcomes, and the values and probabilities associated with these outcomes (Kahneman and Tversky 1979). This includes the determination of the reference point, to which gains and losses are relative. While the reference point is often associated with the status quo (the current asset position), this does not necessarily have to be the case (Kahneman and Tversky 1979; Levy 1992). Possible reference points include positions an individual had expected to obtain, whereby a discrepancy between this point and the actual asset positions may arise from recent changes (Kahneman and Tversky 1979). The specification of a suitable reference point is therefore essential for a successful application of the prospect theory (Dhami and Al-Nowaihi 2007). In the second, the evaluation phase, the prospects are evaluated and the preferred prospect is selected (Kahneman and Tversky 1979; Levy 1992).

Income Effect One way that natural disasters affect the risk-taking propensities of individuals is through their effect on income and wealth, by destroying physical property and reducing future opportunities for earning income (Cameron and Shah 2015). Traumatic events such as disasters also change the production function of households in a structural way (Nguyen et al. 2012).

In the expected utility theory, the effect of changes of wealth on risk behaviour depends on the specific form of the utility function. For concave utility functions, the changing of risk aversion with wealth can be analysed using the Arrow-Pratt measure of risk aversion (Pratt 1964). Studies investigating the effect of natural disaster on risk aversion empirically (see below) assume utility functions with

Fig. 3.2 Value function in the prospect theory

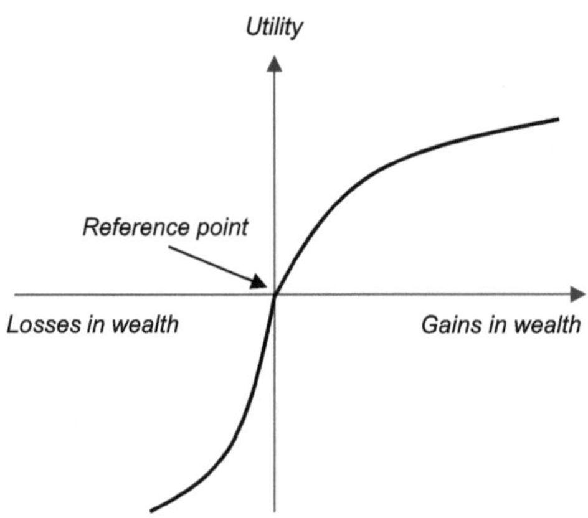

constant relative risk aversion (CRRA). In this case, a decrease in wealth through an external shock will increase absolute risk aversion. The basic model of expected utility theory also assumes that assets are fully replicable. However, a disaster might affect personal health or other state-dependent assets, and the ex post risk utility function therefore has a lower level for a given level of wealth (Zweifel and Eisen 2012).

In order to apply the prospect theory to the relationship between losses in wealth and change in risk behaviour, the determination of a reference point is significant. However, the reference point is subjective and also depends on expectation and aspiration levels, which can differ from the actual status quo (Kahneman and Tversky 1979). Furthermore, this includes cases when the individual experienced a recent change in wealth—for instance due to a natural disaster—and has not yet adapted to it (Kahneman and Tversky 1979). In this case, when assessing the ex post risk behaviour, gains and losses are determined relative to the ex ante reference point (status quo before the disaster). Therefore, the prospect theory predicts risk-seeking behaviour following losses and risk-averse behaviour after gains (Kahneman and Tversky 1979; Page et al. 2014).[1]

Furthermore, economic losses due to disasters could also be reduced by receiving gifts or aid from other members of the community, governments or non-governmental organisations. Cameron and Shah (2015) find that remittances mitigate the negative effect of floods on risk-taking.

Update of Information Given perfect information, individuals would have accurate expectations about the probability and damage of a natural disaster (Cameron and Shah 2015). However, individuals are facing a world with limited information, where their expectation about the likelihood of a disaster may not be adequate. Therefore a shock provides new information about the risk faced by the individual household (Nguyen et al. 2012; Cameron and Shah 2015). As a consequence, a rational agent is able to adjust individual risk perceptions as well as mitigation and adaptation plans for natural disaster (Said et al. 2015).

Furthermore, the literature discusses different heuristics, which individuals use given imperfect information, to determine the individual risk. Hereby the 'availability' heuristic, the 'representativeness' heuristic and the 'conservatism' heuristic should be mentioned. In the first, individuals assess the frequency and probability of an event on the basis of prominent information. In the second heuristic, individuals assess the likelihood of an event based on corresponding parameters compared to a sample event. The third 'conservatism' heuristic causes individuals to underestimate high values. For all three heuristics, the experience of a disaster updates the

[1] Compatible with the prospect theory, Li et al. (2011) also show highly domain-specific behaviour of people's degree of risk-taking. In addition, the so-called 'disposition effect' from finance literature aligns with prospect theory, which investigates risk behaviour after a change in wealth and indicates the risk-seeking behaviour of shareholders after price drops (Page et al. 2014). In contrast, Gheyssens and Günther (2011) investigate risk behaviour in the negative domain in a field experiment and found a strong deviation towards risk aversion.

personal information and leads to a reassessment of risk, which impacts both expected utility and prospect theory. Furthermore, heuristics are an important part in the edition phase of the prospect theory (Tversky and Kahneman 1974; Asgary and Levy 2009; Eiser et al. 2012; Turner et al. 2014; Said et al. 2015).

Perception of Risk Psychological factors might play an important role in the determination of risk choices, especially how individuals perceive risk (Said et al. 2014). The experience of natural disaster might change the perception of risk and therefore has impacts on economic activities (Ingwersen 2014). Botzen et al. (2009) show that in flood-prone areas in the Netherlands, risk perceptions of households differ from the actual risk and play an important role in undertaking mitigation.

The experience or observation of disaster can change the perception of risks and therefore impact the risk-taking propensity of individuals (Reynaud et al. 2013; Ingwersen 2014; Page et al. 2014; Cameron and Shah 2015). As described in the section above, this process can also be interpreted as an update of information about the specific disaster risk or background risk (Nguyen et al. 2012; Cameron and Shah 2015).

Psychological studies have found that people have the tendency to underestimate the probability of an event when this event has recently occurred, a phenomenon called 'Gambler's Fallacy' (Tversky and Kahneman 1974; Ayton and Fischer 2004; Page et al. 2014). In contrast to this, studies have shown that after such an event, people report unrealistically high probabilities that another event will happen again soon, an effect known as 'hot hand' (Gilovich et al. 1985; Ayton and Fischer 2004; Cameron and Shah 2015). Li et al. (2011) show that households in China which have been affected by natural disasters tend to overweigh small probabilities after the disaster. However, the impact of a natural disaster on risk behaviour might change during the years after the disaster, with changing expectations in the short term but a shading effect in the long term (Eckel et al. 2009; Cameron and Shah 2015).

Personal beliefs or perceptions of risk can be implemented in both expected utility and prospect theory models. For the former, subjective expected utility models allow probabilities to be subjective (Savage 1954; Fischhoff et al. 1983). For the prospect theory, the decision weights measuring the impact of events on the desirability of prospects and are often interpreted as perceived probabilities (Kahneman and Tversky 1979; Tversky and Kahneman 1992; Hallegatte 2012).

Emotions Apart from the economically cognitive approach of utility maximisation, emotions and their more intuitive and automatic aspects of individual decision-making play an important role (Loewenstein et al. 2001; Nguyen et al. 2012; Said et al. 2014; Hanaoka et al. 2015). Loewenstein et al. (2001) draft the risk-as-feelings hypothesis, which observes the reactions of people toward the prospect of risk at two levels: a cognitive evaluation (sensitive to probabilities and outcomes) and an emotional reaction (sensitive to associated imagery, proximity in time, etc.). Although emotions respond to a cognitive analysis, they are more intuitive, faster, automatic and not so open to conscious awareness (Nguyen et al. 2012). Therefore, the risk behaviour of individuals may differ from the rational utility maximisation approach due to the role of emotions, and post-trauma, individuals might place greater emphasis, both positive and negative, on emotions (Said et al. 2014). Eckel et al. (2009) found an increase in risk-loving behaviour after a natural disaster and explain this through a greater importance of emotions immediately after the event; risk-loving behaviour is therefore seen as an instrument to escape the situation of poverty. These findings are in contrast to the expected outcome under the utility theory and may occur, depending on the way in which cognitive and emotional systems are involved in decision-making (Nguyen et al. 2012).

Eckel et al. (2009) note that risk preferences might generally be driven by psychological attitudes and mention stress and post-traumatic experiences as determinants for risk behaviour through their effect on the psychological state of the individual. Therefore persons under extreme stress might be less likely to analyse the prospects in a cognitive way and instead use simple emotional rules. Pat-Horenczyk et al. (2007) found for individuals exposed to terrorism in Israel that risk-taking behaviour is associated with post-traumatic stress. These findings would suggest that disaster-affected individuals show a higher risk-taking propensity than unaffected households. In contrast, anxiety and fear are found to lead to more risk-averse behaviour, whilst sadness and angriness affect risk-taking behaviour positively (Raghunathan and Pham 1999; Lerner and Keltner 2001; van den Berg et al. 2009).

Conclusion Theoretically, the impact of an experience of natural disaster on the individual's risk-taking propensity remains unclear. Several channels were presented, though the distinction between the separate effects may not always be completely clear. Firstly, the income effect focuses on the change in wealth, whereby the change in risk behaviour depends on the choice of theoretical model (expected utility, prospect theory) and on the specification of it (assumption about utility function, definition of reference point). Secondly, in a world of limited information, a disaster might update the individual's information about the likelihood and frequency of disaster. Therefore, a new assessment of the individual's risk behaviour is possible. Thirdly, it is not necessary for the perception of risk to be aligned with the actual risk due to psychological factors in the decision-making process. This may have impacts on probabilities and decision weights in expected utility and prospect theory respectively. Fourthly, the role of emotions is highlighted, which indicates a higher likelihood of risk-taking behaviour after disasters due to post-traumatic experiences.[2]

[2]In the literature, background risk—as a risk not under the control of the agent—is analysed both in the context of expected utility theory as well as emotions and risk perception, since possible disasters in the future may create background risk (Page et al. 2014). Studying classical expected utility models with concave utility functions under the existence of background risk, Gollier and Pratt (1996) found increasing risk aversion to other independent risk if background risk is added to wealth, an attribute defined as 'risk vulnerability'. However, empirically ambiguous results of background risk on an individual's risk decision can be found (Gollier and Pratt 1996; Quiggin 2003; Guiso and Paiella 2008; Said et al. 2014). The mixed results show the challenges for the economic theory in clearly predicting the relationship between background risks and risk aversion (Ingwersen 2014; Page et al. 2014).

To conclude, the presented theory predicts widely ambiguous changes of risk behaviour after the experience of a natural disaster. Changes may also result from a new composition of cognitive and emotional systems and the way in which they are involved in the decision-making process (Nguyen et al. 2012).

Although the following discussion concentrates on the experience of natural disaster, the observation of losses of neighbours or the community due to disasters could also be a powerful mechanism, with similar impacts on the individual's risk behaviour (Said et al. 2015). Furthermore, decision-making under uncertainty is determined by the environment (Nguyen et al. 2012; Said et al. 2015). Apart from financial and psychological constraints, individual heterogeneity might vary levels of risk-taking behaviour (Said et al. 2015). Finally, in addition to the approaches mentioned above, evolutionary arguments are used to explain risk preferences, which will be neglected here due to their focus on the long run (Nguyen et al. 2012).

Empirical Results in the Literature

There is a limited variety of literature published in recent years that investigates the impact of the experience of natural disasters on an individual's risk-taking propensity. However, various methods were used to elicit risk attitudes. The specific measurement of risk aversion and risk-taking behaviour therefore depends on the methods used in the research, which include simple one-shot gambles or more extended choices of various risky options. However, risk aversion usually implies less risky choices by participants when presented with various outcomes (concavity of utility function).

Ahsan (2014) uses the same experimental methods as in the following research (described in Sect. 3.3) and finds that cyclone-affected households in Bangladesh are more risk-averse (smaller share bet in risk game) on average than non-affected individuals. Cameron and Shah (2015), though using a different setting to Ahsan (2014), also show that individuals who suffered a flood or earthquake in Indonesia during the past three years exhibit higher levels of risk aversion (household specific parameter based on risk game choices). Nguyen et al. (2012) also report that individuals in villages in Vietnam who were exposed to a flood exhibit more risk aversion than individuals in unaffected villages. Said et al. (2015) do not find significantly different choices between individuals who have or have not experienced a loss through floods in Pakistan. However, individuals who live in areas which are designated as flood clusters make more risk-averse choices than individuals outside these areas. Cassar et al. (2012) also found evidence that subjects living in villages that were impacted by the 2014 tsunami in Thailand showed higher risk aversion than subjects in other villages. Dang (2012) shows that rural households in Vietnam that experienced more natural disasters show a significantly higher level of risk aversion. Similar results are also reported by van den Berg et al. (2009), who show higher levels of risk aversion for individuals exposed to natural disasters in Nicaragua and Peru.

In contrast to these studies, Ingwersen (2014) finds, based on the analysis of a longitudinal study of households and individuals, that physical exposure towards a tsunami in Indonesia leads, on average, to increased risk-taking behaviour. The findings of Page et al. (2014) also suggest that individuals who suffered directly from a flood in Australia are more willing to accept a risky gamble than unaffected households in the immediate neighbourhood. Similar results are predicted by Eckel et al. (2009), who investigated the demographic and psychological conditions of hurricane Katrina evacuees in the United States. Hanaoka et al. (2015) use panel data in Japan, investigating the choice of risky gambles by the same respondents before and after an earthquake in 2011, finding more risk-taking behaviour of men after the experience of the disaster (and more risk-averse attitudes for women, although this result is not very robust). Li et al. (2011) investigate a heavy snowstorm and an earthquake in 2008 and observe a tendency towards risk aversion for losses and risk-seeking for gains, following the prospect theory of Kahneman and Tversky (1979). Table 3.1 gives an overview of the results in the presented studies.

3.2.2 The Impact of Disaster Exposure on Individual Levels of Trust and Trustworthiness

Theoretical Background

The assumption may be reasonable that natural disasters could influence the cultural identity and emotional state of individuals and therefore have an impact on different economic variables (Toya and Skidmore 2012). However, the effect of this impact is not clear: on the one hand, disasters could overwhelm society and thus induce decreasing social capital. On the other hand, such shocks could increase the appreciation of social capital through opportunities for individuals to work together and have common challenges (Toya and Skidmore 2012). In the literature, there are theoretical arguments for both possibilities, which will be presented in the next paragraph.

Cassar et al. (2012) describe four channels through which natural disasters positively impact the levels of trust and trustworthiness:

- Necessary and extensive interaction between individuals in the reconstruction period after a disaster can foster trust within society.
- Receiving support from other members of the community (solidarity between neighbours) can increase an individual's belief in trustworthiness.
- Disasters will update an individual's own information about the frequency and severity of disasters. Therefore, the potential need for help in the future becomes more clear and could create trustworthiness.
- Alesina and La Ferrara (2002) found evidence that more homogeneous communities with lower income inequality tend to display more interpersonal trust. Since disasters may lower the degree of income disparity due to the destruction of assets, this could create higher levels of trust.

Table 3.1 Results of studies regarding risk-taking propensity

Reference	Effect[a]	Main results of study
Eckel et al. (2009)	+	Higher risk-taking behaviour of evacuees compared to reference group
van den Berg et al. (2009)	–	Higher level of risk aversion of individuals exposed to natural shocks in the past
Li et al. (2011)	±	Higher level of risk aversion for losses and increased tendency towards risk-seeking for gains
Dang (2012)	–	Higher level of risk aversion of households that have experienced a higher volume of natural disasters
Cassar et al. (2012)	–	Higher level of risk aversion of persons from affected villages
Nguyen et al. (2012)	–	Higher individual level of risk aversion in affected villages
Ahsan (2014)	–	Higher level of risk aversion of affected households
Ingwersen (2014)	+	Higher risk-taking behaviour of individuals with personal physical exposure
Page et al. (2014)	+	Higher risk-seeking behaviour of flood-affected individuals
Cameron and Shah (2015)	–	Higher level of risk aversion of affected households
Hanaoka et al. (2015)	+	More risk-taking behaviour of men after earthquake occurrence
Said et al. (2015)	–	No difference for affected and non-affected individuals; higher risk aversion for households in designated flood clusters

[a]Effect of natural disaster on risk-taking propensity, with (+) indicating risk-taking and (–) risk-averse behaviour

In contrast, Fleming et al. (2014) mention aftermath conditions of natural disasters which negatively affect the levels of trust and trustworthiness:

- Due to constraints on physical and technical transport, the availability of recovery resources in the community can be limited. Therefore, rivalry within the community to receive scarce relief can arise.
- Aftermath moral hazard: a large disaster in a community can increase information asymmetries between households about damages and income losses. Therefore, excuses to break social contracts, which had been established before the disaster, are provided. This can limit agents to demand the fulfilment of a contract and could yield to decreasing trustworthiness. In line with this finding, Kanagaretnam et al. (2010) show that complete information (and therefore transparency) significantly increases the level of trust in a one-shot game and is also important for trustworthiness.
- Natural disasters have large impacts on migration between different regions, which affects the social structure within a community and can reduce the local levels of trust.
- Migration within regions or communities is also created by the impact of natural disasters, e.g. through offering temporary shelter to families who lost their

homes. However, social displacement within communities can affect trust and trustworthiness negatively.

Toya and Skidmore (2012) found evidence of both positive and negative impacts of disasters on countrywide levels of trust, dependent on the disaster type: while experiencing storms increases the level of trust, the impact of floods decreases it. The authors explain this through the influence of the disaster type on social cooperation: while storms affect different income classes in the same way and therefore cooperative measures are undertaken across social classes to prepare and respond to storms, floods often occur in low-lying areas which are more easily affordable for low-income groups. Thus, cooperation takes place more within certain communities and social classes (Toya and Skidmore 2012).

From the theoretical perspective, both positive and negative impacts of natural disaster on levels of trust and trustworthiness are conceivable. The following section presents the existing empirical findings in the recent literature, although the results are also mixed.

Empirical Results in the Literature

Various studies implemented trust games in economic experiments, with a focus on developing countries (Cardenas and Carpenter 2008). However as far as is known, only four studies have investigated the impact of natural disaster experiences on the levels of individual trust at the household level. Ahsan (2014) finds no significant impact in an analysis of cyclone-affected and non-affected households in Bangladesh. The same result is found by Fleming et al. (2014) for earthquakes in Chile. In contrast, Cassar et al. (2012) analyse the 2004 tsunami in Thailand and found a positive link between affected households and trust. Castillo and Carter (2011) studied 1998's Hurricane Mitch in Central America and also found a positive but non-linear relation between the severity of the disaster and trust.

Whitt and Wilson (2007) investigated cooperation in a public good game with evacuees from Hurricane Katrina and found increased group cooperation within the groups of affected participants, which implies a higher level of trust in the aftermath of a disaster. Toya and Skidmore (2012) analysed in a cross-country study a positive and significant impact of storms on trust and a negative and significant impact of floods on trust. However, only countrywide levels of trust are investigated. Solnit (2009) investigates five disasters between and including the 1906 earthquake in San Francisco to Hurricane Katrina in 2005 and shows that disasters often yield a general increase of trust and social capital.

Fleming et al. (2014) found a significant negative impact of the experience of natural disasters on trustworthiness. In contrast, Cassar et al. (2012) and Castillo and Carter (2011) report a positive link between natural disasters and reciprocity. Table 3.2 gives an overview of the results in the presented studies.

Table 3.2 Result of studies regarding trust and trustworthiness

Reference	Effect on trust[a]	Effect on trustworthiness[a]
Castillo and Carter (2011)	+	+
Cassar et al. (2012)	+	+
Ahsan (2014)	No significant effect	No significant effect
Fleming et al. (2014)	No significant effect	–

[a]Effect of natural disaster on trust and trustworthiness, with (+) indicating a positive link and (–) for a negative relation

3.2.3 Research Hypotheses

Based on the theoretical and empirical evidence presented above, the following hypotheses H1 to H3 will be formulated. Due to the proximity of the research methods, the hypotheses partially take the hypotheses of Ahsan (2014) and Schechter (2007) into account and fit these into the presented research complex.

There are mixed results on how the experience of natural disasters affects the individual's risk-taking propensity, both from theoretical and empirical points of view. The classical theory of expected utility suggests higher risk aversion, however theoretical work regarding risk perception and emotional responses can also explain higher risk-taking behaviour. Even if the direction of the effect may be unclear, the various theory approaches suggest an impact of disaster on individual risk behaviour. Therefore, the hypothesis H1—experiences of natural disasters have no significant influence on an individual's risk-taking propensity—should be rejected by the following analysis.

Results regarding the impact of natural disaster on the individual's level of trust and trustworthiness are also unclear. On the one hand, disasters could overwhelm society and thus induce decreasing social capital. On the other hand, such shocks could increase the appreciation of social capital through opportunities for individuals to work together and tackle common challenges. Empirically, there is evidence for a positive relationship between the experience of a natural disaster and the individual level of trust; however other studies cannot show significant connections. Regarding the impact on trustworthiness, there are mixed empirical results. The hypotheses H2 and H3 therefore concentrate on the impact of experiencing natural disasters on the individual's level of trust and trustworthiness and claim that there is no significant effect.

Table 3.3 presents the three hypotheses regarding the impact of natural disaster on individual behaviour. Section 3.3 explains the methods used in the experiment. Thereby two more hypotheses, H4 and H5, regarding the interaction of risk behaviour and trust will be introduced. Sections 3.4 and 3.5 present the results of the experiment and present statistical evidence for the five research hypotheses.

Table 3.3 Research hypotheses regarding impact of disasters on individual behaviour

Hypotheses	
H1	The experiences of natural disasters have no significant influence on an individual's risk-taking propensity
H2	The amount sent in a trust game will not depend on the sender's experience of natural disasters
H3	The level of trustworthiness will not depend on experiences of natural disasters

3.3 Description of the Experiment

The research consists of a household survey in combination with instruments of experimental economics to investigate the various problems described above and build a foundation for the following considerations. An experiment was conducted in rural Cambodia in September 2014 in order to gather the necessary data.

The first part of this section presents the methodology and the design of the experiment, followed by a description of the scope and study area. In the Appendix, a comprehensive procedure of the experiment, as well as detailed descriptive statistics of the households are presented, showing livelihoods and the ability to cope with natural disasters in rural Cambodia.

3.3.1 Methodology and Theoretical Framework

An experiment with a trust game and a risk game to measure personal risk aversion was performed with populations in rural areas of Cambodia's Battambang province. Similar games are frequently referenced in related academic literature and have been conducted several times in developing countries to measure trust, trustworthiness, and risk aversion.

In the following literature, there are various examples of how behavioural experiments have been conducted. In a survey article, Cardenas and Carpenter (2008) present multiple behavioural experiments conducted in the field in developing countries. A frequently cited instance is that by Schechter (2007), which will also form part of the basis for this research. Ahsan's (2014) experiment in Bangladesh is similar to the following experiment, and based its experiments on Schechter (2007). The experiment by Schechter (2007) was conducted in rural Paraguay and provides a detailed game protocol including advice for dealing with typical problems arising due to lack of literacy and numeracy in the rural areas of some developing countries. Ahsan (2014) notes that the risk and trust game with real money favours the creation of real risk and trust decisions.

The proposed trust game (also known as the 'investment game') is based on the experiment by Berg et al. (1995) and has become a trademark for measuring trust in behavioural experiments. There are two players, where player 1 is endowed with a certain sum of money. In the first move, he is given the possibility to either keep all the money or to send a certain share to an anonymous player 2. Any money sent is tripled. Player 2 is then to decide how much money, if any, to send back to player 1. Money sent by player 1 is used as an indicator of the level of trust that money will be received in return, while money returned by player 2 is used to measure trustworthiness (Schechter 2007).

According to the classical game theory and the assumption of selfish players, the only sub-game perfect Nash equilibrium for player 2 is to send nothing back. Using backward induction, player 1 realises this and will not send anything in the first game. However, empirical results show that participants in different experiments do not follow this expectation (Schechter 2007; Ahsan 2014).

Every player plays the game twice, to measure trust and trustworthiness once each. Burks et al. (2003) suggest that playing both roles reduces both overall trust and reciprocity.[3] The pay-off is dependent on two different interactions, whereby the players feel less responsible for the counterpart. A detailed description of this game including an account is provided in the Appendix.

Schechter (2007) writes that results from a trust game might confuse different levels of trust with different levels of risk aversion. Karlan (2005) also reports similar results, finding that individuals who were more trusting in the investment game were also more likely to default on their microfinance loans. He concluded that they may actually just be ‘more willing to take on risks’. Therefore Schechter (2007) adds a risk game to measure the risk aversion of the participants. This allows her to disentangle actual trust from risk aversion. Different findings regarding the influence of risk behaviour on trust could also depend on varying designs of the risk game. Therefore, a similar design of the risk and trust game is recommended.

For the risk game in Schechter (2007), the player is endowed with a certain sum of money, from which he or she bets a share. The payoff is determined by the roll of a die, whereby a roll of 1 or 2 leads to a negative result for the player, a roll of 3 has a neutral result, and a roll of 4, 5 or 6 has a positive outcome for the player. The pay-out follows the design of Schechter (2007). A detailed description of this game including an account is provided in the Appendix. Risk attitudes are measured by the share bet in the risk game and are therefore relative measurements, thus a participant who bet a relatively small share of the endowed money is characterised as more risk-averse than another participant who bet a larger share.

Section 3.1.3 analyses the theoretical interaction between risk perception and level of trust (especially subjective trust). Furthermore, Schechter (2007) assumed that risk aversion may affect the trust game, but trust does not affect play in the risk game. This seems reasonable as play in the risk game does not depend on expectations of the actions of other people. The impact of risk behaviour on trust and

[3]The reduction in trust and reciprocity is explained by a reduced feeling of obligation toward the counterparts, due to the counterparts’ equal opportunities to make money in the game (Burks et al. 2003).

Table 3.4 Research hypotheses regarding the impact of risk behaviour on trust and trustworthiness

Hypotheses	
H4	Risk preference has no influence on individual levels of trust
H5	The level of trustworthiness will not depend on an individual's risk behaviour

trustworthiness will be investigated by this study and is formalised in hypotheses H4 and H5 (Table 3.4).[4]

Through her experiments, Schechter (2007) highlights that participants should receive and play with amounts of money that are of significance to them, e.g. participants receive large pay-outs of more than 2 days' wages. Participants should also be those who face risk decisions in real life. Therefore, their decisions in the games reflect more closely their risk and trust behaviours in real situations.

The survey considers household characteristics, experiences with natural disasters, disaster risk management activities and questions about prevention and preparedness toward flood risks. Furthermore, by applying a discrete choice experiment, demand for microinsurance products will be considered. The questionnaire was developed based on previous surveys in the literature (Schechter 2007; Reynaud and Nguyen 2012; Ahsan 2014) and was discussed with local researchers in Cambodia.

3.3.2 Scope of the Research and Preparation

The experiment was conducted in cooperation with the University of Battambang (UBB), Cambodia. The preparation in Battambang took place between 5th and 9th September 2014. Both the experiments and the survey were conducted with populations living in six villages in rural areas of Battambang province between 10th and 17th September 2014. The University of Battambang provided four members of the research department and three graduates to conduct the experiments in the local Khmer language.[5] All parts of the research team received extensive instructions and training before the experiment and the author observed all experiments. The description of the experiments for the participants and the questionnaires were given in Khmer.

The Thma Koul district in Battambang province was selected for the experiment due to the existence of villages both affected and unaffected by the severe flooding in October 2013. Contact with multiple administrative levels of government was provided through a letter of support from the Rector of the University of

[4]Some doubts exist about a 'framing' for the player by playing the risk game first. However, Ahsan (2014) alternates the order of the games in different villages and shows that the game order has no significant effect.

[5]Hereby the author wishes to thank the following research staff from the University of Battambang: Yoeurn Nin, Moeurng Chamroeun, Morm Sophany, Run Sorphorn, and the students Mao Sela, Chhuoy Saneth, Leap Channy.

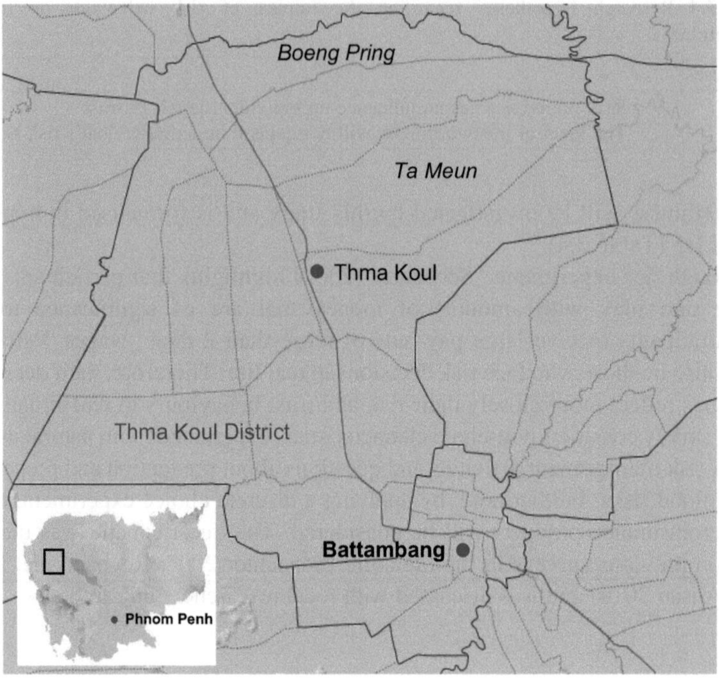

Fig. 3.3 Location of research area in Thma Koul district. Author's illustration, using Open Development (2016)

Battambang. Personal contact with the district, commune and village administrations was necessary to gain access to the villages. However, the head of each village was given only general information about the research and the necessary size of the sample. Every participant was guaranteed a 'show-up' fee and provided with the information that they could win more through the experiment. Only one member per household was accepted for participation. The experiment, including introductory explanations, both games and the questionnaire, took approximately four hours. It was conducted both in the morning and in the afternoon. Figure 3.3 shows the communes Boeng Pring and Ta Meun (both in Thma Koul district), in which the research villages are located.

3.4 The Impact of Natural Disasters on Individuals' Risk-Taking Propensity in Rural Cambodia

Section 3.2 provided theoretical explanations and empirical evidence for the impact of natural disasters on individuals' risk-taking propensity. The following section presents the results of the risk game in rural Cambodia and explains the observed risk-taking behaviour of the participants in the context of an experience of natural

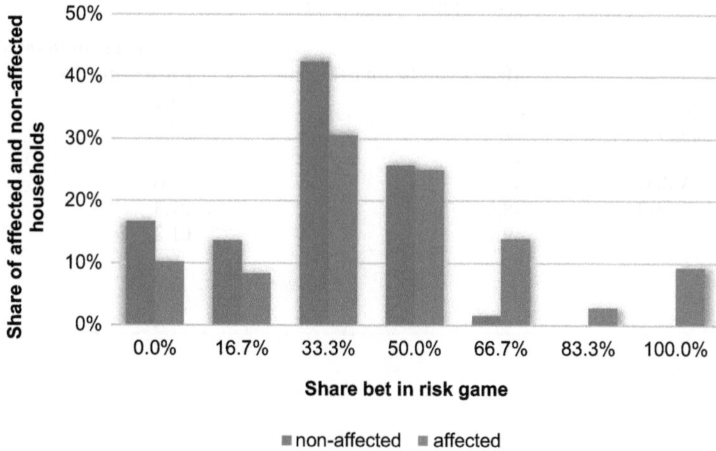

Fig. 3.4 Share bet in the risk game for affected and non-affected households as a percentage of total number of affected or non-affected households

disaster. The outcomes will be explained in the light of the existing literature and statistical evidence regarding the hypotheses H1 and H4 will be presented.

The average amount bet in the risk game was 2,344 Cambodian Riel (39.1% of the participant's endowment). 10.5% of the households (22 out of 174) bet nothing and 4.8% (10 out of 174) bet everything.

Figure 3.4 demonstrates the distribution of the share bet in the risk game (between 0 and 1) for affected and non-affected households. The mean share bet in the risk game in this research in rural Cambodia is smaller than experiments with a similar design in Paraguay with 42.9% (Schechter 2007) and Bangladesh with 51.6% (Ahsan 2014). Table 3.5 shows the results at the village level.[6]

The following empirical investigation explains the participants' individual risk behaviour by personal and village characteristics. One key consideration is the impact of the experience of natural disasters on the individual level of risk (see hypothesis H1 in Sect. 3.2). Table 3.5 therefore also shows the share of affected people in each village next to the amount bet.

A parametric t-test of the share that individuals bet in the risk game shows that the means of both samples are significantly different ($t = 3.950$, $p = 0.000$). Figure 3.5 shows that the average share bet in the risk game is higher for participants who were affected by floods than participants who were unaffected.

[6]The explanation for the risk game in village A did not meet expectations and yielded biased results. Therefore, the results for the risk game are based on 174 observations in 5 villages only.

Table 3.5 Results of the risk game at the village level

Village	Mean share bet in risk game (%)	Percentage of flood-affected participants (%)
Snoul Koenig (Village B)	31.9	2.8
Tasei (Village F)	31.9	20.0
Ang (Village E)	43.4	90.9
Tom Pong (Village D)	39.5	94.6
Boeng Pring (Village C)	48.6	97.3
Average	39.1	61.2

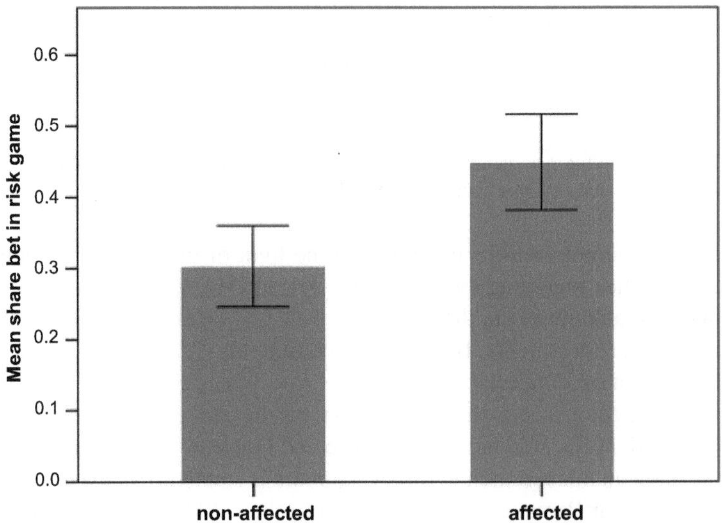

Fig. 3.5 Comparison of means for affected and non-affected households. *Error bars* for 99% confidence interval

Description and Results of Regression An ordinary least-squares (OLS) regression was conducted to investigate the influence of socio-economic variables and attitudes towards floods and prevention on the participants' individual risk behaviour. More specifically, the OLS regression

$$R_i = \alpha + \beta_1 A_i + \beta_2 X_i + \gamma + \varepsilon_i \quad (3.1)$$

is estimated, where i indicates the individuals. The dependent variable R_i is the share bet in the risk game (measuring risk-taking propensity). The coefficient β_1 measures the impact of experiencing a natural disaster A_i (binary variable), while β_2 indicates the role of control variables X_i (see below). Additionally, village dummies γ were used in the regression.

Table 3.6 Descriptive statistics for risk game

Variable	Mean	Standard deviation	Number of observations
Share bet in risk game[a]	0.39	0.24	167
Affected[b]	0.62	0.49	167
Age	50.68	13.77	167
Age squared[c]	27.57	14.42	167
Gender[d]	0.37	0.49	167
Married state[e]	0.97	0.17	167
Financial literacy[f]	1.68	1.27	167
Number of people living in the household	5.45	2.35	167
Number of children under 15 years in the household	1.23	1.45	167
Total income per capita in US Dollars (2013)[g]	2.84	5.78	167
Consequences of flood[h]	3.83	1.25	146
Vulnerability of household[i]	1.89	0.82	146
Importance of prevention[j]	4.21	1.20	146
Ability to prevent[k]	2.12	1.26	146

[a]Share of given endowment of 6000 Riel, which was bet in the one-shot risk game
[b]Measured as a dummy with 1 if household was affected by flood and 0 otherwise
[c]Age squared as age times age divided by 100
[d]Measured as a dummy with 1 for male and 0 for female
[e]Measured as a dummy with 1 for married and 0 otherwise
[f]Measured as the number of right solutions for four simple mathematical questions
[g]Income in US Dollars, divided by 100
[h]Question in the survey with the following choices: 1 'No consequences at all' to 5 'Extremely severe consequences'
[i]Question in the survey with the following choices: 1 'Less vulnerable' than other households in the village, 2 'As vulnerable as others' and 3 'More vulnerable'
[j]Question in the survey with the following choices: 1 'Not important at all' to 5 'Extremely important'
[k]Question in the survey regarding own ability to protect, with the following choices: 1 "I cannot protect myself at all" to 5 "I can protect myself completely"

The choice of the socio-economic variables follows the literature (Schechter 2007; Eckel et al. 2009; Nguyen et al. 2012; Ahsan 2014; Cameron and Shah 2015; Said et al. 2015). The inclusion of various questionnaire answers respecting consequences and vulnerability, as well as prevention measures, follows the stated research questions based on comparable studies. Table 3.6 presents the descriptive statistics for the included variables. For all regressions, village dummies are used.

Regressions (1) and (2) of Table 3.7 present the results when only socio-economic variables are included in the estimation, controlling for income classes in regression (2). Regressions (3) and (4) present the results when answers of the questionnaire regarding the expectation of future floods and prevention measures are included. Several robustness checks were conducted to confirm the validity of

Table 3.7 Regression for risk game

	Share bet in risk game			
	(1)	(2)	(3)	(4)
(Constant)	0.225	0.225	0.057	−0.014
	(0.204)	(0.211)	(0.256)	(0.287)
Affected	0.169**	0.169**	0.241***	0.348*
	(0.072)	(0.073)	(0.083)	(0.193)
Age	0.015*	0.014*	0.020**	0.021**
	(0.007)	(0.008)	(0.008)	(0.008)
Age squared	−0.015**	−0.014*	−0.019**	−0.019**
	(0.007)	(0.007)	(0.008)	(0.008)
Gender	0.037	0.035	0.057	0.062
	(0.040)	(0.041)	(0.044)	(0.044)
Married state	−0.251**	−0.240**	−0.259**	−0.261**
	(0.114)	(0.116)	(0.116)	(0.116)
Financial literacy	0.030*	0.032*	0.031*	0.026
	(0.016)	(0.016)	(0.017)	(0.018)
Number of people living in the household	−0.017*	−0.016*	−0.015	−0.017*
	(0.009)	(0.009)	(0.010)	(0.010)
Number of children under 15 years in the household	0.038**	0.038**	0.037**	0.038**
	(0.015)	(0.015)	(0.015)	(0.015)
Total income per capita in US Dollars (2013)	−0.002	−0.004	−0.009	−0.008
	(0.003)	(0.004)	(0.006)	(0.006)
Importance of prevention			0.033	0.032
			(0.022)	(0.024)
Ability to prevent			−0.028	−0.027
			(0.019)	(0.019)
Consequences of flood			−0.016	−0.026
			(0.021)	(0.031)
Vulnerability of household			−0.047*	0.029
			(0.026)	(0.050)
Consequences * Affected				0.016
				(0.040)
Vulnerability * Affected				−0.104*
				(0.058)
Income classes	No	Yes	Yes	Yes
Village dummy	Yes	Yes	Yes	Yes
Number of observations	167	167	146	146

Standard errors in parentheses
***$p < 0.01$, **$p < 0.05$, *$p < 0.10$

the OLS regression presented below. A detailed description of the robustness checks can be found in the Appendix.[7]

[7]Hereby the author wishes to thank Danny Wende from the TU Dresden for his comments regarding the robustness checks, especially the propensity score matching.

Experience of Natural Disasters The exploration of effects of natural disasters on the individual risk perception is relatively new in the economic literature and limited research exists. Section 3.2 presents an in-depth introduction into the theoretical background and empirical results from previous studies. This study finds that experiencing natural disasters has a significant positive impact on risk-taking propensity. Participants exposed to natural disasters bet 16.9% more on average than non-affected participants (regressions 1 and 2); when controlling for individual assessments of vulnerability and flood consequences 24.1% was bet on average (regression 3). Therefore, the proposed hypothesis H1 can be rejected.

In the theoretical analysis in Sect. 3.2, four main channels are presented through which an exposure to natural disasters can affect individuals' risk preferences. Risk behaviour can be altered through changes to income and wealth, the upgrade of information about probabilities and outcomes, the perception of risks, and emotional responses. Altogether, widely ambiguous changes of risk behaviour after the experience of natural disasters can be expected. Additionally, changes may also result from a new composition of cognitive and emotional systems and their involvement in the decision-making process (Nguyen et al. 2012). The following section bring the results in line with the theoretical explanations.

The income effect can be investigated within both expected utility and prospect theory. As outlined above, the effect of a change in wealth in the expected utility model depends on the specific form of the utility function. However, previous research investigating the link between disaster and risk attitudes assumes mostly a concave utility function with constant relative risk aversion, in which case the result presented above contradicts the expected utility model (Ingwersen 2014; Page et al. 2014). Applying the prospect theory, the way in which risk behaviour reacts to a loss in wealth depends on the definition of the reference point. As discussed above, a reference point which still reflects the pre-disaster status quo leads to risk-seeking behaviour after the disaster, due to the perception of the flood damage as loss in wealth relative to the reference point. In this specific case, the presented results can be aligned with the prospect theory. However, this does not hold if the disaster experience creates a new reference point.

In a world of imperfect information, natural disasters update individuals' expectations about probability and damage and provide new information about the risk to be faced by the household (Nguyen et al. 2012; Cameron and Shah 2015). The positive impact of natural disasters on risk-taking behaviour in Cambodia may be a result of this update process, showing that the damages of flooding are less devastating or more manageable than previously expected.

Due to psychological factors, the perception of risk may change through the experience of natural disasters (Ingwersen 2014; Said et al. 2014). A risk-seeking behaviour after a disaster could be explained by an underestimation of the probability for an event (Gambler's Fallacy). There are empirical studies showing this effect in the context of casinos, lotteries and investment decisions (Terrell 1994; Croson and Sundali 2005; Huber et al. 2010), as well as in the context of natural disasters when affected populations were questioned within 2 days of the event (Shanteau 1992). Although there is empirical evidence for the contrary effect as well (Croson and Sundali 2005; Huber et al. 2010), a higher risk-taking behaviour after a natural disaster—as found in rural Cambodia—can be interpreted as a lower perception of another disaster risk and therefore supports the theory of the Gambler's Fallacy empirically. These perceptions can therefore change the subjective probabilities and decision weights in the expected utility model and prospect theory, respectively.

Expected risk behaviours of individuals may also differ from the channels presented above due to the role of emotions (Loewenstein et al. 2001; Eckel et al. 2009). Persons under extreme stress or with post-traumatic experiences might analyse the prospects in a less cognitive way and tend to be more risk-taking (Pat-Horenczyk et al. 2007; Eckel et al. 2009). These psychological results may also explain the observed risk-taking of affected households in comparison to unaffected households in rural Cambodia.

The positive impact found in Cambodia aligns with Ingwersen (2014) in Indonesia, Page et al. (2014) in Australia, Hanaoka et al. (2015) in Japan and Eckel et al. (2009) in the US, which also found a higher risk-taking propensity for affected households. However, this is in contrast to the studies of Ahsan (2014) in Bangladesh, Cameron and Shah (2015) in Indonesia, Cassar et al. (2012) in Thailand, Nguyen et al. (2012) in Vietnam and Said et al. (2015) in Pakistan. Although a wide range of methods were used in these studies to measure risk attitudes, no evidence is found that risk behaviour after disasters depends on research methods used.

The regression was repeated by including the individual heights of water in participants' yards and houses due to annual and extreme flooding. Additionally, the income difference between 2012 and 2013 (when the flood occurred) was taken into the regression as a dummy for flood damage. However, no significant impact of these measures on the individual risk behaviour could be found. In contrast, Said et al. (2015) show that both severity and frequency of disasters lead to significantly more risk-averse behaviour.[8]

Said et al. (2015) also report that change in risk behaviour depends on the type of loss experienced. Risk aversion is lower for participants with flood damage to their house structure, while no significant change is reported for individuals with losses to crops, livestock or personal belongings (Said et al. 2015). In contrast, Ingwersen

[8]A problem of endogeneity could arise if households with higher risk-taking behaviours are more likely to choose a location in a more risk-prone area. However, location decisions are made long-term (the average time living in a village is 41.1 years, whereby 61.7% have always lived there and only 9.6% have arrived during the last 15 years), while more severe effects of disasters in this specific area have risen during the last 10 years (see Chap. 2). If such an endogeneity problem exists, more risk-taking households would be more likely to have moved to these villages in the last decade, when these locations became more risk-prone. However, no significant difference in the mean average of those 'Affected' can be found between people living longer or shorter than 15 years in a village.

However, a problem which cannot be excluded in these types of studies is that particularly risk-averse individuals moved away shortly after the disaster occurred. Panel data with individual risk measurements of several years is needed in order to control for this effect (Hanaoka et al. 2015).

(2014) does not find an impact of asset losses and concludes that the impact of exposure to the disaster is not driven by personal economic losses. However, when controlling for damage-specific effects (damage on household property or production assets), no significant effects could be found in the regression.

Socio-Economic Variables The presented outcomes show a non-linear connection between risk behaviour and age in the study presented above, with an increase of risk-taking behaviour until the age of 50, 52.6 and 55.3 for regressions (1) and (2), regression (3) and regression (4), respectively. Thereafter, the risk-taking propensity decreases with higher age. Similarly, Riley and Chow (1992) found that risk aversion initially decreases with age but began to increase again after the age of 65. Halek and Eisenhauer (2001) also found a non-linear relationship.

Said et al. (2015) found a negative relationship between risk aversion and age. Ingwersen (2014) did not find that age had a large impact except for individuals above 50, who displayed a larger decrease in risk aversion due to their experience of natural disasters. In contrast, there is a broad literature around the 'life-cycle risk aversion hypotheses', which states that risk aversion increases with age (Bakshi and Chen 1994; Wang and Hanna 1997). This result is also found by Cameron and Shah (2015), who found that older people tend to be more risk-averse. Diverse evidence of the relation between risk behaviour and age is also presented by van den Berg et al. (2009).

The gender of the participant in the investigation in Cambodia has no significant impact on the average share bet in the risk game, although previous studies on risk behaviour found significant, but mixed results. Eckel and Grossman (2008), Ahsan (2014), Cameron and Shah (2015), van den Berg et al. (2009), Hanaoka et al. (2015), and Eckel et al. (2009) find that women are more risk-averse than men in the middle and long term after a disaster, which is supported by the evolutionary theory (Ahsan 2014). In contrast, Eckel et al. (2009) and Schechter (2007) show that women exhibit more risk-taking prosperity than men in the short term after a disaster.

Participants in Cambodia who were married bet less on average in the risk game than unmarried individuals, a result which is also shown by Ahsan (2014) and can be explained by the fact that married persons usually hold a greater degree of responsibility to their families. Married participants bet approximately 25% less on average than single participants.

Financial literacy as a proxy for education is significantly positive, a result also found by Cameron and Shah (2015). Studies with similar settings found no significant impact of education on the risk behaviour (Schechter 2007; Ahsan 2014), although other studies show mixed results in the literature (see Said et al. (2014) for an overview).

Individuals from larger households are more risk-averse on average than participants from smaller families. This result contrasts with Ahsan (2014), who found that members of larger families are less risk-averse. In contrast to previous studies, the number of children under 15 will be analysed in the estimation. Participants with more children are on average more risk-taking than individuals with fewer children. However, these effects are relatively small compared to those of disaster exposure, age and married state.[9]

There is a broad literature on the interaction between income and natural disasters, however mostly on the aggregate level (see Sect. 3.2). On the household level, Schechter (2007) found in the same experimental setting that wealthier households are more risk-taking, which implies decreasing absolute risk aversion. However, the presented outcomes do not show a significant impact of income per capita on the risk behaviour of the participants. The implementation of income classes does not alter the results from the regression.[10]

Vulnerability, Flood Consequences and Prevention Participants' own assessments of vulnerability in comparison to other households have a negative and significant impact on the share bet (regression 3). The more vulnerable an individual perceives himself to be, the less he bets on average in the risk game. The connection between vulnerability and risk-taking behaviour becomes clearer when including an interaction term between vulnerability and affection (regression 4): while the experience of natural disaster itself leads to much more risk-taking (the share bet in the risk game was 34.8% higher on average than by non-affected households), this effect decreases as perception of own household vulnerability increases (compared to other households in the village). In addition to vulnerability, the individual consequences of floods on the household were investigated. However, no significant effect in explaining risk attitudes could be found.

Said et al. (2015) has shown for participants in Pakistan that individuals who believed the floods would be worse in the future (in terms of intensity), tend to make more risk-averse choices. In this context, Page et al. (2014) highlight the importance of background risk of future disasters; they also mention the possibility that the observation of the effects of floods on neighbours increases the perception of background risk for non-affected individuals. However, regressions that include expectations about future floods show no significant impact on risk-taking propensity in this experiment.

Questions on the individual assessment of the importance of prevention measures as well as the ability for prevention were included in the questionnaire and results are reflected in the regression. As shown in regressions (3) and (4), both variables have no significant effect in explaining risk attitudes.

[9]Furthermore, Gheyssens and Günther (2011) find a strong influence of religion on risk preferences, with stronger faith increasing risk-taking behaviour. However, this effect cannot be considered in this experiment due to limited variability of different religions (96.2% of participants were Buddhist).

[10]Income classes as quintiles. Differences to other studies may also be explained by the data collection, particularly regarding income data, which had to be calculated based on different individual statements and assumptions. See Sect. 3.3 and Appendix for a detailed description of the data collection.

3.5 The Impact of Natural Disaster on Trust and Trustworthiness in Rural Cambodia

The following section presents empirical results for the impact of the experience of natural disaster on the participants' levels of trust and trustworthiness. The outcomes will be explained in light of the existing literature and statistical evidence regarding the hypotheses H2, H3 and H5 will be presented.

As described in Sect. 3.3, all participants played both roles in the trust game, as player 1 (sender) and player 2 (receiver). While the amount sent can be interpreted as trust, the amount sent back measures trustworthiness (reciprocity).

Trust The average amount sent as player 1 in the trust game was 4,038 Riel (67.3% of their endowment). 1.9% of the households (4 out of 209) sent nothing, and 22.5% (47 out of 209) sent everything to an anonymous player 2. Figure 3.6 demonstrates the distribution of the share sent in the risk game. The mean amount sent in the trust game, and therefore the levels of trust in these Cambodian villages, is higher than in similar experiments elsewhere; for example, a mean of 46.8% was found in Paraguay (Schechter 2007) and 48.8% in Bangladesh (Ahsan 2014). Table 3.8 shows the results at the village level.

Trustworthiness The money sent by player 1 was tripled and player 2 could decide which share they wanted to send back. On average, 63.7% of the money was sent back. 1.9% of the households (4 out of 209) sent nothing back, and 15.8% (33 out of 209) sent everything back to the anonymous player 1. The share returned in the trust game in rural Cambodia is also much higher than in similar experiments: 43.4% sent back in Paraguay (Schechter 2007) and 34% in Bangladesh (Ahsan 2014). Despite the high level of trustworthiness in Cambodia, differences between experiments in various developing countries are not uncommon and are dependent

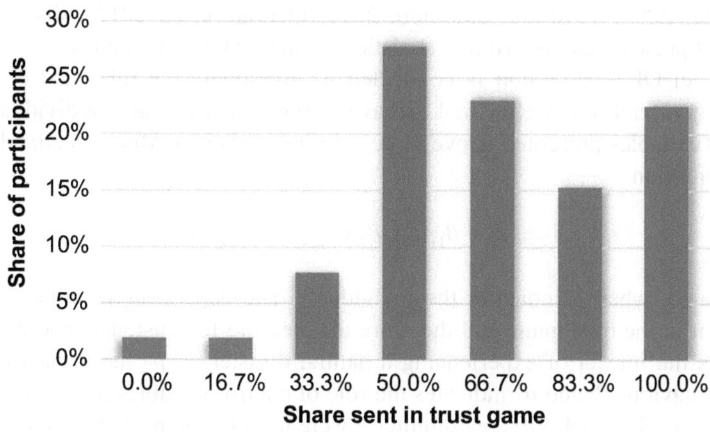

Fig. 3.6 Distribution of share sent in trust game

Table 3.8 Results of the trust game at the village level

Village	Mean share sent in trust game (Player 1, %)	Mean share returned in trust game (Player 2, %)	Percentage of flood-affected participants
Snoul Koenig (Village B)	71.4	73.6	2.8
Tasei (Village F)	56.7	65.7	20.0
Ang (Village E)	58.1	67.3	90.9
Tom Pong (Village D)	88.1	67.0	94.6
Boeng Pring (Village C)	71.2	66.2	97.3
Pory Ta Sek (Village A)	57.4	41.7	100.0
Average	67.3	63.7	67.5

on the particular community [see Cardenas and Carpenter (2008) for a survey]. Table 3.8 shows the results for each village.

The following empirical section explains the individual levels of trust and trustworthiness through personal and village characteristics. As before, the key considerations are the influence of experiencing natural disasters on individual behaviour (see also hypotheses H2 and H3 in Sect. 3.2) as well as the impact of risk behaviour on the individual's level of trust.

3.5.1 Description of Regression and Results

In the following section, OLS regressions are conducted to explain trust and trustworthiness, investigating the influence of socio-economic individual and village characteristics. The choice of these variables is based on the existing literature (Schechter 2007; Toya and Skidmore 2012; Fleming et al. 2014; Ahsan 2014). Table 3.9 presents the descriptive statistics for the included variables.

First, an OLS regression is conducted to investigate the influence of socio-economic variables as well as risk behaviour on the participant's individual level of trust (variables presented above in descriptive statistics). More specifically, the OLS regression

$$T_i = \alpha + \beta_1 A_i + \beta_2 R_i + \beta_3 X_i + \gamma + \varepsilon_i \qquad (3.2)$$

is estimated, where i indicates the individuals. The dependent variable T_i is the share sent in the trust game and therefore the measure for trust. The coefficient β_1 measures the impact of experiencing a natural disaster A_i, β_2 the impact of risk-taking behaviour R_i and β_3 indicates the role of control variables X_i. As in the risk regression in Sect. 3.4, village dummies γ were used to control for village-specific effects.

Table 3.9 Descriptive statistics for trust game

Variable	Mean	Standard deviation	Number of observations
Share sent in trust game[a]	0.67	0.24	202
Share returned in trust game[b]	0.63	0.24	202
Affected[c]	0.68	0.47	202
Age	50.97	13.48	202
Age squared[d]	27.79	14.12	202
Gender[e]	0.38	0.49	202
Married state[f]	0.98	0.16	202
Financial literacy[g]	1.69	1.26	202
Number of people living in the household	5.54	2.31	202
Number of children under 15 years in the household	1.20	1.38	202
Total income per capita in US Dollars (2013)[h]	2.64	5.32	202
Win in risk game[i]	64.31	28.88	167
Share bet in risk game	0.39	0.24	167

[a]Share of given endowment of 6000 Riel, which was sent as player 1 in the trust game
[b]Share of money returned by player 2. For a share higher than 0.33, trust has a positive pay-out because money sent by player 1 was tripled
[c]Measured as a dummy with 1 if household was affected by flood and 0 otherwise
[d]Age squared as age times age divided by 100
[e]Measured as a dummy with 1 for male and 0 for female
[f]Measured as a dummy with 1 for married and 0 otherwise
[g]Measured as the number of correct solutions for four simple mathematical questions
[h]Income in US Dollars divided by 100
[i]Income in US Dollars divided by 100 Money in Riel won in the risk game divided by 100

Second, trustworthiness (reciprocity) will be analysed by the OLS regression:

$$TW_i = \alpha + \beta_1 A_i + \beta_2 T_i + \beta_3 X_i + \gamma + \varepsilon_i \tag{3.3}$$

Hereby, the dependent variable TW_i is the share returned in the trust game (as a measure for trustworthiness). Mostly, the regression for trustworthiness is similar to that for trust, except for using trust instead of risk as an explaining variable.

Regressions (5) and (6) in Table 3.10 present the results for the individuals' behaviour as player 1, and therefore the share of the given endowment sent in the game (trust), while regressions (7) and (8) show the results for behaviour as player 2 (trustworthiness).

3.5.2 *Trust*

The results for trust, presented in regressions (5) and (6), will be analysed. Hereby the impact of a disaster experience as well as risk behaviour and socio-economic variables will be investigated.

Table 3.10 Regressions for trust and trustworthiness

	Share sent in trust game		Share returned in trust game	
	(5)	(6)	(7)	(8)
(Constant)	0.602***	0.621***	0.652***	0.315
	(0.197)	(0.196)	(0.201)	(0.215)
Affected	−0.179*	−0.184*	−0.119***	−0.076
	(0.103)	(0.100)	(0.038)	(0.071)
Age	0.013*	0.010	−0.007	−0.004
	(0.007)	(0.007)	(0.008)	(0.007)
Age squared	−0.012*	−0.009	0.005	0.003
	(0.007)	(0.006)	(0.007)	(0.007)
Gender	0.080**	0.084**	0.028	0.033
	(0.037)	(0.036)	(0.037)	(0.036)
Married state	−0.115	−0.095	0.175	0.242**
	(0.105)	(0.103)	(0.116)	(0.113)
Financial literacy	−0.004	−0.004	−0.012	−0.008
	(0.014)	(0.014)	(0.015)	(0.014)
Number of people living in the household	−0.005	−0.001	0.002	0.006
	(0.008)	(0.008)	(0.008)	(0.008)
Number of children under 15 years in the household	−0.018	−0.017	0.014	−0.001
	(0.014)	(0.013)	(0.014)	(0.014)
Total income per capita in US Dollars (2013)	0.000	−0.004	0.001	0.001
	(0.003)	(0.004)	(0.003)	(0.003)
Win in risk game	−0.002*	−0.002		
	(0.001)	(0.001)		
Win in risk game * Affected	0.003**	0.002**		
	(0.001)	(0.001)		
Income class: very poor		−0.168***		
		(0.053)		
Income class: poor		−0.115**		
		(0.051)		
Income class: wealthy		−0.065		
		(0.050)		
Income class: very wealthy		0.004		
		(0.057)		
Share bet in risk game	0.137*	0.118		
	(0.074)	(0.072)		
Share sent in trust game			0.115*	0.030
			(0.115)	(0.075)
Village dummy	Yes	Yes	No	Yes
Number of observations	167	167	202	202

Standard errors in parentheses
***p < 0.01, **p < 0.05, *p < 0.10

Experience of Natural Disaster The experience of a natural disaster has a significant negative effect on the share sent in the trust game. Therefore, hypothesis H2 can be rejected. This result is in contrast to Castillo and Carter (2011) and Cassar et al. (2012), who found a positive connection between the experience of a natural disaster and the individual level of trust.

The theory suggests both positive and negative effects due to the impact of disasters on social capital as well as the challenges and opportunities in the aftermath situation (see Sect. 3.2 for a broader theoretical discussion). The negative effect of the experience of natural disaster on the level of trust follows the argumentation by Fleming et al. (2014). Lower levels of trust could arise from rivalry within the community to receive scarce recovery resources in the aftermath of a disaster. Natural disasters additionally have a large impact on migration, both within and between regions and communities. This changes the social structure of a community and can therefore negatively affect the levels of trust (Fleming et al. 2014).

Impact of Risk Behaviour There is empirical evidence that the results from the trust game might confuse different levels of trust with different levels of risk aversion (Karlan 2005; Schechter 2007). Theoretically it can be shown, in Sect. 3.1.3 that there is an interaction between behavioural risk and risk-taking of an individual (Das and Teng 2004).

Therefore, the share bet in the risk game is included as an explaining variable. Indeed, an individual's behaviour in the risk game has a significant influence on the share sent in the trust game. The more risk-taking a participant is, the higher the average amount they send in the trust game; thus, hypothesis H5 can be rejected. By including this variable, the risky part of trust is separated from the pure level of trust. This study therefore confirms the results of Ahsan (2014) and Schechter (2007).

Socio-Economic Variables The results indicate that participants become more trusting with increasing age until the age of 54.2 (regression 5), albeit at a decreasing rate. Thereafter, a higher age decreases the level of trust. However, this effect is no longer significant when controlling for income classes. The significance of age aligns with the results found by Fleming et al. (2014) in Chile and Cassar et al. (2012) in Thailand.

In comparison, gender is a significant variable in explaining the individual level of trust: men are more trusting on average than women. Male participants sent ca. 8% more on average in the trust game than their female counterparts. This result agrees with studies using the same methods for their risk and trust games (Schechter 2007; Ahsan 2014).

Total income has no significant effect in explaining the trust behaviour of the individual. However, when including income classes, very poor and poor households (as compared to the medium quantile) sent substantially less in the trust game, on average.

Robustness Checks Schechter (2007) highlights a concern that participants may have sent more in the trust game if they had a lucky roll of the die in the risk game. Indeed, Said et al. (2015) report that participants who had won a higher amount in round 1 made more risk-taking decisions in round 2. Indeed, the amount won in the risk game has an effect on the level sent in the trust game. The more money that was won in the first game, the lower the level of trust (regression 5), which contrasts with the results in the literature. Interestingly, the effect changes with the experience of a disaster: the more an affected participant won in the risk game, the smaller the amount they sent in the trust game (regression 6).

In addition to the regressions presented above, other control variables were added. Neither the type of damage (household property, production assets) nor the source of received help (government, charity) are significant in explaining trust behaviour. Moreover, no significant impact of income distribution (Gini coefficient within a village), mean village income, or amount of time a participant lived in the village can be found.

3.5.3 *Trustworthiness*

After interpreting the results from the first round of the trust game, regressions (7) and (8) analyse the second round of the game. The share sent back in the trust game measures trustworthiness, also referred to as reciprocity in the literature. Again, the impact of a disaster experience as well as socio-economic variables will be investigated.

Experience of Natural Disaster In the regression (7), the experience of a natural disaster has a significant and negative effect on the share returned by player 2 in the trust game. People who experienced a natural disaster return less to player 1 on average, and therefore show a lower level of trustworthiness. However, when village effects are included in the regression (8), there is no longer a significant effect, while village dummies become highly significant. Therefore, the village-specific characteristics are the dominating explanatory variable for trustworthiness of participants; exposure to natural disaster can no longer explain differences in trustworthiness. Thus, hypothesis H3 cannot be rejected.

This result aligns with Ahsan (2014), who also did not find any significant effect of exposure towards natural disaster on trustworthiness. The initial negative effect can be explained by aftermath moral hazard, which arises through increasing information asymmetries about damages and losses after a disaster (Fleming et al. 2014). The positive effect of a natural disaster on trustworthiness found in other studies cannot be confirmed (Castillo and Carter 2011; Cassar et al. 2012).

Impact of Risk Behaviour The regressions shown above were repeated by including the share bet in the risk game. No significant impact of the risk behaviour on the share returned in the trust game could be found (see Table 3.11). This was to be expected, since decisions behind trustworthiness are not made under uncertainty (Schechter 2007). Therefore, hypothesis H5 cannot be rejected.

Socio-Economic Variables When including village dummies, the married state is significant and positive for explaining the trustworthiness of a household. Participants who are married returned 24.2% more to player 1 on average than individuals who are not.

Table 3.11 Including share bet in risk game in regression for trustworthiness

	(7)	(8)
Share bet in risk game	−0.044 (0.079)	−0.044 (0.080)
Number of observations	167	167

Each column represents the regressions (7) to (8) for trustworthiness (above) with the share returned in trust game as dependent variable. Control variables included as in Table 3.7
Standard errors in parentheses
***p < 0.01, **p < 0.05, *p < 0.10

In regression (7), the behaviour as player 1 has a positive and significant impact on the behaviour as player 2. Participants who have trusted more, and therefore sent more as player 1, are on average more trustworthy. This result was also found in other studies (Schechter 2007; Fleming et al. 2014). The impact of the behaviour in the first game disappears again when controlling for village-specific characteristics in regression (8).

Fleming et al. (2014) found a positive impact of individual income on trustworthiness. However, in this study, income cannot explain trustworthy behaviour. The effect stays insignificant when income classes are included.

Robustness Checks In addition to the regressions presented above, other control variables have been tested. On average, damages to household property reduce trustworthiness. However, the damage type-specific impact disappears again when village-specific characteristics are considered. The source of received help has no significant effect.

3.6 Conclusion

This chapter has presented the outcomes of a regression analysis, investigating the impact of experiencing natural disasters and socio-economic characteristics on the risk-taking propensity and levels of trust and trustworthiness of participating households. Several linear regressions and robustness checks were conducted in order to investigate the proposed hypotheses. Table 3.12 summarises the results regarding the five hypotheses.

Risk Aversion This study found a significant positive impact of the experience of natural disasters on risk-taking propensity, whereby hypothesis H1 can be rejected. Thus, this empirical evidence can be added to the relatively new literature investigating the experience of natural disaster on individuals' risk behaviour with ambiguous results. Several theoretical channels are analysed (income effect, update of information, perception of risks, emotions), whereby the perception of risks as well as the emotional state seem to be important in explaining risk behaviour after the experience of a natural disaster. Under specific circumstances of the underlying reference point, prospect theory may also be able to explain this behaviour due to a

Table 3.12 Result of analysis regarding hypotheses about risk and trust behaviour

Hypotheses		Result of analysis
H1	The experiences of natural disasters have no significant influence on an individual's risk-taking propensity	Rejected
H2	The amount sent in a trust game will not depend on the sender's experience of natural disasters	Rejected
H3	The level of trustworthiness will not depend on experiences of natural disasters	Not rejected
H4	Risk preference has no influence on individual levels of trust	Rejected
H5	The level of trustworthiness will not depend on an individual's risk behaviour	Not rejected

loss in wealth. These results also support the Gambler's Fallacy: after a disaster, future events appear less likely. In conclusion, psychological factors play an important and often neglected role in explaining changing individual behaviour due to adverse shocks.

A non-linear effect between age and risk-taking behaviour can be found, initially with less and later with more risk-averse behaviour following the experience of a disaster. Individuals with better financial literacy are less risk-averse, whilst married individuals and those from larger households tend to be more risk-averse. Participants who assess their own vulnerability higher than other households in the village are on average also more risk-averse in the risk game. This effect is more noticeable when the household was affected by the disaster.

Trust and Trustworthiness The experience of a natural disaster has a significant and negative effect on the individual's level of trust, therefore hypothesis H2 can be rejected. Several theoretical explanations were found to explain this observation. Lower levels of trust may arise from rivalry within the community to receive scarce recovery resources in the aftermath of a disaster. Furthermore, natural disasters have a large impact on internal and external migration, changing the social structure of the community. Additionally, the gender of the participant has been found to have a significant effect on the level of trust, showing that men are more trusting than women. Trust behaviour is significantly impacted by the risk behaviour of the participant; thus, hypothesis H4 can be rejected. Furthermore, a lower level of trust can be reported for poor households.

Experiencing a disaster has a significant negative effect on trustworthiness; however, the effect disappears when controlling for village-specific characteristics. It is apparent that village-specific attributes significantly determine the level of trustworthiness of the individual household. The risk behaviour does not significantly impact the level of trustworthiness. Therefore, hypotheses H3 and H5 cannot be rejected. On average, participants who are married returned more in the trust game than non-married individuals.

Implications The results presented above provide important implications for natural disaster policy and show the relevance of deeper and broader analyses of the effect of disasters on individual behaviour. Social capital—trust and trustworthiness—can be a key factor in the economic and social recovery of communities and therefore plays a vital role for aftermath policies, specifically in the design of efficient aid and recovery mechanisms (Fleming et al. 2014; Said et al. 2015).

A lower level of trust due to the experience of a disaster—observed in the experiment in Cambodia—might lead to decreasing social capital. Higher rivalry for recovery resources and less support within the village could be the result and delay the accomplishments of the restoration process. Additionally, less trust could yield lower productivity and economic growth (Knack and Keefer 1997; Zak and Knack 2001; Ahsan 2014). A lower level of trustworthiness may also have a significant impact on the efficiency of aid provided to communities.

The results presented above indicate a higher risk-taking behaviour from those affected by natural disaster. This may have important implications for decisions about investments in productive activities, namely entrepreneurship, agriculture technologies, etc. (Said et al. 2015). Therefore, providing opportunities for local investment may be a successful and efficient aftermath policy, particularly given the positive long-term effects on economic development.

To conclude, significant changes in risk, trust or trustworthiness may have relevance for the design and efficiency of aftermath policies. Therefore, these effects should be addressed in more detail in further academic research and considered in the design of policy programmes.

Limitation of Research and Critical Appraisal Most of the studies investigating the impact of natural disaster are focused on measuring the short-term effects. Therefore, it is difficult to assess if the measured behaviour originates from one specific shock or from background risk, composed of past experiences in the long-term (Dang 2012).

Due to the single experiment and questionnaire at one point in time, no dynamic effects of natural disaster on individual behaviour can be analysed. The recurrent experience of certain extreme weather events could improve the individuals' ability to cope by creating learning effects. By updating individual information regarding future events and learning about aftermath behaviour in their community, another disaster might have a smaller or different effect on the individuals' risk behaviour and levels of trust. There is also evidence that an increased perception of the probability for future events may lead to higher discount rates (Cassar et al. 2012).

Several robustness checks have been conducted to consider possible misleading effects within the regressions. Nevertheless, the collection of data along with experiments in developing countries contain certain problems (see Sect. 3.3 and Appendix for a detailed description of the data collection).

Although the questionnaire is relatively comprehensive as compared to other studies, there are particular challenges for empirical analysis. Specifically, it was necessary to calculate the income of the participants based on various individual statements and assumptions for a broad ranch of income sources (see descriptive statistics in the Appendix). Additionally, individual information on economic losses due to the disaster lacks detail and comparability. Due to a lack of data about gifts and provided services within the community, a deeper consideration of how levels of trust might be confounded with kindness or altruism (Barr 2003; Schechter 2007) is not possible. Although comparable with other field research regarding the question, the number of households participating in the study is too small to investigate specific sub-groups. Altogether, a broader and deeper database could therefore strengthen the empirical research. Additionally, as described previously, it was necessary to conduct the experiments in the Khmer language. Linguistic competence of all research parties is strongly preferable in order to smoothly conduct the experiment.

Further Impact: Microinsurance Demand The following chapter directs its focus on the demand side of microinsurance. Besides other social and structural factors, risk aversion and individual levels of trust are found in the literature as important determinants for microinsurance demand. Therefore, an indirect impact of the experience of natural disaster on the demand for microinsurance can be assumed. The following chapter will analyse this link, investigate individual behaviour in the context of microinsurance and evaluate the impact of risk behaviour and trust on the demand for microinsurance products in rural areas of Cambodia.

References

Ahsan D (2014) Does natural disaster influence people's risk preference and trust? An experiment from cyclone prone coast of Bangladesh. Int J Disaster Risk Reduct 9:48–57

Alesina A, La Ferrara E (2002) Who trusts others? J Public Econ 85:207–234

Asgary A, Levy J (2009) A review of the implications of prospect theory for natural hazards and disaster planning. Int J Environ Res 3:379–394

Ayton P, Fischer I (2004) The hot hand fallacy and the gambler's fallacy: two faces of subjective randomness? Mem Cognit 32:1369–1378

Bakshi GS, Chen Z (1994) Baby boom, population aging, and capital markets. J Bus 67:165–202

Barr A (2003) Trust and expected trustworthiness: experimental evidence from Zimbabwean villages. Econ J 113:614–630

Berg J, Dickhaut J, McCabe K (1995) Trust, reciprocity, and social history. Games Econ Behav 10:122–142

Bjørnskov C, Méon P-G (2010) The productivity of trust. CEB Working Paper 10/042, Brussels

Bjørnskov C, Méon P-G (2013) Is trust the missing root of institutions, education, and development? Public Choice 157:641–669

Botzen WJW, Aerts JCJH, van den Bergh JCJM (2009) Willingness of homeowners to mitigate climate risk through insurance. Ecol Econ 68:2265–2277

Burks SV, Carpenter JP, Verhoogen E (2003) Playing both roles in the trust game. J Econ Behav Organ 51:195–216

Butler JK, Cantrell SR (1984) A behavioral decision theory approach to modeling dyadic trust in superiors and subordinates. Psychol Rep 55:19–28

Cameron L, Shah M (2015) Risk-taking behavior in the wake of natural disasters. Hum Resour 50:484–515

Cardenas JC, Carpenter J (2008) Behavioural development economics: lessons from field labs in the developing world. J Dev Stud 44:311–338

Cassar A, Healy A, von Kessler C (2012) Trust, risk, and time preferences after a natural disaster: experimental evidence from Thailand. University of San Francisco, San Francisco
Castillo M, Carter M (2011) Behavioral responses to natural disasters. GMU Interdisciplinary Center for Economic Science, Arlington
Cavallo E, Noy I (2010) The economics of natural disasters—a survey. IDB Working Paper Series 124, Washington, DC
Clarke DJ, Grenham D (2013) Microinsurance and natural disasters: challenges and options. Environ Sci Policy 27:S89–S98
Cole S, Giné X, Tobacman J et al (2013) Barriers to household risk management: evidence from India. Am Econ J Appl Econ 5:104–135
Croson R, Sundali J (2005) The gambler's fallacy and the hot hand: empirical data from casinos. J Risk Uncertain 30:195–209
Dang DA (2012) On the sources of risk preferences in rural Vietnam. MPRA Paper 38058, Munich
Das TK, Teng B-S (2004) The risk-based view of trust: a conceptual framework. J Bus Psychol 19:85–116
De Bock O, Gelade W (2012) The demand for microinsurance: a literature review. Microinsurance Innovation Facility Research Paper 26, Geneva
Dhami S, Al-Nowaihi A (2007) Why do people pay taxes? Prospect theory versus expected utility theory. J Econ Behav Organ 64:171–192
Dillenberger D, Rozen K (2015) History-dependent risk attitude. J Econ Theory 157:445–477
Eckel CC, Grossman PJ (2008) Forecasting risk attitudes: an experimental study using actual and forecast gamble choices. J Econ Behav Organ 68:1–17
Eckel CC, El-Gamal MA, Wilson RK (2009) Risk loving after the storm: a Bayesian-network study of Hurricane Katrina evacuees. J Econ Behav Organ 69:110–124
Eiser RJ, Bostrom A, Burton I et al (2012) Risk interpretation and action: a conceptual framework for responses to natural hazards. Int J Disaster Risk Reduct 1:5–16
Fischhoff B, Goitein B, Shapira Z (1983) Subjective expected utility: a model of decision-making. Adv Psychol 16:183–207
Fleming DA, Chong A, Bejarano HD (2014) Trust and reciprocity in the aftermath of natural disasters. J Dev Stud 50:1482–1493
Fukuyama F (1995) Trust—the social virtues and the creation of prosperity. The Free Press, New York
Gambetta D (1988) Can we trust trust? In: Gambetta D (ed) Trust: making and breaking cooperative relations. Blackwell, Oxford, pp 213–237
Gheyssens J, Günther I (2011) Risk experiments in gains and losses: do rural villagers want microinsurance? ETH Discussion paper, Zurich
Gilovich T, Vallone R, Tversky A (1985) The hot hand in basketball: on the misperception of random sequences. Cogn Psychol 17:295–314
Gollier C, Pratt JW (1996) Risk vulnerability and the tempering effect of background risk. Econometrica 64:1109–1123
Guiso L, Paiella M (2008) Risk aversion, wealth, and background risk. J Eur Econ Assoc 6:1109–1150
Halek M, Eisenhauer JG (2001) Demography of risk aversion. J Risk Insur 68:1–24
Hallegatte S (2012) An exploration of the link between development, economic growth, and natural risk. The World Bank Policy Research Working Paper 6216, Washington, DC
Hallegatte S, Bangalore M, Bonzanigo L et al (2016) Shock waves: managing the impacts of climate change on poverty. The World Bank, Washington, D.C.
Hanaoka C, Shigeoka H, Watanabe Y (2015) Do risk preferences change? Evidence from panel data before and after the great East Japan earthquake. NBER Working Paper Series 21400, Cambridge, MA
Huber J, Kirchler M, Stöckl T (2010) The hot hand belief and the gambler's fallacy in investment decisions under risk. Theory Decis 68:445–462

Ingwersen N (2014) Impact of a natural disaster on observed risk aversion. Duke University, Durham
James HS (2002) The trust paradox: a survey of economic inquiries into the nature of trust and trustworthiness. J Econ Behav Organ 47:291–307
Kahneman D, Tversky A (1979) Prospect theory: an analysis of decision under risk. Econometrica 47:263–292
Kanagaretnam K, Mestelman S, Nainar SMK, Shehata M (2010) Trust and reciprocity with transparency and repeated interactions. J Bus Res 63:241–247
Karim A, Noy I (2016) Poverty and natural disasters – a qualitative survey of the empirical literature. Singapore Econ Rev 61:1640001
Karlan DS (2005) Using experimental economics to measure social capital and predict financial decisions. Am Econ Rev 95:1688–1699
Kee HW, Knox RE (1970) Conceptual and methodological considerations in the study of trust and suspicion. J Confl Resolut 14:357–366
Kellenberg DK, Mobarak AM (2008) Does rising income increase or decrease damage risk from natural disasters? J Urban Econ 63:788–802
Knack S, Keefer P (1997) Does social capital have an economic payoff? A cross-country investigation. Q J Econ 112:1251–1288
Lerner JS, Keltner D (2001) Fear, anger, and risk. J Pers Soc Psychol 81:146–159
Levhari D, Weiss Y (1974) The effect of risk on the investment in human capital. Am Econ Rev 64:950–963
Levy JS (1992) An introduction to prospect theory. Polit Psychol 13:171–186
Lewicki RJ, McAllister DJ, Bies RJ (1998) Trust and distrust: new relationship and realities. Acad Manage Rev 23:438–458
Li J-Z, Li S, Wang W-Z et al (2011) Are people always more risk averse after disasters? Surveys after a heavy snow-hit and a major earthquake in China in 2008. Appl Cogn Psychol 25:104–111
Loewenstein GF, Weber EU, Hsee CK, Welch N (2001) Risk as feelings. Psychol Bull 127:267–286
MacCrimmon KR, Wehrung D, Stanbury WT (1988) Taking risks. Simon & Schuster, New York
Malmendier U, Nagel S (2011) Depression babies: do macroeconomic experiences affect risk taking? Q J Econ 126:373–416
March JG, Shapira Z (1987) Managerial perspectives on risk and risk taking. Manag Sci 33:1404–1418
McKnight DH, Cummings LL, Chervany NL (1998) Initial trust formation in new organizational relationships. Acad Manage Rev 23:473–490
Narayan D, Pritchett L (1999) Cents and sociability: household income and social capital in rural Tanzania. Econ Dev Cult Chang 47:871–897
Nguyen M-H, Reynaud A, Thomas A, Thanh ND (2012) Do natural disasters modify individual preferences: evidences from a field experiment in Vietnam. School of Economics, Toulouse
Open Development (2016) Open Development mapping kit. http://www.opendevelopmentcambodia.net/maps/. Accessed 29 Apr 2016
Page L, Savage DA, Torgler B (2014) Variation in risk seeking behaviour following large losses: a natural experiment. Eurasian Econ Rev 71:121–131
Pat-Horenczyk R, Peled O, Miron T et al (2007) Risk-taking behaviors among Israeli adolescents exposed to recurrent terrorism: provoking danger under continuous threat? Am J Psychiatry 164:66–72
Pratt JW (1964) Risk aversion in the small and in the large. Econometrica 32:122–136
Quiggin J (2003) Background risk in generalized expected utility theory. Econ Theory 22:607–611
Raghunathan R, Pham MT (1999) All negative moods are not equal: motivational influences of anxiety and sadness on decision making. Organ Behav Hum Decis Process 79:56–77
Reynaud A, Nguyen M-H (2012) Monetary valuation of flood insurance in Vietnam. Vietnam Center of Research in Economics, Management and Environment 01-2012, Hanoi, Ho Chi Minh City

Reynaud A, Aubert C, Nguyen M-H (2013) Living with floods: protective behaviours and risk perception of Vietnamese households. Geneva Pap Risk Insur Issues Pract 38:547–579
Riley WB, Chow KV (1992) Asset allocation and individual risk aversion. Financ Anal J 48:32–37
Rousseau DM, Sitkin SB, Burt RS, Camerer C (1998) Not so different after all: a cross-discipline view of trust. Acad Manage Rev 23:393–404
Said F, Afzal U, Turner G (2014) Attitudes towards risk in the wake of a rare event: evidence from Pakistan. CREB Working Paper 02-14, Lahore
Said F, Afzal U, Turner G (2015) Risk taking and risk learning after a rare event: evidence from a field experiment in Pakistan. J Econ Behav Organ 118:167–183
Savage LJ (1954) The foundations of statistics. Courier Corporation, Chicago
Schechter L (2007) Traditional trust measurement and the risk confound: an experiment in rural Paraguay. J Econ Behav Organ 62:272–292
Schmidt U, Starmer C, Sugden R (2008) Third-generation prospect theory. J Risk Uncertain 36:203–223
Schoemaker PJH (1982) The expected utility model: its variants, purposes, evidence and limitations. J Econ Lit 20:529–563
Shanteau J (1992) Decision making under risk: applications to insurance purchasing. Adv Consum Res 19:177–181
Shaw KL (1996) An empirical analysis of risk aversion and income growth. J Labor Econ 14:626
Sheppard BH, Sherman DM (1998) The grammars of trust: a model and general implications. Acad Manage Rev 23:422–437
Sitkin SB, Pablo AL (1992) Reconceptualizing the determinants of risk behavior. Acad Manage Rev 17:9–38
Sitkin SB, Roth NL (1993) Explaining the limited effectiveness of legalistic "remedies" for trust/distrust. Organ Sci 4:367–392
Solnit R (2009) A paradise built in hell: the extraordinary communities that arise in disaster. Penguin Publishing Group, London
Tamura H (2005) Behavioral models for complex decision analysis. Eur J Oper Res 166:655–665
Terrell D (1994) A test of the gambler's fallacy: evidence from pari-mutuel games. J Risk Uncertain 8:309–317
Toya H, Skidmore M (2012) Do natural disasters enhance societal trust? CESifo Working Paper 3905, Munich
Turner G, Said F, Afzal U (2014) Microinsurance demand after a rare flood event: evidence from a field experiment in Pakistan. Geneva Pap Risk Insur Issues Pract 39:201–223
Tversky A, Kahneman D (1974) Judgment under uncertainty: heuristics and biases. Science 185:1124–1131
Tversky A, Kahneman D (1992) Advances in prospect theory: cumulative representation of uncertainty. J Risk Uncertain:297–323
van den Berg M, Fort R, Burger K (2009) Natural hazards and risk aversion: experimental evidence from Latin America. In: International Association of Agricultural Economists conference 2009, Beijing
Wang H, Hanna SD (1997) Does risk tolerance decrease with age? Financ Couns Plan 8:27–32
Whitt S, Wilson RK (2007) Public goods in the field: Katrina Evacuees in Houston. South Econ J 74:377–287
World Bank (2013) World development report 2014: risk and opportunity—managing risk for development. World Bank, Washington, DC
Zak PJ, Knack S (2001) Trust and growth. Econ J 111:295–321
Zweifel P, Eisen R (2012) Insurance economics. Springer, Berlin, Heidelberg

Chapter 4
The Demand for Microinsurance Products Against Disaster Risk

The previous chapters have shown both enormous social and economic effects as well as significant impacts on individual behaviour. Therefore, beyond the immediate and direct effects, there are compelling impacts on economic activities and human capital. For instance, disaster risk and the anticipation of shocks leads to an engagement of households in strategies with lower productivity in order to decrease income variability and vulnerability (Skees 2008; Oviedo and Moroz 2014; Karim and Noy 2016).

As seen in Chap. 2, these economic and social impacts have increased through weather variability and climate extremes, and are likely to increase further due to climate change and its regional effects. The adverse effects of natural disasters are particularly harmful for less resilient countries and deeply affect poor and more vulnerable individuals and households. In addition, the poor are limited in their access to coping mechanisms such as insurance, savings, social safety nets and others. Suitable risk management tools are necessary to remove or reduce the financial risk arising from natural hazards and to limit the adverse impacts on poverty alleviation and development processes. Insurance is one promising instrument to cope with financial risks, which can further encourage investments in prevention measures and therefore risk reduction (Mechler et al. 2006; Surminski and Oramas-Dorta 2014).

With the focus on developing countries, microinsurance models were developed as an instrument for low-income clients to compensate losses caused by natural disasters and to strengthen their ability to cope with the consequences. Furthermore, positive side effects arise from the higher creditworthiness of insured households and small businesses as well as a higher likelihood of investing in productive assets (Mechler et al. 2006).

Hereby these instruments are intended to provide easily accessible and affordable insurance against the impact of natural disasters such as floods, droughts, storms, and others. Dependent on the specific insurance project, life, health, property and crops are covered. Nevertheless, limitations of this instrument arise in the context of disaster risk from the covariant appearance of the hazard as well as from

O. Fiala, *Natural Disasters and Individual Behaviour in Developing Countries*, Contributions to Economics, DOI 10.1007/978-3-319-53904-1_4

moral hazard, asymmetric information and the immature nature of microinsurance markets (Churchill 2006a; Mechler et al. 2006; Clarke and Grenham 2013).

Even if microinsurance in general appears to be a promising tool to reduce vulnerability for low-income households, the overall enrolment rates in specific projects remain relatively low (Cole et al. 2007; Mahul and Skees 2007; Giné and Yang 2009; Cole et al. 2013; Eling et al. 2014). Possible explanations for this can be found on the supply as well as on the demand side.

On the supply side, traditional actors such as insurance companies, re-insurance companies, as well as governments and non-governmental organisations are included. However, significant volumes of insurances will only be offered if these are profitable for companies, meaning that the charged premiums exceed the costs of covering the risk as well as the administration costs. Given that microinsurance targets low-income households with relatively small premiums and overheads, the insurer must develop cost-effective distribution channels; community-based models, cooperation with microfinance organisations or new technologies such as mobile phones used for financial transactions are used in developing countries (Clarke and Grenham 2013).

Furthermore, the limited availability of modelling tools and data for various hazards at the local level are challenges for providing adequate products at affordable prices (Surminski and Oramas-Dorta 2014). In addition, proper regulation for these specific kinds of insurance as well as extension of the contract term (currently often only one year), could help to better manage the negative effects of adverse selection and provide a more sustainable microinsurance supply (Clarke and Grenham 2013). A comprehensive and more detailed consideration of the supply side for microinsurance products is provided by Churchill (2006a) and Churchill and Matul (2012).

On the demand side, a variety of factors play a crucial role. Summarising various studies, Eling et al. (2014) identify 12 key factors affecting microinsurance demand. Social factors include risk aversion, levels of trust and financial literacy. Structural factors include informal risk-sharing instruments and the individual risk exposure. Beside these effects, economic factors include the price of insurance and the wealth and income of households, while personal factors highlight the importance of age and gender of the individual (Eling et al. 2014).

In contrast to traditional insurance markets, a negative correlation between risk aversion and the demand for microinsurance products is evident, whereby the literature often concludes that insurance itself may be viewed as risky by households (Cole et al. 2007; Giné et al. 2008; De Bock and Gelade 2012; Eling et al. 2014). This can be explained by the anticipated or actual non-performance in the case of losses, including basis risk for index-based insurances (Clarke 2011).

In addition, the individual level of trust is seen as a crucial factor. Various studies see the 'non-performance' risk as a core reason for lack of trust (Giné et al. 2008; Cole et al. 2013). The importance of trust in insurance contracts is affected by the enforcement of property rights which is especially relevant in environments with weak legal systems (Eling et al. 2014). Furthermore, trust is a significant factor for the decision to participate in community-based informal insurance networks (World Bank 2013).

Furthermore, risk exposure has a significant impact on the demand for microinsurance products. Given that the experience of natural disasters also indirectly affects the levels of risk and trust (see Chap. 3), a crucial role of disaster experience on the demand for microinsurance products can be assumed. Therefore, a deeper analysis of the relationship between disaster experience and microinsurance demand is needed. Based on a comprehensive literature review as well as the experiment and survey conducted in rural Cambodia, this chapter will provide evidence of a significant impact of disaster experience on the household demand for microinsurance products. For this reason, the following analysis focuses on the demand side and ignores supply-side effects.

Section 4.1 provides an introduction into insurance as an instrument of disaster risk management, its potential and a broader description of microinsurance and its characteristics. The chapter will provide an overview of the microinsurance landscape in Cambodia. Following this introduction into microinsurance in general, Sect. 4.2 provides a comprehensive overview of the individual determinants of microinsurance demand and their interactions, with a particular focus on the impact of disaster experience. Building on this, Sect. 4.3 provides the empirical analysis of the impact of individual preferences and exposure to natural disaster on the demand for microinsurance products. Section 4.4 concludes the analysis.

4.1 Microinsurance as an Instrument of Disaster Risk Management

The following section introduces microinsurance products as instruments of disaster risk management against natural hazards. Section 4.1.1 describes insurance as an instrument for coping with disaster risk, with a focus on insurance in developing countries. Section 4.1.2 defines and describes microinsurance and its characteristics, including delivery models as well as the emerging instrument of index-based insurance. Section 4.1.3 concludes with a brief overview of the microinsurance landscape, particularly in Asia.

4.1.1 Insurances for Disaster

Disaster Risk Management and Risk-Financing Strategies

Chapter 2 introduced the concept of disaster risk management and presented the four components of knowledge, protection, insurance and coping (World Bank 2013). Aside from the presented framework, the literature often consolidates various financial instruments as risk-financing strategies, distinct from risk reduction (prevention and mitigation in order to reduce exposure and vulnerability); hereby risk-financing strategies manage the residual risk and provide appropriate relief and effective recovery (Linnerooth-Bayer et al. 2011). However, a balance between risk reduction and risk transfer as well as effective disaster preparation and management of disaster impact is needed (IPCC 2012; Linnerooth-Bayer and Hochrainer-Stigler 2015).

Traditional risk-financing instruments comprise governmental and donor assistance, reallocation of expenditures, ex ante savings and ex post credits, informal risk-sharing arrangements (reciprocal exchange, community self-help) and insurances as well as capital markets (World Bank 2007; Linnerooth-Bayer and Hochrainer-Stigler 2015).[1] The specific design of each instrument, its feasibility and limitations depend largely on the local preconditions and framework conditions.

Insurance as Risk Transfer Instrument
Risk transfer is a well-established instrument to manage the risk of uncertain losses by shifting the financial risk.[2] It is mostly used in its basic form of insurances, where an individual or organisation (the insured) transfer—in return for a payment—part of their risk to another party (the insurer). In case of a loss, the insurer pays out a pre-defined amount. Insurance does not reduce the immediate damage of the disaster itself, but by pooling the risk it provides compensation for losses. Hereby, the contributions of a larger group benefit the insured victim. The willingness to pay for insurance arises from the aversion to large losses and the concern of an individual about the volatility of possible outcomes (Mechler et al. 2006; Surminski and Oramas-Dorta 2011; Linnerooth-Bayer et al. 2011).

Potential of Insurance
Insurance has the potential to provide a defence against social and financial exclusion for individuals whose existing coping mechanism struggles (Mosley 2009). The access to insurance markets and the provision of effective protection through the reduction of uncertainty about a future economic status can therefore encourage investment in productive activities to increase growth and sustainable development (Skees 2008; Cai et al. 2009; Mosley 2009).

---

[1]More recently, capital markets as an alternative to traditional types of cover have been developed. So-called 'catastrophe bonds' and other instruments spread the risk of a disaster directly to capital markets instead of pooling it within the community (World Bank 2007; Botzen et al. 2009; Surminski and Oramas-Dorta 2011; Chhibber and Laajaj 2013; Linnerooth-Bayer and Hochrainer-Stigler 2015). Many of these bonds are designed parametrically, thus using measurable indices which trigger payments (Skees et al. 2005). In addition, the role of indexed catastrophe bonds in providing disaster relief to developing countries has been discussed (Goes and Skees 2003).

[2]The advantages of a risk transfer mechanism include less pressure on fiscal balances after a disaster, increased government control over financing the disaster, greater capacity for the countries to set their own priorities as well as increased transparency for relief and reconstruction funding and the promotion of mitigation (Benson and Clay 2004).

Especially in developing countries, risk transfer—and particularly insurance—can play a cost-effective role to increase resilience and can be an important part of a country's adaptation against disaster risk (Surminski and Oramas-Dorta 2011). Due to the dependence on agriculture in these countries, weather or disaster insurance could play an important role in helping rural households to mitigate risk, providing quick access to disaster relief and recovery needs, and improve their creditworthiness and therefore general access to financial resources (Mechler et al. 2006; Skees 2008).

In detail, insurances against disaster risks reduce poverty by protecting rural livelihoods, the productive capacity of farm households and small enterprises, and financial institutions against disaster-related defaults of loans, as well as financing disaster relief. Furthermore, investments in higher-return activities are promoted, rural access to credit and other financial services is improved and better public spending is enabled through the provision of a mechanism to manage the most costly source of risk (Skees 2008). In addition, insurance significantly reduces the probability of selling livestock during a drought and therefore improves the recovery process (Janzen and Carter 2013). By improving stability and opportunities for growth in the agricultural and financial sectors, economic development should be stimulated (Skees 2008). The benefits of microinsurance products as effective instruments of disaster risk management will be discussed further in Sect. 5, in light of the empirical results.

Informal Insurances

Without existing or affordable insurance systems, households in developing countries rely on informal insurance mechanisms. These includes savings, access to credit through microfinance institutions or money lenders, the reliance on public and international aid, as well as the depleting or mortgaging of land and assets. Furthermore, there are arrangements based on the principles of kin and reciprocity, such as family support, community self-help and remittances. Due to the direct observation of others within communities and frequent personal communication, informal insurance systems based on social ties reduce problems of information asymmetry and moral hazard. While some of this locally-based funding works reasonably well for small, localised (idiosyncratic) events, they are problematic for disasters affecting an entire risk-sharing community (common or systemic risks)[3] (Cohen and Sebstad 2005; de Weerdt 2005; Dercon 2005; Skees et al. 2005; Mechler et al. 2006; Linnerooth-Bayer et al. 2011; World Bank 2013).

Despite the positive effects of community-based informal insurance systems, uncertainty about the actual protection from the adverse effects of disaster risk through these instruments and their inefficiency reduces investments in productive activities (ex ante disaster impact); this can lead to a poverty trap, where assets and livelihoods cannot be equivalently restored, making households even more vulnerable to future risks (Dercon 2005; Mechler et al. 2006; Barnett et al. 2008; Skees

[3]However, in practice few risks are purely idiosyncratic and common (Dercon 2005; Mechler et al. 2006; Linnerooth-Bayer et al. 2011).

2008). In particular, very poor households have limited options for proactive risk management and have to leave informal group-based systems if they cannot satisfy reciprocal obligations. If no governmental system of social protection exists, they depend on often inadequate self-insurance mechanisms (Cohen and Sebstad 2005; World Bank 2013). Furthermore, insurance arrangements which rely on social ties and shared norms often exclude minorities and are easily challenged by in-migration (World Bank 2013).

Insurances in Developing Countries

The emergence of new insurance instruments as well as the possibility of transferring disaster risk to global financial markets have motivated governments and organisations in developing countries to consider financial instruments and insurance as disaster risk management approaches (Linnerooth-Bayer et al. 2011). However, traditional disaster insurances used in higher income countries are often not suitable for lower income countries (Skees 2008).[4] Incomplete or non-existing insurance markets endure due to financial restraints, moral hazard, adverse selection, asymmetric information, high transaction costs and a lack of effective legal systems (Skees et al. 2005; Barnett et al. 2008; Dror and Piesse 2014).

Insufficient resources to control information asymmetries as well as lack of data, undersized risk pools and excessive transaction costs are significant problems, especially for health and agriculture insurance. Furthermore, insurance markets in developing countries often lack institutional stability, public confidence and trust, and need competent regulatory bodies to enable the market to provide sustainable insurance contracts. Finally, existing insurance schemes are often limited in their scalability and geographic spread with uncorrelated risks (Mechler et al. 2006; Linnerooth-Bayer et al. 2011; Biener and Eling 2012; Hochrainer-Stigler et al. 2012; Gehrke 2014).

Disaster risks are characterised by the difficulty in estimating them, the effect on large parts of the population (and therefore the effect on the risk pool at the same time), the breakdown of informal safety nets (family and friends), the covariant nature of the disaster with multiple simultaneous losses to life, health, property and crops (Brown and Churchill 2000). Therefore, disaster risk insurances are much more complex than health or life insurances because of disaster impact on large regions with multiple losses, the covariant nature of risks and the large capital resources needed to avoid insolvency (Mechler et al. 2006; Linnerooth-Bayer et al. 2011).

Insurances should be implemented within a broader disaster risk scheme and can be combined with other transfer and mitigation mechanisms (Reinhard and Qureshi 2013). Linking community-based informal instruments to formal insurance systems

[4]While 30% of households and businesses in high-income countries have insurances against disaster risks, only 1 and 3% in low- and middle-income countries, respectively, have such a financial instrument against natural hazards (data from Munich Re, cited by Mechler et al. (2006) and Linnerooth-Bayer and Mechler (2006)).

can help to overcome the shortcomings of both formal and informal insurance arrangements (World Bank 2013). Given the high costs of formal insurance, Reinhard and Qureshi (2013) suggest that extreme, low-probability shocks should be insured by formal products, and that informal insurance approaches such as credit, savings or risk-sharing with relatives should be used for less extreme, but frequent shocks.

Insurances in developing countries are often restricted by limited access to capital markets for reinsurance or alternative financial instruments, particularly for coping with disaster risk (Elbers et al. 2007; Clarke and Dercon 2009; Kouame and Kouam 2012; Janzen and Carter 2013; Clarke and Grenham 2013). Moreover, due to the potential insurance offers (financial inclusion, encouragement of investments, reduction of uncertainty, disaster financing, etc.) and a lack of widespread social safety nets for poor households, insurance products in developing countries are additionally considered from a humanitarian point of view; they are often seen as possible instruments for social protection as they reduce vulnerability and build resilience (Jacquier et al. 2006; Deblon and Loewe 2012). Programmes started in recent years are therefore often supported by governments, non-governmental organisations and international donors, and are often organised as a public-private insurance system (Linnerooth-Bayer et al. 2011; Clarke and Grenham 2013).

4.1.2 Description of Microinsurance

A cluster of different insurance programmes has emerged in the last 20 years—known as microinsurance—in order to provide easily accessible and affordable insurance instruments in developing countries. While these instruments mainly focus on life and health risks, there is a growing interest in weather and disaster risk instruments to reduce the long-term consequences of disasters by providing financial assistance (Mechler et al. 2006; Mosley 2009).

A variety of different definitions can be found in the literature. The first and most common definition is given by (Churchill 2006a), who defines microinsurance as the "protection of low-income people against specific perils in exchange for regular premium payments proportionate to the likelihood and cost of the risk involved". The significant difference in this definition to traditional insurance instruments is described by the target market: low-income people (Churchill 2006a; Mechler et al. 2006; Clarke and Grenham 2013). A second way the term 'micro' can be understood is as characteristic of the product by focusing on the size of premiums and benefits (Clarke and Grenham 2013; Dror and Piesse 2014). However, over the years the definition of microinsurance has become more operational by focusing on target groups, product definitions (definition based on sum assured or premium), provider definition (definition based on the type of provider) and distribution channels (Churchill and McCord 2012).

Although the definitions are apparently very similar to traditional insurances, the product itself is often quite different in many respects given its focus on people who are generally excluded from access to conventional insurance due to social, financial, cultural or other constraints (Clarke and Grenham 2013; Gehrke 2014). First-movers in microinsurance markets often simply downsized traditional insurance products for low-income markets, however this was not efficient; in fact, a specific design understanding the needs and living situations of the customers is needed for a much more effective insurance market (Biener and Eling 2012). To create sustainable microinsurance systems, low-priced insurances should be offered (with low transaction costs implied), accompanied by investments in customer education and understanding of the product as well as innovative distribution channels and the use of new technologies (Churchill 2006a).[5]

Another common feature of microinsurance is the group-based nature of contracts: households or farmers with similar risks share one contract to reduce the cost of issuing contracts and processing premiums and claims (Brown and Churchill 2000; Cohen and Sebstad 2005; Hochrainer-Stigler et al. 2012). Furthermore, the group-based nature of microinsurance products can exploit information advantages and therefore overcome moral hazard and adverse selection problems by peer monitoring, etc. (Heenkenda 2014). In some cases, classical indemnity-based insurances against weather risks are given out by local community groups or organisations, then pooled and again re-insured as group contracts with international insurers. Therefore, it is possible to provide protection against systemic risks—such as disaster risks—at an acceptable cost (Clarke and Grenham 2013; Dercon et al. 2014). Following Lloyd's and Microinsurance Centre (2009), Table 4.1 provides a distinction between traditional insurance and microinsurance products.

Delivery Models

A diverse range of delivery models are an additional and important characteristic for microinsurance instruments, which also helps to distinguish them from traditional insurance markets (Mechler et al. 2006). The literature distinguishes several provider models, whereby the full-service model, the community-based model, the partner-agent model, and the provider model are the most common (Cohen and McCord 2003).

In the full-service model, one commercial or public institution (commercial insurance company, microfinance institution, charity organisation) provides the full range of services, including product design, marketing, servicing and absorbing the risk. A large insurance company is usually better able to provide a large risk pool, offering access to reinsurance and capital markets; however, their social and geographical distance to the clients results in a lack of proper observation of risk profiles and behaviour (Cohen and McCord 2003; Gehrke 2014).

[5]Although the definitions of microinsurance—as well as this thesis—often concentrate on the demand side, there are certain conditions for insurability on the supply side: large numbers of similar units exposed to a certain risk; limited control of policy holder over the insured event; insurable as well as determinable and measurable interest; losses which are not catastrophic; a calculable chance of loss; economically affordable premiums (Brown and Churchill 2000).

Table 4.1 Comparison between microinsurance and traditional insurance

Characteristic	Microinsurance	Traditional insurance
Clients	High risk exposure/high vulnerability; weak insurance culture	Low risk environment; established insurance culture
Distribution models	Sold by non-traditional intermediaries to clients with little insurance experience	Sold by licensed intermediaries or by insurance company directly to clients or companies with insurance experience
Policies	Simply-formulated policies, with no or only few exclusions; often group policies; often index-based insurances	Complex policy documents with many exclusions; indemnity-based insurances
Premium calculation	Little historical data; group pricing; very price sensitive markets	Good statistical data; pricing based on individual risk
Premium collection	Frequent and irregular payments adapted to cash flows of clients; often linked with other transactions	Monthly to yearly payments; often paid via invoices or debit orders
Control of insurance risk (adverse selection, moral hazard, fraud)	Broad eligibility; Insurance risk included in premiums rather than controlled by exclusions; link to other services (e.g. credit)	Limited eligibility; significant documentation required, screenings may be necessary
Claims handling	Simple and fast procedures for small sums; efficient fraud control	Complicated processes, extensive documentation verification

Lloyd's and Microinsurance Centre (2009)

In the community-based model, a local community, microfinance organisation or other non-governmental organisation develops, distributes and manages the product. The risks are shared amongst the members of the local group, either ex ante by contributing to a fund or ex post by providing support to one member. Due to organisation by the local community, information about needs and risks is more easily accessible. However, broader knowledge about the effective design and management of insurance is lacking. In addition, the local coverage of risks prevents this distribution model from covering covariant events such as disaster or weather risks (Cohen and McCord 2003; Fonteneau and Galland 2006; Gehrke 2014).

The partner-agent model is characterised by a collaboration between a commercial or public insurer and a local microfinance institution or other organisation in the development of the product. While the public insurer (as the partner) is responsible for the product design and risk management, the local agent provides access to the clients' needs and risk information as well as an effective existing interface. By combining the advantages of the previous models, important synergies can be created through cooperation (Cohen and McCord 2003; McCord 2006; Gehrke 2014).

Finally, in the provider model, banks or microfinance institutions can directly offer insurance contracts or require them. These organisations often couple insurance products with credits or other services to reduce their own risk, for instance through disaster-related credit default (Cohen and McCord 2003; Mechler et al. 2006).

Mechler et al. (2006) note that cover against disaster risk can be provided as a public good, for instance through social protection, designated parts of governmental budgets or catastrophe funds. Hereby, no premium must be paid or needs to be collected.

Index Insurance

For traditional insurance and microinsurance products, claims are paid by the insurer based on actual losses which occur to households, small businesses and farmers. These indemnity-based insurances require an extensive network of employees who assess individual losses following a disaster as well as extensive marketing and servicing. Thus, such programmes are costly, particularly for crop insurance against extreme weather events, and are therefore not easily applicable and often unsuccessful in developing countries (World Bank 2005; Mechler et al. 2006; Clarke and Grenham 2013).

Such indemnity-based products also come with the classical market failures of insurances: moral hazard, adverse selection and fraud. The risk of moral hazards could be reduced, but not eliminated, by intensive control or deductible contracts (Mechler et al. 2006; Clarke and Grenham 2013). Both approaches are cost intensive and lower trust and understanding of the product for inexperienced clients. The risk of adverse selection can be mitigated by making insurance compulsory for farmers, for instance in combination with microfinance credit (Clarke and Grenham 2013). Further problems arise from fraud, where high costs occur from detection and investigation, as well as from high reinsurance costs due to limited access to global financial markets (Mechler et al. 2006; Clarke and Grenham 2013).

However, even if it may be possible to offer indemnity-based microinsurance products for some climate-related disasters, it is important to develop new approaches for lowering transaction and contract costs in order to provide affordable insurance products for the poor (Skees 2008; Clarke and Grenham 2013).

In contrast to indemnity-based insurances, so-called index-based insurances or index insurances emerged both in the academic literature and development projects to overcome the described shortcomings. An index insurance is written against a specific risk, represented by physical or economic triggers, for instance rainfall measured at a local weather station. The pay-out of the insurance depends only on the realisation of the index and is equal to the amount agreed to in the insurance contract (Mechler et al. 2006; Skees 2008; Linnerooth-Bayer et al. 2011).

Therefore, index-based insurance is not against the loss itself, but against the event which causes the loss (Linnerooth-Bayer et al. 2011). Hereby, the index serves as an proxy for the actual loss and the payment rate is the same for each policyholder with the same contract, regardless of their actual loss (Skees 2008). In fact, a compensation to a household who experienced a loss caused by a disaster may be too high, too low, or either, depending on the triggered index (Clarke and Grenham 2013).[6]

By conditioning the pay-out on an objective and cheaply observable index, which cannot be controlled by the policyholder, index insurances have the potential to significantly reduce problems of moral hazard, adverse selection and fraud (Clarke and Grenham 2013). In addition, as the claims are pre-fixed in the contract and the assessment of damage becomes irrelevant, transaction costs are much lower, while the transparency of these contracts is much higher than traditional insurance products; both make the administration of these insurances much simpler and allow for lower costs (Mechler et al. 2006; Skees 2008; Linnerooth-Bayer et al. 2011). As mentioned, index insurances are not only able to reduce moral hazard: as the actual payment is not directly connected to the individual's losses, they also provide incentives to reduce potential losses and increase awareness of risk reduction mechanisms (Mechler et al. 2006).

The significant disadvantage of index insurance is the insufficient correlation between the actual loss and the index, called 'basis risk' (Mechler et al. 2006; Skees 2008; Linnerooth-Bayer et al. 2011). Therefore, a disaster may lead to significant losses by the policy holder, which are not compensated because the index is not triggered (e.g. weather station to measure the index does not record same extent of an event as the individual household). In fact, from a household perspective, an individual who is suffering from basis risk is even worse-off than one without insurance at all: not only are no indemnities received, the insurance premium must also be paid (Clarke and Grenham 2013). However, basis risk can be minimised through appropriate product design and application (Skees 2008). Hereby, the availability of sufficient historical data for the chosen region is crucial to create an appropriate index, which correlates highly with the actual losses experienced by the households (Skees 2008; Clarke and Grenham 2013).

Experience with index insurance against extreme weather events in developing countries is still limited despite a rapidly growing number of pilot projects and some sustainable solutions. After the first successful pilot was implemented by the microfinance institution BASIX in the Indian state of Andhra Pradesh in 2003, several schemes at the individual level were started in Bangladesh, Burkina Faso, Ethiopia, Ghana, India, Kenya, Malawi, Mali, Mongolia, Nicaragua, Peru, Rwanda, Senegal, Tanzania and Thailand (Skees et al. 2007; Hellmuth et al. 2009; Cole et al.

[6]Index insurance can be offered on the macro level to governments and relief agencies, on the meso level to farmers' associations, non-governmental organisations or financial service providers, and on the micro level directly to farmers and individuals (Hazell et al. 2010). However, the focus in this thesis is on household decisions and therefore on index insurances at the micro level.

Furthermore, index insurance can be intended for disaster relief against catastrophic losses as well as for development, helping farmers to protect their investments; even if these two roles are not independent, the product objective and design will differ (Hazell et al. 2010). However, as mentioned, the following analysis will concentrate on microinsurance as an instrument against disaster risk.

2012; Leblois et al. 2013; Carter et al. 2014). Leblois and Quirion (2013) provide a survey about projects, methodologies, used indices and experiences of weather index insurance.

Clarke and Grenham (2013) note that despite the growth of index insurances in developing countries, little analysis is available about their actual benefits for the clients and the existing information is typically not so positive. Reliable and accessible data, education (particularly financial literacy), the ability to finance large losses and affordable reinsurance systems are crucial in order to offer successful index insurance products (Skees 2008). In particular, the focus is on the intelligent design of insurance contracts in order to reduce basis risk, but a more systematic interlinking with credits or other financial services is also discussed in order to offer households a superior risk-financing choice other than pure self-insurance (Carter 2012).

Conclusion

To conclude, microinsurance is the provision of cover to the specific market segment of low-income persons (Churchill 2007). Since the failure of traditional disaster insurance in many developing countries, mainly due to high transaction and insurance costs, microinsurance products in general and index based schemes in particular have been seen as innovative and promising instruments to provide a more efficient risk management approach to low-income households (Mechler et al. 2006; Clarke and Grenham 2013). Although similar limitations arise for both approaches offering insurance products for disaster risk, new innovative solutions (customised delivery models, index based insurance systems) may help to overcome some of these shortcomings. Furthermore, due to the lack of public safety nets and the lower capability of developing countries to cushion the adverse effects of disasters, microinsurance products as well as other accompanying financial services in developing countries are seen as promising instruments in order to provide resilience for low-income households, reduce poverty and support economic development.

4.1.3 Microinsurance Landscape

The following section provides available data to give an impression of the microinsurance market worldwide, in Asia and in Cambodia in particular. Although the availability of reliable data and estimations are very limited and differ between existing studies, the market potential of microinsurance instruments as well as their growth in recent years has become increasingly apparent.

Worldwide

According to Roth et al. (2007), formal microinsurance (non-social security) was provided in 2007 in 77 of the poorest 100 countries and covers a total of 78.5 million people in Asia, the Americas and Africa. Lloyd's and Microinsurance Centre (2009), institutions reporting on opportunities in the microinsurance market, state that 135 million, or 5%, of low income people in developing countries are using this instrument. Furthermore they calculate a potential of 1.5 to 3 billion policies (Lloyd's and Microinsurance Centre 2009).

In a comprehensive landscape study of microinsurance, the Munich Re Foundation (2013) calculates a total of 261.9 million customers in Africa, Latin America and the Caribbean as well as in Asia and Oceania. Other studies suggest up to 500 million clients throughout the developing world (Dror and Piesse 2014). Even if there are fundamental differences in specific numbers of clients, the data shows an immense market for microinsurance with high growth rates.

With the focus on microinsurance products against disaster risk, agricultural crop and property insurance are of special interest. However, Roth et al. (2007) show that both the supply and demand are significantly lower than for health and life insurance and find only 5.4 million policy holders with crop insurance and 40,000 with livestock insurance. As described above, these products suffer from the threats of moral hazard and fraud as well as carrying high transaction costs for administration, claim validation and the fact that they are sold more often to individuals rather than to groups (Roth et al. 2007). In a comprehensive survey, the Munich Re Foundation (2013) found a total of 38.2 million policy holders of agriculture and property insurance in Africa, the Americas and Asia combined.

Asia

Approximately 70% of microinsurance products can be found in Asia (Dror and Piesse 2014). Roth et al. (2007) estimate that 67.2 million people are covered by microinsurance, 57.9 million of them living on less than USD 2 per day. However, by the end of 2012, according to the Munich Re Foundation (2013), 170.4 million low-income people were covered in 24 countries, representing 4.3% of the population.[7]

The Asian market is still highly dynamic with annual growth rates of 30% and 47% between 2010 and 2012 for numbers of people covered and premiums generated. In this context, India is the dominant market from every perspective: within the continent of Asia, it contributes 65.2% of microinsurance clients (111.1 million), 66% of premiums, 72% of the growth in coverage and 80% of the growth in premiums. In terms of coverage, the countries that follow are the Philippines (19.9 million), China (11.9 million) and Bangladesh (9.4 million). However, even if India dominates in absolute terms, it is only third in coverage ratio (9% of the population have microinsurance products). In Thailand and the Philippines, 13.9% and 10.6% of the population respectively are covered by an insurance scheme. Malaysia and Mongolia as well as Indonesia, Fiji, China, Nepal, Sri Lanka, Cambodia and Pakistan have a rate of more than 50% annual growth either in coverage, premiums or both (Munich Re Foundation 2013).

The Munich Re Foundation (2013) found 507 microinsurance products through their survey, with life insurance as the key product, even if health and agriculture products were found to be growing rapidly with annual growth rates of 131.8% and

[7]The Munich Re Foundation (2013) determines the market size for microinsurance by the proportion of the people living from more than USD 1.25, but less than USD 4 per day.

67.3% respectively. Furthermore, commercial insurers were found to have the largest outreach, whilst community-based organisations or other member-based schemes are the most commonly used distribution channels. However, in contrast to Africa and the Americas, Asian providers do not participate so heavily in mobile technology-based insurance distribution.[8] (Munich Re Foundation 2013)

Agricultural and property insurance together cover 31.5 million people, with agricultural insurance showing particularly high growth rates, with the number of policies rising by 130% between 2010 and 2012. Furthermore, they contribute to nearly half of the premiums generated (USD 382.6 million in 2012, representing 46.2%), even if coverage sits at a mere 10.5%. In comparison, property insurance—which focus on the damage or destruction of homes or businesses—is still in its early stages with USD 31.5 million generated in premiums (Munich Re Foundation 2013).

Cambodia

In Cambodia, the insurance industry is still at an embryonic stage. The concept of insurance is a new phenomenon and not always well-understood. While a majority of the population is poor and face particularly high levels of risk from various devastating events including floods, droughts and other natural disasters, only 2% of the population or 0.3 million people are equipped with insurance coverage. Since 2005, the insurance industry has been liberalised to foster the development of the private insurance sector (Roth et al. 2007; Hong 2013; Munich Re Foundation 2013).

UNDP (2013) estimated that by mid-2013, 641,000 microinsurance policies would exist in Cambodia, almost all of them health or credit life insurances. Despite the country's heavy dependence on agriculture and the high associated risk level, there is currently no significant market for agriculture and property insurances and a lack of research on the industry. Nevertheless, there is a growing market for microinsurance in Cambodia with premium growth rates of more than 50% (Munich Re Foundation 2013; UNDP 2013).

4.2 Determinants of Microinsurance Demand

Academics and practitioners view microinsurance as a promising instrument to manage risk for the poor in developing countries (De Bock and Gelade 2012; Biener and Eling 2012; Clarke and Grenham 2013; Eling et al. 2014). Following microfinance, insurance for the poor is considered the 'next revolution' and huge

---

[8]The Munich Re Foundation (2013) mentions that 1.7 billion individuals are served by various government-run social microinsurance programmes, particularly in the health and agriculture sectors. These schemes are characterised by commercial insurance companies underwriting the risk, while the premiums are paid by the government. They are therefore a blend between traditional social security schemes and conventional microinsurance, however they carry the implication of microinsurance (Munich Re Foundation 2013).

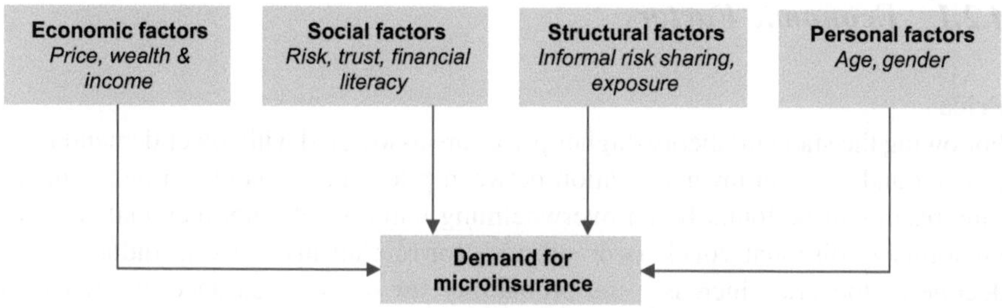

Fig. 4.1 Determinants of microinsurance demand. Following the structure of Eling et al. (2014) and Outreville (2013)

investments have been made in recent years by development agencies (Morduch 2006; De Bock and Gelade 2012).

Frequent adverse shocks as well as imperfect risk-pooling and self-insurance mechanisms make new instruments necessary and desirable. However, microinsurance as a concept is even more complex than microfinance and the demand for this instrument remains relatively low, even if highly subsidised (Giné et al. 2008; De Bock and Gelade 2012; Cole et al. 2013).[9]

In contrast to traditional insurance markets, a negative correlation between risk aversion and microinsurance demand can be found in the literature. In addition to individual risk preferences, factors such as the level of trust and risk exposure, among others, are found to have a significant impact on the demand (Cole et al. 2013; Eling et al. 2014).

In order to investigate the relevant determinants of microinsurance demand, this thesis follows a framework of insurance demand by Outreville (2013) and Eling et al. (2014). The framework consists of four categories which summarise the relevant factors for insurance demand: economic, social, structural and personal factors (see Fig. 4.1).

In the following section, the 12 determinants of microinsurance are presented, supported by comprehensive empirical evidence regarding their impact and theoretical explanations of the various observations. Furthermore, the impact of natural disasters on the various determinants will be highlighted. These results will be the backbone of the empirical analysis of microinsurance demand in rural Cambodia in Sect. 4.3.[10]

[9]The higher complexity of microinsurance over microfinance arises from the (often unfamiliar) idea of insurance itself (uncertainty of a pay-out despite a regular premium being paid; compensation of some participants, while others do not benefit; heterogeneous market) (De Bock and Gelade 2012).

[10]Due to the topicality of the issue, the references investigating microinsurance demand presented above are less than 4 years old on average, and are therefore often only available as working papers.

4.2.1 Economic Factors

Price

Following the standard theory, higher prices are associated with lower demand for a product and thus, an inverse relation between price and demand can be assumed. This result can be found by an overwhelming majority of empirical analyses. By randomising discount vouchers or subsides for rainfall insurance in India, a 10% decline of the price increases the probability for buying insurance by 10.4% to 11.6% (Cole et al. 2013). Cutting the price for rainfall insurance in different regions in India by half (relative to the actuarially fair price) increases the take-up probability by 17.6% (Mobarak and Rosenzweig 2012). Similar results can be shown for rainfall insurance in Ghana, where a 50% decline of the actuarially fair price increases the probability of buying the insurance by 31% (Karlan et al. 2014). The premium also has a negative effect on the willingness to pay for catastrophe insurance in flood prone areas in Bangladesh (Brouwer and Akter 2010) and for flood insurance in Pakistan (Arshad et al. 2016). In addition, high prices are also given as a significant reason by smallholder farmers in rural India for not buying insurance (Giné et al. 2008). The cost of the premium was also found to be an important factor in the decision for disaster insurance in Indonesia (Viverita et al. 2010). In contrast to previous results, the offer of a full refund of the insurance premium in India, in case the rainfall insurance failed to pay-out, found no effect on demand (Gaurav et al. 2011). Nghiem and Duong (2012) found no significant effect of the price on the hypothetical demand for microinsurance in Vietnam and explain this observation by the already minimal premiums.

Although demand can be increased by reducing costs and lowering premiums, overall take-up rates may remain low (Eling et al. 2014). Cole et al. (2013) find insurance take-up rates at less than half, even for prices significantly below the actuarially fair price and suggest heavy initial subsidies. However, there is evidence for very low retention rates after the subsidies expire (Thornton et al. 2010).

One explanation for low take-up rates, even for subsidised insurances, may be the existence of transaction costs, such as costs of time and effort (Thornton et al. 2010; De Bock and Gelade 2012). The payment and renewal process must become easier and less complex in order to keep transaction costs low on the demand side. Microfinance institutions with their existing microfinance networks already play a role in decreasing transaction costs and improving demand (Akotey et al. 2011; Eling et al. 2014).

Unless permanent subsidies are available, discounts on the premium can help to offer access to insurances in the short run—and therefore experience with insurances—but are not a sustainable long-term strategy (Matul et al. 2013). The modalities and timing of the payment are important, particularly for low-income clients, to make insurance policies affordable (De Bock and Gelade 2012). Providing small monthly instalments instead of one large one every year and collecting premiums after the harvest season can help smooth the burden of the premium (Akotey et al. 2011; De Bock and Gelade 2012; Clarke and Grenham 2013).

Income and Wealth

Wealth provides higher levels of liquidity (availability of assets beyond basic household expenditures) or access to credit (opportunity to borrow) and makes the purchase of insurance more feasible (Eling et al. 2014). However, the effect is not clear a priori. Households without any access to credit are less able to smooth consumption in the case of a shock, which could increase households' value of an insurance; in contrast they might not have enough funds to buy insurance even if they are more vulnerable to shock (Giné et al. 2008; Matul et al. 2013; Eling et al. 2014). However, higher levels of wealth may allow households to choose self-insurance instruments instead of formal insurance products.

There is also empirical evidence for the hypothesis that wealthier households are more likely to buy rainfall insurance (Akter et al. 2008; Giné et al. 2008; Giné and Yang 2009; Akotey et al. 2011; Gaurav et al. 2011; Cole et al. 2013; Arshad et al. 2016; Yeboah and Obeng 2016). Households with no access to liquidity or credit simply have no resources to buy insurance, at least at the time when premiums are due (Eling et al. 2014). Cole et al. (2013) show in an experimental setting that providing households with a positive liquidity shock increases insurance demand, and therefore suggest that liquidity constraints are significant barriers. Similar deductions can be gained from empirical evidence by Giné et al. (2008) and Brouwer et al. (2013). In terms of willingness to pay for flood insurance, farm income is especially relevant, whilst off-farm income has no statistically significant effect (Arshad et al. 2016).[11]

In contrast, Karlan et al. (2014) and Thornton et al. (2010) found no significant effect of wealth and income respectively, on insurance demand. However, income is particularly difficult to measure in developing societies, characterised by marginal wage income and unreliable self-reporting measures, and furthermore has a high correlation with other household characteristics (Thornton et al. 2010; Eling et al. 2014). Clarke and Kalani (2012) found a non-linear relationship between wealth and index-insurance take-up, with low demand for the poorest and richest households. However, Liu et al. (2013) found a negative effect of wealth on the probability to purchase rainfall index insurance and explain this by the greater ability for self-insurance.[12]

Acknowledging liquidity constraint as an important decision factor for purchasing microinsurance products, demand can be increased by adjusting the payment of premiums, either by delaying it to a later point in time (e.g. after the harvest period or at the end of the insurance contract) or by breaking the payment up into smaller monthly or even weekly premiums (Matul et al. 2013; Eling et al. 2014). Furthermore, insurances are often offered in bundles together with savings or loans;

[11] Despite the complex relationship between wealth, income, credit and liquidity, this thesis follows the usual method in the literature of considering these factors together in order to investigate the demand for microinsurance (De Bock and Gelade 2012; Matul et al. 2013; Eling et al. 2014).

[12] Self-insurance works here as a substitute for market insurance (Ehrlich and Becker 1972).

however savings, at least, seem not to change the demand for insurance significantly (Matul et al. 2013). Mixed results can be found in empirical studies regarding the relationship between credit and insurance demand.[13]

Microinsurance demand is not only determined by the levels of wealth and income, but also by the effects that changes of wealth have on the individual's risk attitudes, which depend on the specific utility function.[14] The following section investigates the role of risk aversion on microinsurance demand in detail.

4.2.2 Social Factors

Risk Aversion

In contrast to the observation in traditional insurance markets and predictions of the expected utility theory, various studies for the microinsurance market show a negative relationship between risk aversion and demand. Therefore, more risk-averse households are less likely to purchase insurance (Giné et al. 2008; Giné and Yang 2009; Dercon et al. 2011; Giesbert et al. 2011; Cole et al. 2013). Table 4.2 presents the main results of the empirical studies.

Measurement of Risk Aversion Different methods exist to measure risk aversion in an experimental setting. Mostly the designs to measure risk attitudes follow either the lottery game by Binswanger (1981) or the survey questions proposed by Holt and Laury (2002). In order to reveal the true risk attitude, both concepts propose that subjects must make a choice between more risky lotteries and a safer alternative (De Bock and Gelade 2012). However, both approaches consider gains and neglect losses. Although it may be important in light of the prospect theory, Dercon et al. (2011) find no significance in regard to insurance demand by observing risk attitudes across the two domains.

Expected Utility Theory Following the classical expected utility theory, risk aversion is the reason why insurance is valuable and the demand for insurance increases with the individual level of risk aversion. Given the concave utility function with decreasing marginal utility, an individual will always prefer a definite amount (average of his income) over a risky outcome (De Bock and Gelade 2012). However, the higher demand for individuals with a higher level of risk aversion is the opposite of what is shown by the empirical evidence. The prospect theory is

[13]Giné et al. (2008) and Akter et al. (2008) find complementary effects between the access to credit and insurance. In contrast, Giné and Yang (2009) show that demand for credit falls if bundled with insurance and explain these findings by the over-insurance of farmers.

[14]Given decreasing absolute risk aversion (DARA), wealthier households show lower levels of absolute risk aversion facing the same risk and therefore have a lower demand for insurance (following the traditional insurance theory). However, assumptions of increasing, constant, and decreasing relative risk aversion predict that wealthier households demand more, the same, and less, respectively (De Bock and Gelade 2012).

Table 4.2 Results of studies regarding microinsurance demand and risk aversion

Reference	Effect[a]	Main results of study
Giné et al. (2008)	–	Risk-averse households are less likely to purchase rainfall insurance (India)
Giné and Yang (2009)	–	Take-up of an uninsured loan is negatively associated with farmers' self-reported risk aversion (Malawi)
Giesbert et al. (2011)	–	Risk-averse households are less likely to participate in microinsurance (Ghana)
Dercon et al. (2011)	–	Demand for insurance (under limited trust) is negatively correlated with measures of risk aversion (Kenya)
Reynaud and Nguyen (2012)	(+)	Risk-averse respondents value high level of insurance cover positively; no information about insurance take-up (Vietnam)
Cole et al. (2013)	–	Measured household risk aversion is negatively correlated with insurance demand (India)

[a]Effect of risk aversion on microinsurance demand, with (+) indicating a positive and (–) a negative relation

Brief descriptions of research designs for these references can be found in the Appendix

often used in order to explain the deviation of insurance demand from traditional expectations (De Bock and Gelade 2012; Carter et al. 2014; Hwang 2016; Schmidt 2016).[15]

Prospect Theory Section 3.2 introduced the prospect theory as an alternative approach to the expected utility theory in order to explain decision-making under risk. Following the prospect theory, the value of an insurance rises from the overweighting of small probabilities, whereby overweighting refers to a property of decisions weights and not to the overestimation of probabilities (Kahneman and Tversky 1979; Levy 1992; Carter et al. 2014). However, Clarke and Kalani (2012) argue that decisions regarding insurance take-up can be better explained by underweighting (instead of overweighting) extreme events.

Furthermore, loss aversion (the different valuation of losses and gains) can explain the demand for insurance: sensitivity to losses make individuals more likely to demand an insurance product which protects losses (e.g. insurance against damage to invested capital) than possible gains of the same size (e.g. income gains) (Kahneman and Tversky 1979; Carter et al. 2014). Loss aversion highlights the importance of framing in particular: marketing an insurance as a prevention against losses rather than offering a gain increases an individual's perception of the insurance value (De Bock and Gelade 2012; Matul et al. 2013). Cole et al. (2013) find empirical evidence for higher take-up rates of insurances following negative framing of the product.

[15]Individuals' intrinsic discount rate, and therefore the preference for present consumption, can also impact the demand for microinsurance. While the premium is often paid at the beginning of the contract period, a possible pay-out is in the future, which implies opportunity costs (De Bock and Gelade 2012). However, the evidence for discounting on take up is weak and is rarely discussed further in the relevant literature (Giné et al. 2008; Morsink 2012; Eling et al. 2014).

Finally, the prospect theory postulates risk-seeking behaviour in the dimension of losses and risk-averse attitudes in the dimension of gains, relative to a reference point. However, various discussions regarding the definition of a reference point exist in the relevant literature, as discussed in Chap. 3 (Hwang 2016; Schmidt 2016). Moreover, the new literature of the prospect theory introduces state-dependent reference points (dependent on the realisation of a damage) and therefore finds the status quo (without insurance) leading to neither losses nor gains (Schmidt et al. 2008; Schmidt 2016). However, Schmidt (2016) argues that the safe option (wealth after the purchase of insurance) may be a more reasonable reference point.

Hwang (2016) attempts to analyse the low insurance demand of risk-averse individuals, showing that loss aversion and reference points are important determinants for insurance demand. Under the assumption of a reference point before the purchase of insurance and 'narrow framing', a negative relationship between loss aversion and insurance demand can be shown theoretically (Hwang 2016). Narrow framing refers to the tendency of individuals to consider decision problems partly in isolation, ignoring pre-existing risks (Kahneman and Lovallo 1993; Barberis et al. 2006). In this case, individuals evaluate insurance in the narrow frame of gain and losses (neglecting the hedging value of the insurance), whereby the gain-loss structure appears similar to a risky gamble. Therefore, the expected value is negatively associated with loss aversion, theoretically explaining the low demand of risk-averse individuals (Hwang 2016).

Traumatic Events Although classical economic theory generally assumes that individual risk preferences are fixed and only constraints are changed by traumatic or impactful experiences, there is a large literature in psychology regarding the potential of behavioural learning (Turner et al. 2014; Hanaoka et al. 2015).[16] Furthermore, Tversky and Kahneman (1974) discuss behavioural heuristics as an instrument of decision-making under uncertainty (see Sect. 3.2). The specific impact of disaster experience and exposure will be considered in more detail below.

Finally, trust in the insurance provider or in the insurance itself interacts with risk aversion and will impact the demand for microinsurance. These impacts will be discussed in more detail in the following two sections.

Non-Performance and Basis Risk

One possibility to explain the negative relationship between risk aversion and demand for microinsurance products is the existence of non-performance risk, and therefore insurance itself as a risky element. This uncertainty regarding the insurer may arise, for instance, from contract exclusions or insurer bankruptcy (Eling et al. 2014). This ambiguity can also accrue from a limited understanding of the product (Cole et al. 2013).[17] The aversion to ambiguity is often seen as a

[16] Voors et al. (2010) discuss the relevant literature regarding behavioural changes in preferences following conflicts. Like conflicts, natural disasters can be traumatic events, which can therefore shift expectations of future risk (Turner et al. 2014).

[17] Hereby, the level of financial literacy is a relevant factor for insurance demand (see section below).

factor as to why the most risk-averse individuals dislike insurance. Bryan (2010) finds that negative effects of risk aversion on demand are driven by ambiguity averse individuals. Empirical evidence for a negative impact of non-performance expectations on microinsurance demand can be found by Dercon et al. (2011).

A particularly important and relevant topic is non-performance risk in index insurance markets. As explained in Sect. 4.1, basis risk arises from the imperfect correlation between the insurance pay-out and the underlying losses due to the linkage of payments on an objectively measurable index (e.g. level of rainfall), rather than actual losses experienced by the insured household (Eling et al. 2014). While this mismatch can lead to a situation where the insured individual receives payments without experiencing a loss, the opposite effect—experiencing a loss without receiving pay-outs—is particularly important for the demand of index insurance products. While the particularly low demand for the most risk-averse individuals was originally explained by a lack of understanding and unwillingness to experiment on the part of farmers, Clarke (2011) explains this observation by rational choices regarding basis risk (Giné et al. 2008; Clarke 2011; Clarke and Kalani 2012). Mobarak and Rosenzweig (2012) show robust evidence for the effect of basis risk on demand. They find, in the absence of informal risk-sharing coverage, that for every kilometre's increase in a farmer's perceived distance from the weather station, the demand falls by 6.4% (Mobarak and Rosenzweig 2012; Eling et al. 2014). In order for a successful index insurance product, the pay-outs must be closely, negatively correlated with agricultural yields (Cole et al. 2012).

Trust

The decision to buy or not to buy insurance is essentially an individual decision as to whether or not to accept disbursing a regular payment (premium) in return for a possible, but uncertain, future pay-out (De Bock and Gelade 2012). Therefore, it can be expected that trust has a significant impact on the demand for microinsurance products. In particular, when formal insurance products are not familiar, the assessment of benefits and costs may be difficult (De Bock and Gelade 2012). When households do not have complete trust in the product, the insurance itself becomes risky (Cai et al. 2009). Trust becomes especially relevant in countries and environments with weak legal systems and protections, particularly with respect to the enforcement of contracts (Cole et al. 2013; Eling et al. 2014). Countries with better creditor rights, law enforcement and accounting information are found to have more developed financial intermediaries (Levine et al. 2000; Hussels et al. 2005).

Theoretical Background Patt et al. (2009) distinguishes three kinds of trust: trust in other people (closely related to information one receives from other people), trust in other information and products, and trust in oneself. The latter is relevant for the way that people take in new information, make decisions and believe in their own ability to make successful changes. All of these types of trust matter for insurance markets: clients need to trust the people they are paying, they need to trust the structure of the contract and potentially an index, and they need to believe that their decision can positively influence their livelihoods (Patt et al. 2009).

Following the theoretical background of trust, De Bock and Gelade (2012) and Patt et al. (2009) highlight trust in the product and institution and interpersonal trust as two decisive factors which potentially impact the demand for microinsurance products. In this context, trust in the product and institution involves the understanding of insurance in general and the product specifically, as well as risks connected to the insurance, such as basis risk (Patt et al. 2009). It also involves trust in the providing institution and the belief that the external institution will pay-out in case a loss occurs. However, as insurances often involve several institutions, distrust towards any actors can have negative effects (De Bock and Gelade 2012). Trust can be built over time and through experiences; however, there are successful examples of delivering through existing institutions, such as farmer organisations (Patt et al. 2009).

The second dimension comprises interpersonal trust, both as an indicator of trust towards others in general as well as an instrument of obtaining advice and information from trusted intermediaries, also called peer effects (De Bock and Gelade 2012). The latter can be useful in spreading information to others and can also help to reach financially illiterate households (De Bock and Gelade 2012). Particularly in communities without insurance experience, advice from trusted sources about the quality of the product and the reputation of the institution is likely to influence the household decision (Cole et al. 2013). However, Patt et al. (2009) note that trust in other people varies according to cultural backgrounds and social factors.

Empirical Evidence Both quantitative and qualitative research for various risks provides overwhelming evidence that trust is a significant determinant of higher microinsurance demand (Giné et al. 2008; Cai et al. 2009; Dercon et al. 2011; De Bock and Gelade 2012; Cole et al. 2013; Liu et al. 2013; Eling et al. 2014). The detailed presentation of the empirical evidence hereby follows the distinction of Patt et al. (2009).

Most discussed in the literature is the dimension of trust in the institutions and products, where trust depends, amongst others factors, on experience with the product and institution, as well as trust in the management of the institution (De Bock and Gelade 2012). Demand is found to be significantly higher if a recommended and trusted insurance educator is involved in the process (Cole et al. 2013). The importance of trust in an institution is highlighted by Cai et al. (2009), using a large randomised natural field experiment in China to indicate that the lack of trust for government-sponsored insurances acts as significant barrier for the farmers' willingness to pay. Furthermore, confidence in the provider has a significant and positive impact on microinsurance demand (Akotey et al. 2011; Reynaud and Nguyen 2012).[18] In contrast to the previous studies, Yeboah and

[18]For micro health insurances, trust in the management of the scheme was found as an important factor (De Bock and Gelade 2012; Matul et al. 2013).

Obeng (2016) found a negative correlation between insurance demand and the respondent's trust and confidence in the contract.[19]

As raised previously, interpersonal trust is a significant factor in the demand for insurances.[20] In this context, the involvement of known and trusted individuals as well as social networks is highlighted, an effect often described as the peer effect (De Bock and Gelade 2012; Morsink 2012; Eling et al. 2014). Individuals are more likely to purchase insurance when they know the insurance vendor personally, receive advice from more progressive farmers and village officials or observe other trusted farmers buying insurance (Giné et al. 2008). Furthermore, the experience of pay-outs both for the insured person as well as for others in his social network increases demand (Karlan et al. 2014), as does attendance at village meetings where insurance products are presented (Cai et al. 2011). Strong peer effects can also be found by Grislain-Letrémy (2015) for French overseas departments and by Yeboah and Obeng (2016) in Ghana (despite the negative effect of trust in the product, presented above). Table 4.3 concludes the main outcomes of the empirical evidence.

Furthermore, trust is also closely connected to risk aversion, as described in more detail in Sect. 3.1. Dercon et al. (2011) show through a model that limited trust can reduce insurance demand for the most risk-averse individuals. Aligned with this, Giné et al. (2008) find that the negative effect of risk aversion on insurance demand is particularly concentrated amongst people with no knowledge of the microfinance institution selling the insurance. The role of limited trust as a factor for the negative correlation between risk aversion and the insurance purchasing decision can also be shown by Kouame and Kouam (2012).

Trust Building Based on this evidence, building trust in insurance contracts and providers is important in order to reach out to more clients in developing countries. Clients must trust the insurance provider to pay-out in the case of an experienced loss; reinsurance for the insurance company in order to secure the insurer's survival may enable this (Eling et al. 2014). Changing the payment timing from the beginning to the end of an insurance period is also seen as a way in which to build trust. Furthermore, encouraging familiarities with the general concept as well as with the product increases understanding and thus trust (Eling et al. 2014). Cai et al. (2011) and Cohen and Sebstad (2005) highlight the importance of financial education as well as experience with insurance pay-outs.

Conclusion The role of trust is very likely to be particularly relevant in an environment where formal legal protection as well as household education and financial literacy are low (Cole et al. 2013). As further discussed in the context of

---

[19]However, in contrast to the previous presented studies, Yeboah and Obeng (2016) measure trust as a binary variable, whereby no more information about collection of data and underlying method are available.

[20]This aspect of trust is often measured by the trust game initiated by Berg et al. (1995), see Sect. 3.3.

Table 4.3 Results of studies regarding microinsurance demand and trust

Reference	Effect[a]	Main results of study
Giné et al. (2008)	+	Trust in insurance provider increases the participation in insurance scheme
Cai et al. (2009)	+	Lack of trust in government-subsidised microinsurance is significant barrier for insurance take-up
Akotey et al. (2011)	+	Improvement in the perception of insurers increases demand for microinsurance
Cai et al. (2011)	+	Importance of social networks in insurance take-up (peer effects)
Dercon et al. (2011)	+	Significant impact of insurers' creditability on purchase decision for insurance
Reynaud and Nguyen (2012)	+	Trust and confidence in institution plays important role in insurance adoption
Cole et al. (2013)	+	Significantly higher demand for insurance if individuals trust insurance educator
Liu et al. (2013)	+	Significant insurance take-up if option is given to pay premium at the end of the insurance period
Karlan et al. (2014)	+	Demand for microinsurance increases with observation of insurance pay-out within the social network (peer effects)
Grislain-Letrémy (2015)	+	Take-up rate in the neighbourhood directly increases the individual probability of purchasing insurance (peer effects)
Yeboah and Obeng (2016)	–/+	Negative impact of respondents' confidence in the contract on insurance demand; positive peer effects

[a]Effect of trust on microinsurance demand, with (+) indicating a positive and (–) a negative relation

Brief descriptions of research designs for these references can be found in the Appendix

informal risk-sharing, trust is also a significant factor for the stability and efficiency of informal and community-based risk-sharing systems. As a consequence, there is an important role for the regulation of the insurance market, either by the government or the insurance industry itself, in order to ensure that contracts are fair and information is promoted transparently (Patt et al. 2009; Clarke and Grenham 2013). The important role of trust for decision-making processes will be further discussed in light of the empirical evidence from rural Cambodia in Sect. 4.3.

Religion

In some cases, religion is considered in relation to risk behaviour as well as a sign of solidarity within a community; related to this the 'fatalism' factor measures to which extent individuals view events as outside of their control (Zelizer 1979; Eling et al. 2014). Empirically, ambiguous results can be found: Gheyssens and Günther (2011) show a positive relation between religion (independent of any specific religion) and risk-taking behaviour. Cole et al. (2013) investigate the role of flyer messages and thereby framing on the take-up of microinsurance products. They find that households identifying themselves as Muslim have a significantly lower take-up rate for insurance, when the flyer includes Hindu symbols, and vice versa (Cole et al. 2013). However, Turner et al. (2014) do not find any significant effect of religious views on microinsurance demand in Pakistan.

Financial Literacy and Education

As previously indicated in the sections on non-performance risk and trust, an important precondition for any insurance demand in developing countries is the fundamental understanding of a core concept of insurance—the expenditure of money in return for an uncertain pay-out in case of a hypothetical event. This concept is in contrast to traditional risk-sharing mechanisms, which are usually guided by the principle of balanced reciprocity (De Bock and Gelade 2012).

Following the theory of behavioural change postulated by Tower and McGuinness (2011), as the process is initiated, awareness of insurance as an instrument of disaster risk management should be raised. This is followed by learning about the terms of insurances and evaluating different policies; this changes the general attitude towards insurance and it is seen as beneficial and important to the individual. Finally, this leads to a behavioural change and an increase in demand (Tower and McGuinness 2011). However, these changes take place in the long term. De Bock and Gelade (2012) and Matul et al. (2013) note that low demand is often attributed to problems of understanding, both of the general concept as well as of the specific product.

Following these preliminary remarks, financial literacy is expected to increase insurance demand (Eling et al. 2014). Giné et al. (2008) as well as Cole et al. (2013) found the lack of understanding as a core reason for not purchasing insurance and financial literacy as a significant and positive factor for microinsurance demand. The significance of financial literacy and insurance knowledge were also found by Akotey et al. (2011), Heenkenda (2014), Brata et al. (2014), Qin et al. (2016) and Yeboah and Obeng (2016). Furthermore, various studies found that financial literacy trainings or initiatives have a positive impact on insurance demand (Patt et al. 2009; Cai et al. 2011; Gaurav et al. 2011; Dercon et al. 2014).

However, a few studies cannot confirm a link between financial literacy and insurance demand. Clarke and Kalani (2012) and Dercon et al. (2012) find no significant effect of a mathematical measurement for financial literacy and financial literacy training, respectively. In addition, Turner et al. (2014) have not found that previous experience with insurance significantly drives behaviour in the experiment towards insurance demand.

Although education (often measured as years of schooling) was used in several studies as a proxy for financial literacy, they have subtle differences (Eling et al. 2014). Mixed results can be found for the relationship between education and insurance demand (Akter et al. 2008; Nghiem and Duong 2012; Arshad et al. 2016).

To address a possible lack of financial education, insurance literacy training is seen as a fundamental part of implementing insurances in developing countries, often in the form of games, plays and a variety of media (De Bock and Gelade 2012). Additionally, existing frameworks should be exploited to use peer effects to influence individuals' decisions (Cai et al. 2011). It should also be noted that underinsurance—specifically against disaster risk—is not only an issue in developing countries and arises in particular from the low value of personal experience for decisions regarding disaster risks (Kunreuther 1996; Kunreuther and Pauly 2004; Clarke and Grenham 2013).

4.2.3 Structural Factors

Informal Risk-Sharing

Informal risk-sharing networks are an important instrument that enable households in developing countries to cope with risk. Traditional methods of reducing and transferring risks include diversification of crops, existence of various income sources, access to remittances from family members in cities or abroad, amongst others, as well as various kinds of community-based risk-sharing measures (De Bock and Gelade 2012; Clarke and Grenham 2013; Eling et al. 2014).

Natural disasters affect entire communities at the same time and informal strategies often break down due to their limited risk-sharing pool (Skees 2008; Matul et al. 2013; Clarke and Grenham 2013). Furthermore, informal risk-sharing activities are in no case costless. The damage of farming outputs induces the purchase of food, the sale of livestock (for depressed prices after a major disaster) or the migration of the household; all informal risk-coping strategies which come at a high cost to the household (Skees et al. 2005). In addition, other informal risk-sharing instruments (e.g. income diversification) create opportunity costs (Skees et al. 2005).

Insurance as a formal method of risk transfer can be a complement or a substitute to these existing traditional methods, especially for such risks which cannot be easily managed at the community level (Clarke and Grenham 2013).[21] However, the level of informal risk-sharing activities can have a significant impact on the demand for formal insurance (De Bock and Gelade 2012; Eling et al. 2014). On the one hand, informal strategies may crowd-out microinsurance products and lower the demand. On the other hand, the demand for microinsurance can be increased through learning effects from informal risk-sharing activities and formal insurance as a complement to existing informal instruments. However, the issue of informal risk-sharing instruments in developing countries is complex and considered more in depth in a broad variety of publications (Dercon 2002; de Weerdt 2005; Mobarak and Rosenzweig 2012). In the following section, the main point of interest is the possible interaction between informal risk-sharing activities and the demand for microinsurance, with a specific focus on credit and savings due to the relevance of bundling insurance with either credit or savings schemes.

[21]Following the terminology by Dercon et al. (2014), determinants/factors are described as complements (substitutes) in the sense that an increase in one factor will increase (decrease) the marginal utility of the other (see also Mobarak and Rosenzweig 2012; Jowett 2003).

Crowding-out of Insurance Informal risk-sharing arrangements in the form of community risk-pooling or family transfers have the advantage that members can closely monitor each other and can crowd-out formal insurance (Arnott and Stiglitz 1991; De Bock and Gelade 2012). Evidence for this observation can be found for health and disaster insurance schemes in developing countries. Jowett (2003) finds that individuals living in cohesive communities are less likely to be interested in buying health insurance. Brata et al. (2014) show that the individual's membership in a farmer association significantly impacts their probability to buy disaster insurance, supporting the argument that local associations play a role as existing risk-sharing instruments.[22]

In addition, households with access to agriculture extension services are less interested in flood insurances in Pakistan (Arshad et al. 2016). Finally, Akter et al. (2008) show that households which have a large number of non-agricultural dependent income sources (as a kind of informal self-insurance mechanism) are less likely to participate in a formal insurance scheme.

Credit and savings (either in the form of cash or alienable assets) have a secondary function as instruments to cope with the consequences of disasters due the role of consumption smoothing. However, savings in particular suffer from limitations when several shocks occur in a short period of time and come at a cost in the form of forgone investments (De Bock and Gelade 2012; Lashley and Warner 2015). Finally, remittances, a significant income source in developing countries, are found to reduce the demand for formal insurance because they are by nature self-insurance instruments (Giesbert et al. 2011; Crayen et al. 2013).

Learning Effects Experiences with informal risk-sharing networks provide a wider community with extended insurance knowledge, which can in turn increase demand for formal insurance products (Cai et al. 2011; Clarke and Kalani 2012; Eling et al. 2014). Indeed, Giné et al. (2008) and Cole et al. (2013) show that membership in social groups has a positive impact on the take-up of insurances.

Risk-Sharing Networks and Insurance as Complements Mobarak and Rosenzweig (2012) investigate the interaction of informal risk-sharing networks and the demand for microinsurance products, with a focus on index insurance. They find evidence for a positive relationship between informal networks and index insurance: when a formal insurance makes a pay-out, informal mechanisms spread these pay-outs to the farmers who suffered the most. Therefore, informal risk-sharing networks of a community undertake administrative tasks in order to deliver the pay-out to the individuals (Mobarak and Rosenzweig 2012; Eling et al. 2014).

Similarly, Dercon et al. (2014) find a complementary relationship between microinsurance demand and informal risk-sharing. They explain this by the ability of groups to mitigate the existing basis risk, which are always present with index-based insurances (Dercon et al. 2014).

[22]However, the opposite effect can be found for breeder associations; this is explained as being due to their differing organisation or level of importance to the client (Brata et al. 2014).

As discussed above, wealth is an important determinant for microinsurance demand. Offering credit therefore overcomes liquidity constraints and households which were not able to afford insurances are then able to purchase contracts (De Bock and Gelade 2012). Credit itself is a highly imperfect insurance instrument. Although the negative effect of a disaster can be spread over time, credit does not provide the opportunity for risk-sharing. Furthermore, risk-averse individuals prefer smooth consumption, both over time and states of nature (Clarke and Dercon 2009; De Bock and Gelade 2012).

The absence or limitations in market insurances in developing countries are seen as credit market imperfections, which may deter individuals from taking on loans due to the risk of high default costs, for instance in the case of an adverse weather event (Giné and Yang 2009; Galarza and Carter 2011). By offering default insurance in combination with credit, both the risk for the bank and the customer as well as the interest rate for the credit taker can be reduced. Therefore, interlinking credit and insurance products has become more popular in developing countries. However, the combination between both types of products has shown mixed effects on the take-up of insurance.

Galarza and Carter (2011) find that interlinking credit and insurance can increase demand for both insurance and credit. Moreover, Arshad et al. (2016) find that the demand for flood insurance is positively associated with the access to credit. Similar results can be found for savings: offering group savings in combination with index insurance products increases the demand for insurance; savings provide an instrument to cope with basis risk and therefore limit the potentially negative effect of insurance (Clarke et al. 2012).

In contrast, Giné and Yang (2009) show in an experimental setting that households with insurance have a lower demand for credit (and therefore smaller investments in new seeds) than households without insurance; this is in contrast to the expectation that insurance makes the investment less risky and therefore more likely. The authors explain this observation by limited liability (Giné and Yang 2009).

Finally, purchasing insurance changes the dynamics of the group, which again could impact demand (De Bock and Gelade 2012). In addition, risk-sharing groups can—similarly to savings—offer an instrument to cope with basis risk and therefore increase the attraction of insurance (Mobarak and Rosenzweig 2012).

Conclusion Informal risk-sharing activities have complex and ambiguous effects on the demand for microinsurance products. To exploit the positive complementary effects, insurances can be offered to groups (particularly pre-existing risk-sharing groups) instead of individuals and therefore combine their advantages, such as lower transaction costs and less asymmetric information, with the stability against covariate shocks provided by the insurance (Clarke and Dercon 2009; De Bock and Gelade 2012). However, the existence of informal risk-sharing not only impacts the demand for insurance, but the existence of insurances influence the dynamic of risk-sharing groups; insured individuals are better protected against disaster and adverse shocks and are therefore more able to help, thus they are more interesting to the group (De Bock and Gelade 2012).

Microinsurance is introduced into a complex setting of existing risk-coping strategies and therefore it is crucial to understand which risks are covered by existing schemes, where microinsurance products are needed, how they complement existing strategies, and therefore in which context they are most valuable and demanded (De Bock and Gelade 2012). The comparative advantage of microinsurance therefore lies in larger and covariant risks, which existing coping strategies cannot address (Cai et al. 2009; Clarke and Dercon 2009). For smaller and more idiosyncratic risks, formal microinsurance is not necessarily the best approach due to information problems and transaction costs. However due to incomplete existing instruments, insurances may even offer additional value (De Bock and Gelade 2012). Index insurances in particular could exploit their complementary nature to existing risk-sharing schemes, while indemnity insurances and risk-sharing networks are substitutes (Dercon et al. 2014).

Quality of Service

Various studies analyse the impact of product quality and service on insurance demand, however all studies focus solely on health insurance and show a significant and positive link between good product/service and the demand for insurance products (Eling et al. 2014). However, the design of the contract in order to find a subtle mix between simplicity (easier to understand and therefore higher take up rates) and flexibility (meeting the needs of subscribers), is an important topic for all kinds of insurance (De Bock and Gelade 2012). Index insurances are specifically characterised by their amount of basis risk, which can also be seen as a quality indicator. However, the role of non-performance and basis risk is discussed separately above.

Risk Exposure

Risk exposure, particularly the experience and effects of disaster, affects the demand for microinsurance products. Chapter 3 has shown that disaster experience also affects risk behaviour and the individual level of trust. However, the following section analyses the empirical evidence regarding the direct connection between risk exposure and insurance demand, while the complex relationship between disaster experience and the various determinants for insurance demand are analysed later.

Theoretically, the effect of past shocks on microinsurance demand can make an impact in a number of ways and the direction of impact is not clear (Eling et al. 2014). Firstly, people change their beliefs about probability and loss through an adverse shock (update of information). Secondly, previous flood experience may have encouraged households to adopt various strategies (physical, psychological and others). Thirdly, the experience of receiving external aid after a disaster forms future expectations. Altogether, the kind, severity and frequency of a shock provides information about the stability of existing risk management strategies and may affect insurance demand (Clarke and Grenham 2013; Turner et al. 2014).

Update of Information Households learn from rare events and may update their risk perceptions after the occurrence of such an event (Turner et al. 2014). Given that insurance demand depends on the individual perception of expected losses, new information about both the severity and probability of an adverse shock—either real or hypothetical—can change the individual demand (De Bock and Gelade 2012; Turner et al. 2014). Turner et al. (2014) find that individuals residing in a cluster affected by a severe flood show stronger behavioural differences than those who experienced smaller floods, indicating the importance of actual and perceived disaster intensity. Furthermore, the farmers' belief in future floods is a significant factor in explaining interest and willingness to pay for rainfall insurance (Liu et al. 2015).

As mentioned previously in Chap. 3, individuals often use heuristics in order to create subjective beliefs (Tversky and Kahneman 1974; Eling et al. 2014). Due to limited time and resources, people do not necessarily search for the optimal, but for the 'satisfying' option, which adequately meets their needs (Patt et al. 2009). On the one hand, individuals might tend to overweight recent and severe events, which increases the demand for insurance products (Karlan et al. 2014; Eling et al. 2014). On the other hand individuals underestimate autocorrelation and therefore underestimate the risk of future events after the experience of a severe adverse shock (Galarza and Carter 2011; De Bock and Gelade 2012).

Adaptation Strategies The previous experience of floods or other natural disasters may have impacted households, encouraging the adoption of adaptation strategies. These could range from physical coping mechanisms to reduce loss and recover more quickly from damages, to psychological coping strategies which reduce the perception of damages. However, the effect of adaptation strategies in order to cope with adverse effects can have ambiguous effects on insurance demand, dependent on whether the coping strategies are substitutes or complements of insurance products (see the discussion above regarding informal risk-sharing activities) (Turner et al. 2014).

However, households which have changed their flood precautions or adopted new practices are more likely to take up insurances (Turner et al. 2014). Psychological factors such as perception of damages are particularly important determinants in risk mitigation as well as post-disaster recovery (Cole et al. 2013).

External Assistance Finally, the experience or expectation of external assistance after the occurrence of a rare adverse shock impacts risk perceptions and therefore the demand for microinsurance products (Turner et al. 2014). These observations are theoretically discussed—also for developed countries—under the keyword of 'charity hazard': external assistance from governments, charities or others is seen as a substitute to formal insurance, therefore crowding-out the demand for insurance products (Albarran and Attanasio 2005; Schwarze and Wagner 2007; Raschky and Schwindt 2011; Raschky et al. 2012; Kousky et al. 2013).[23]

External assistance for rebuilding house structures or replacing infrastructure significantly lowers the demand for insurance, given a constant value of losses (Turner et al. 2014). Farmers, who were found to be less dependent on government relief than others, are more interested in index insurances and show a higher willingness to pay (Liu et al. 2015). Furthermore, Akter et al. (2008) also suggest that households with access to ex post disaster relief are less likely to participate in a formal insurance programme. Grislain-Letrémy (2015) finds a decreasing probability of purchasing insurance with a higher number of past disasters. She shows evidence for charity hazard through a cumulative effect of the anticipation of assistance; households affected in the area by previous disasters are more aware than others of the scope of assistance and therefore anticipate higher ex post aid (Grislain-Letrémy 2015). In addition, external assistance as a kind of self-insurance instrument is found to mitigate risk aversion towards natural disasters (Nguyen et al. 2012; Cameron and Shah 2015). However, Brouwer and Akter (2010) do not find any significant impact of external aid on flood insurance demand in Bangladesh.

Empirical Evidence Empirically, the three effects are difficult to distinguish and often not considered separately in the empirical literature. However, the empirical evidence reflects the ambiguous relationship between risk exposure and microinsurance demand. Turner et al. (2014) investigate insurance demand in Pakistan, using a unique data set of behavioural experiments and surveys. The results show a positive correlation between disaster experience and insurance demand: individuals who have been affected by floods as well as those in flood-affected villages demand significantly more microinsurance than unaffected households (Turner et al. 2014). Liu et al. (2015) find similar results for rainfall index insurance in China, with a significantly higher demand for rainfall insurance from flood-affected households. Brata et al. (2014) suggest that individuals' perceptions of volcanic risk in Indonesia (which is aligned with experts' risk assessments) have a positive effect on the probability to purchase disaster microinsurance. Furthermore, investigating insurance demand in Bangladesh, Akter et al. (2008) find that participation in an insurance scheme increases with a higher frequency of disasters and decreases with lower household exposure (distance from the river). Arun and Bendig (2010) investigate households' risk assessments and exposure to hazards in Sri Lanka and find a higher probability of using financial instruments (including insurances) for households which perceive themselves as more exposed to risks. Finally, Qin et al. (2016) analyse the farmer demand for forest insurance in China and find a positive impact on disaster frequency and farmers' demand for insurance.

[23]Independent of insurance demand, free disaster aid by governments and non-governmental institutions are discussed regarding their embedded incentives: when households expect compensation for disaster damages, they are more willing to take on additional risks (Kunreuther 1996; Skees et al. 2005).

Table 4.4 Results of studies regarding microinsurance demand and risk exposure

Reference	Effect[a]	Main results of study
Akter et al. (2008)	+	Households with a higher frequency of floods and a smaller distance from the river show higher interest in insurance
Arun and Bendig (2010)	+	Households with higher perception of risk exposure are more likely to use financial instruments, including insurances
Giesbert et al. (2011)	–	Individuals with higher risk exposure show less interest in life insurance
Arun et al. (2012)	–	Households with higher perception of risk exposure are less likely to purchase life insurance
Brata et al. (2014)	+	Individuals with higher perception of disaster risk have higher probability to participate in insurance programme
Turner et al. (2014)	+	Flood-affected households have higher demand for microinsurance in experimental insurance game
Liu et al. (2015)	+	Significantly higher demand for rainfall index insurance by flood-affected households
Grislain-Letrémy (2015)	–	The probability of purchasing insurance decreases with the number of past disasters that have occurred (charity hazard)

[a]Effect of risk exposure on microinsurance demand, with (+) indicating a positive and (–) a negative relation

Brief descriptions of research designs for these references can be found in the Appendix

In contrast to the evidence above which shows a positive relationship between risk exposure and insurance demand, there is also evidence for a negative relationship. Households which perceived themselves as more exposed to risk show a lower demand for life insurance in various studies, a result explained by the households' limited ability to afford insurance after shocks (Giesbert et al. 2011; Arun et al. 2012; Eling et al. 2014).

Conclusion The risk exposure of individuals is likely to impact their interest in formal insurances; however the ambiguous results show that the direction of the effect is unclear. Table 4.4 concludes the main outcomes of the empirical evidence. Furthermore, different factors (adaptation strategies, informal risk-sharing instruments, external assistance) impact the relationship between the two variables. Chapter 3 analyses in depth the impact of disaster experience on risk behaviour and the level of trust, which are significant factors for insurance demand. This complex relationship between disaster exposure and insurance demand will be analysed below (Sect. 4.2.5).

4.2.4 Personal Factors

Age

Age has been included in most empirical studies, although mostly as a control rather than as a variable of interest (Eling et al. 2014). The results are highly ambiguous:

while some studies show a positive effect on insurance demand (Gaurav et al. 2011; Giesbert et al. 2011; Turner et al. 2014), others find negative effects (Giné et al. 2008; Heenkenda 2014; Arshad et al. 2016) or insignificant effects (Cole et al. 2013).

Gender

As previously discussed in Sect. 3.4, there is some empirical evidence for the more risk-averse behaviour of women in the middle and long run after a disaster (Eckel and Grossman 2008; Eckel et al. 2009; van den Berg et al. 2009; Ahsan 2014; Cameron and Shah 2015). In contrast, some evidence shows more risk-taking behaviour in the short-term after traumatic events (Schechter 2007; Eckel et al. 2009). The higher risk aversion of women as well as the specific roles of women in household risk management in developing countries may translate into a higher insurance demand, however the results are mixed (De Bock and Gelade 2012; Eling et al. 2014). Turner et al. (2014) find a positive impact of female household heads on demand for flood insurance in Pakistan. In contrast, Guo (2015) finds that women are less likely to purchase index-based crop insurance. However, research is still needed on intra-household decisions and their role in decision-making processes.

4.2.5 The Impact of Natural Disasters on Determinants of Microinsurance Demand

In addition to assessing the above presented determinants for insurance demand, the present thesis focuses on the effect of disaster exposure on the demand for microinsurance. However, as previously mentioned there is no one direct way in which natural disaster experience affects insurance, but there is a complex interaction between different factors. Therefore, the following section will analyse which of the twelve presented determinants are affected by individuals' disaster experience and explain the possible ways in which they will be affected. Based on this analysis, the possible effects on microinsurance demand will be described and highlighted.

As this present thesis concentrates on demand-side effects; the determinants' price and quality of service will not be considered, but will be assumed to stay constant despite the occurrence of an adverse shock. Furthermore, no effect of individuals' disaster experiences can be seen on the personal factors age and gender. Financial literacy and education are likely to be impacted in the long term (see discussion of long-term effects in Sect. 2.1), however no short-term effect on the decision-making process regarding insurances can be found. The religion of an individual may change due to losing or gaining faith following traumatic events, however no significant short-term effects can be found for developing countries in the respective literature.[24]

Therefore, out of the twelve determinants presented above, six are found to be directly impacted by disaster exposure. Hereby, both personal loss and the observation of others' losses are significant for explaining the demand for insurance products (Turner et al. 2014).

Wealth

The wealth and income of an individual are directly and negatively affected by disaster experience due to losses in assets or income-earning opportunities. However, the consequences of this effect on the demand for insurance is not clear. The empirical evidence suggests that lower levels of liquidity or credit access contribute to a lower demand for microinsurance (Akter et al. 2008; Giné et al. 2008; Giné and Yang 2009; Akotey et al. 2011; Cole et al. 2013; Arshad et al. 2016). However, poor households are less able to smooth consumption or rely on other risk-sharing activities (savings, credit, etc.) and the experience of a disaster may highlight the necessity of an adequate risk-financing instrument (Eling et al. 2014). Although there is evidence that particularly vulnerable households simply cannot afford insurance, the final effect on insurance demand is unclear.

Risk Aversion

In Chap. 3, four main channels of change in risk behaviour through disaster experience could be classified: income effect, which explains changes in risk behaviour due to changes in income and wealth; update of information due to new information about the frequency and impact of disasters; perception of risk, which may change due to psychological factors; emotions, which can play an important role in individual decision-making (Cassar et al. 2012; Dang 2012). A broad analysis of the theory in Chap. 3 has shown that it predicts widely ambiguous changes of risk behaviour after the experience of a natural disaster. In addition, the evidence also shows ambiguous results (Eckel et al. 2009; Li et al. 2011; Cassar et al. 2012; Dang 2012; Nguyen et al. 2012; Ingwersen 2014; Page et al. 2014; Ahsan 2014; Cameron and Shah 2015; Said et al. 2015).[25] Furthermore, this present study found a significant positive impact of the experience of natural disasters on risk-taking propensity in rural Cambodia (see Sect. 3.3).

In contrast to the expected utility theory, more risk-averse households are found to be less likely to purchase microinsurance products (Giné et al. 2008; Giné and Yang 2009; Clarke 2011; Dercon et al. 2011; Cole et al. 2013). However, overweighting of small probabilities, loss aversion and domain-dependent risk attitudes can explain some of the observations made when the prospect theory is

---

[24]Although some long-term effects are possible (e.g. religious comfort hypothesis, risk preferences and religion), more research is needed for an adequate consideration of this issue within the context of insurance demand. Furthermore, this effect cannot be considered in this experiment due to the limited variability of different religions (96.2% of participants were Buddhist).

[25]See Sect. 3.2 for a detailed analysis as well as a theoretical and empirical discussion.

applied. Specifically, under the assumptions of narrow framing and a status-quo reference point (before insurance purchase), insurance demand is negatively related to loss aversion, explaining the low demand for insurance by more risk-averse individuals (Hwang 2016). However, due to the ambiguous effects of disaster experience on risk behaviour, the overall effect on insurance demand remains unclear and must be analysed empirically.

Non-Performance Risk

Non-performance risks arise from uncertainty towards an insurance, for instance due to contract exclusions or insurer bankruptcy, and is particularly important as basis risk in the context of index insurance (Eling et al. 2014). Personal experiences with insurance as well as observations within social networks following a natural disaster can reduce (increase) this non-performance risk, if a pay-out was observed (not observed) as an indemnity for losses experienced. Based on the information gathered in this situation, a more adequate estimation of non-performance risk can be reached. Observations of pay-outs usually increase the take-up of microinsurance (Cohen and Sebstad 2005; Karlan et al. 2014).

Trust

The experience of natural disaster has the potential to increase or decrease the levels of trust. The experience of interactions between individuals in the reconstruction period, receiving support from other members of the community, the understanding of necessary help in the future as well as a more homogenous community, all increase the level of trust (Cassar et al. 2012). In contrast, resource constraints in the recovery period, aftermath moral hazard and migration as a consequence of disasters with effects on social structures decrease the level of trust (Fleming et al. 2014). While the empirical evidence in the literature shows positive or no significant effects for disaster experience on the level of trust, this study finds a negative effect of disaster experience on the individual's level of trust in rural Cambodia (Castillo and Carter 2011; Cassar et al. 2012; Fleming et al. 2014; Ahsan 2014).[26]

Both the theoretical and empirical analysis find consistently positive effects of the level of trust on the demand for microinsurance (Giné et al. 2008; Cai et al. 2009; Dercon et al. 2011; De Bock and Gelade 2012; Cole et al. 2013; Liu et al. 2013; Eling et al. 2014). As this is a constant, the overall effect of natural disaster on the demand for microinsurance therefore depends on the relationship between disaster experience and trust, as discussed in Sect. 3.5.

Informal Risk-Sharing

Self-insurance measures as well as community-based risk-sharing instruments are important methods for households in developing countries to cope with risk (De Bock and Gelade 2012; Clarke and Grenham 2013; Eling et al. 2014). However, their relationship with insurance demand is complex and shows ambiguous results; if insurance products and informal risk-sharing activities are

[26]Section 3.2 analyses the theoretical and empirical discussion in detail. The results of the levels of trust in Cambodia can be found in Sect. 3.4.

complementary to each other, advantages for both instruments can be gained—transaction costs and asymmetric information are decreased for insurances and stability against covariate shocks is provided for informal networks (Clarke and Dercon 2009; De Bock and Gelade 2012). In contrast, if these instruments are substitutes to each other, informal risk-sharing approaches may crowd-out insurance (Arnott and Stiglitz 1991; Jowett 2003; De Bock and Gelade 2012).

The experience of a natural disaster gives individuals information about the utility and stability of existing informal risk-sharing instruments and a better understanding of whether and how formal insurance can work as a complement to informal activities. A priori, no clear effect on the demand for microinsurance can be assumed and empirical evidence is needed to investigate this complex relationship in more detail.

Risk Exposure

The analysis of risk exposure for insurance demand offers various factors which impact the relationship significantly. Individuals' experiences with disasters can update information about frequency, severity and personal impact of adverse shocks as well as show the stability of informal risk-sharing instruments. Furthermore, the experience of external assistance can impact insurance demand significantly. As described above, individuals learn about possible external aid from governments, charities and others as well as their potential dimensions. The expectation to receive help can lead to charity hazard, where external aid is seen as a substitute to formal insurance, which leads to a crowding-out of microinsurance demand (Raschky et al. 2012; Grislain-Letrémy 2015).

Conclusion

The analysis presented above shows the complex relationship between natural disasters and the demand for microinsurance, whereby six determinants were selected and explained in detail. Figure 4.2 concludes the expected impact of disaster experience on microinsurance demand and provides the framework for the following empirical analysis.

4.2.6 Conclusion and Research Hypotheses

The burden of natural disasters heavily affects developing countries, yet insurance penetration as well as the demand for these products remains low. Microinsurance can help the poor to reduce vulnerability and to overcome poverty traps when facing adverse shocks (Cohen and Sebstad 2005; Morsink 2012; Turner et al. 2014).

The previous section analysed, based on the existing academic literature, which factors determine the demand for microinsurance in developing countries, following the structure of Eling et al. (2014) and Outreville (2013). The analysis revealed economic, social, structural and personal determinants. In most studies, price is found to have a negative effect on the demand for microinsurance, while there is empirical evidence that wealth influences insurance demand positively. Social factors consist of risk aversion, non-performance risk, trust, religion and financial

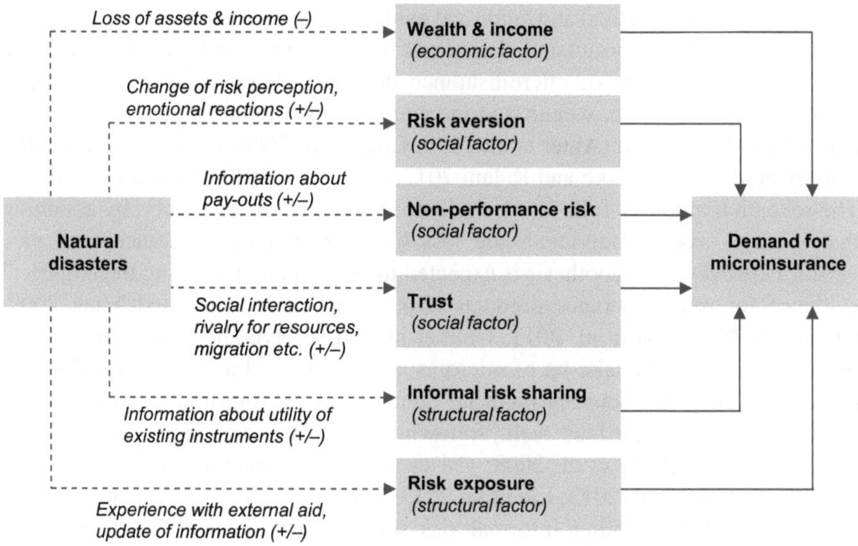

Fig. 4.2 The expected impact of natural disasters on selected determinants of microinsurance demand. Selection of relevant determinants by the author, with (+) indicating a positive and (–) a negative relation.

literacy. The latter increases the understanding of the product and has a mostly positive effect on insurance demand. Risk aversion and trust play a particularly significant role; with risk aversion having a negative impact on microinsurance demand, likely due to the existence of basis risk and the belief that insurance is a risky element itself. Trust in its different dimensions has a positive and significant impact on the demand for insurance products in developing countries. Finally, the structural factors informal risk-sharing and risk exposure have significant impacts on insurance demand, although the direction of the effects remains unclear and depends crucially on the specific circumstances.[27]

The following empirical analysis sheds light on the persistently low demand for microinsurance. A particular focus is given to the complex interaction between the experience of natural disasters and various factors. Factors such as low risk awareness or the expectation of external assistance may explain the low take-up of insurances (Turner et al. 2014).

In this context, the importance of so-called 'status quo bias', the tendency of doing nothing in a decision-making process, must be analysed (De Bock and Gelade 2012). Reynaud and Nguyen (2016) find a strong preference for status quo bias, leading to the decision of not buying insurance.

[27]Ambiguous effects are found for several of the analysed determinants, resulting from different research designs and context-specific framework conditions in various countries. The Appendix provides brief descriptions of research designs for presented studies regarding risk aversion, trust and risk exposure, due to their importance for the following empirical analysis. However, no simple pattern can be found to indicate that certain effects correspond to specific research models.

Based on the theoretical and empirical evidence presented above, the hypotheses H6 to H12 will be formulated. Economic factors are found as significant and important determinants of microinsurance demand. Therefore, hypothesis H6—economic factors (price, wealth and income) are not significant determinants—is expected to be rejected (Akter et al. 2008; Giné et al. 2008; Giné and Yang 2009; Akotey et al. 2011; Clarke and Kalani 2012; Cole et al. 2013; Arshad et al. 2016). The seventh hypothesis follows the traditional expected utility theory, by assuming that less risk-averse individuals are less likely to demand insurance (and vice versa). However, the hypothesis is expected to be rejected, following the empirical evidence for microinsurance products (Giné et al. 2008; Giné and Yang 2009; Clarke 2011; Dercon et al. 2011; Cole et al. 2013). Hypothesis H8—trust has a negative effect on the take-up of microinsurance—as well as hypothesis H9—the negative relationship between financial literacy and microinsurance demand—are expected to be rejected as well, following the significant empirical evidence presented above (Giné et al. 2008; Cai et al. 2009; Akotey et al. 2011; Dercon et al. 2011; Cole et al. 2013; Liu et al. 2013; Brata et al. 2014; Heenkenda 2014).

The impact of existing informal risk-sharing activities on the demand for insurance is unclear, due to the possibilities of formal insurance as a substitute or a complement to these activities. However, following the more prominent empirical evidence of a complementary relationship, hypothesis H10 is expected to be rejected as well (De Bock and Gelade 2012; Clarke and Grenham 2013; Eling et al. 2014). Hypotheses H11 and H12 focus on the experience of external assistance after a disaster as well as the experience of a disaster in general. Empirical evidence suggest that these experiences have a significant impact on disaster microinsurance, therefore it is expected that the hypotheses will be rejected by the following empirical analysis (Viverita et al. 2010; Heenkenda 2014; Turner et al. 2014; Grislain-Letrémy 2015).

The hypotheses regarding the determinants of microinsurance demand are presented in Table 4.5. Section 4.3 explains the method and data of the discrete

Table 4.5 Research hypotheses regarding demand for microinsurance

Hypotheses	
H6	Economic factors, such as price of the insurance and the individual's wealth and income, are not significant determinants in explaining microinsurance demand
H7	Risk-taking behaviour (risk aversion) will have a negative (positive) impact on the demand for microinsurance
H8	Individuals' higher levels of trust have a negative effect on the take-up rate of microinsurance
H9	Individuals' financial literacy has a negative impact on the demand for microinsurance
H10	The availability of informal risk-sharing activities reduces the demand for formal insurance products due to their substitutive relationship
H11	Receiving external assistance following a previous disaster has no significant effect on the demand for microinsurance
H12	The experience of natural disaster in general has no significant effect on the take-up rate of microinsurance against disaster risk

choice experiment and presents the results of this analysis as well as the statistical evidence regarding the seven proposed hypotheses.

4.3 The Demand for Microinsurance in Rural Cambodia

A comprehensive overview in Sect. 4.2 presented the individual determinants of microinsurance demand and several hypotheses were derived. The impact of disaster experience on various determinants and its complex relationship is highlighted.

To analyse the demand-side effects of microinsurance as well as the impact of natural disaster on these determinants in more detail, a survey and two experiments were conducted in rural Cambodia. The following section presents the results of this empirical analysis.

Whilst in Chap. 3 the impact of natural disaster on individual behaviour was investigated, the following section revisits these results and focuses the analysis on insurance demand. The experiment was conducted in the Battambang province of rural Cambodia in September 2014. In addition to the risk and trust games previously described, an extensive interview was conducted. The survey regards household characteristics, experiences with natural disasters, disaster risk management activities and questions about prevention and preparedness toward flood risks. Furthermore, a discrete choice experiment was conducted to investigate the demand for microinsurance products. Section 3.3 provides a detailed description of the experiment, its scope and study area. In addition, a description of the experiment procedure and detailed descriptive statistics of the households are presented in the Appendix.

The first part of this section presents the results of an ordinary OLS estimation in order to gain an initial impression of the effects of the various determinants. However, a discrete choice experiment (DCE) was conducted in the field to elicit individual preferences for microinsurance. Therefore, the following presents the theoretical background and methodology of this approach. The results of the DCE analysis will be presented hereafter.

4.3.1 The Interest in Microinsurance: First Results from a Poisson Regression

Prior to delving into an in-depth analysis of microinsurance demand using a discrete choice analysis (below), a simpler approach is used to identify relevant variables and to present initial results. As will be explained in further detail at a later stage, a discrete choice experiment was conducted in September 2014 in rural Cambodia. Each respondent was presented with six choice sets, consisting of two different

Table 4.6 Frequency of individual choices

Choice	Frequency (%)
Insurance A	37.2%
Insurance B	33.6%
No insurance	29.3%
Insurance A for all six choice sets	2.8%
Insurance B for all six choice sets	0.6%
No insurance for all six choice sets	20.1%

hypothetical insurance products and one option of 'no insurance'. In each choice set, the respondent selected his preferences from amongst these (i.e. Insurance A, Insurance B, No insurance). Table 4.6 reports the frequency of choices in the discrete choice experiment. The last row hereby indicates the relevance of the status quo bias. For the following analysis, the interest in insurance was used as the dependent variable, measured by the amount a respondent chose any insurance contract (out of six choice sets).

A Poisson regression was conducted to investigate the influence disaster experience, risk, trust and other socio-economic variables had on the participants' interest in microinsurance. More specifically, the regression function

$$\log(I_i) = \alpha + \beta_1 A_i + \beta_2 R_i + \beta_3 T_i + \beta_4 X_i + \gamma + \varepsilon_i \tag{4.1}$$

is estimated, where i indicates the individuals. The dependent variable I_i represents the interest in the insurance (measuring the number of choice sets in which an insurance was chosen). The coefficient β_1 measures the impact of experiencing a natural disaster A_i, β_2 indicates the role of the share bet in the risk game R_i (risk-taking propensity), and the coefficient β_3 investigates the importance of trust T_i (share sent in the trust game). The coefficient β_4 indicates the role of control variables X_i (see below). In addition, village dummies γ were used in the regression. The choice of control variables follows the analysis in Chap. 3. Furthermore, dummy variables are included for flood damage towards household property (e.g. house, vehicles, amenities) or household production (e.g. crops, livestock) as well as for money and/or goods received by the government or charities. For both regressions, village dummies were used and robust regressions were estimated. In order to control for over-dispersed data, both an over-dispersed Poisson model as well as a negative binomial model were estimated, whereby the presented results regarding size and significance of the coefficients were confirmed. The results of the regression model are presented in Table 4.7.

Results

In the following section, the main results will be summarised briefly, whilst an in-depth discussion of these effects will follow at a later stage, together with the results of the discrete choice experiment. Households affected by natural disaster are less likely to be interested in insurance than unaffected households. However, the more severely participants anticipate future flood consequences, the smaller this

Table 4.7 Poisson regression for interest in microinsurance

	Interest in insurance	
	(9)	(10)
(Constant)	2.197*** (0.447)	2.356*** (0.421)
Affected	−1.560*** (0.349)	−1.891*** (0.377)
Share bet in risk game	0.504** (0.208)	0.517*** (0.190)
Share sent in trust game	−0.553*** (0.193)	−0.662*** (0.175)
Age	0.012 (0.017)	0.013 (0.017)
Age squared	−0.020 (0.018)	−0.022 (0.018)
Gender	0.173** (0.074)	0.195*** (0.067)
Married state	−0.246 (0.190)	−0.302* (0.155)
Financial literacy	0.046 (0.034)	0.052* (0.030)
Number of people living in the household	−0.015 (0.015)	−0.016 (0.014)
Number of children under 15 years in the household	0.005 (0.024)	0.002 (0.023)
Total income per capita in US Dollars (2013)	−0.00004 (0.00004)	−0.00004 (0.00003)
Consequences of flood	0.013 (0.031)	0.010 (0.033)
Vulnerability of household	−0.056 (0.058)	−0.060 (0.062)
Consequences * Affected	0.307*** (0.072)	0.287*** (0.071)
Vulnerability * Affected	0.020 (0.091)	0.084 (0.090)
Damage to household production		0.377*** (0.105)
Damage to household property		0.238 (0.160)
Received money/goods from government		−0.457*** (0.137)
Received money/goods from charities		−0.102 (0.143)
Village dummy	Yes	Yes
Number of observations	126	126

Standard errors in parentheses, *** $p < 0.01$, ** $p < 0.05$, * $p < 0.10$

effect. Flood damage to household production (e.g. crops, livestock) has a positive effect on insurance, whilst support from the government through money or goods reduces interest significantly. Risk-averse behaviour as well as individual levels of trust have a negative impact on the interest in insurance. Furthermore, men are more likely to be interested in insurance than women. Finally, low significances can be found for the married state (negative) and the level of financial literacy (positive).[28] As mentioned, these effects will be discussed in detail in Sect. 4.3.4, together with the results of the choice experiment.

[28]'Tropical livestock units' (see Appendix) were calculated, which are an appropriate measure of household wealth in rural areas (Clarke and Kalani 2012). However, no significant effect on the interest in microinsurance could be found (see robustness check in Appendix). Due to the lack of another measurement of wealth and in alignment with other studies investigating insurance demand in developing countries, income was used as proxy for wealth (Akotey et al. 2011; Turner et al. 2014).

4.3.2 *Theoretical Background and Methodology of Discrete Choice Experiments*

Discrete choice experiments (DCE) are a quantitative approach used to elicit individual preferences, providing an instrument to uncover how individuals value specific attributes of a product, programme or service. During the experiment, individuals are asked to state their choice over different (hypothetical) alternatives. The methodology recently emerged as an attractive tool for researchers and policy makers in situations where consumer demand for goods and services, as well as the relative importance of specific characteristics, cannot be observed by using revealed preferences based on actual choices. The approach is particularly interesting for products which are not yet available (hypothetical demand) or where there is no variation in the product (and therefore the contribution of separate product attributes cannot be isolated). In addition, the method goes beyond traditional qualitative assessments and allows for information on the strength of preferences, probability of take-up and trade-offs (Mangham et al. 2009; WHO 2012; Navrud and Magnussen 2013; Reynaud and Nguyen 2016).

The following section presents the theoretical framework and methodology of discrete choice experiments. Furthermore, the design for the specific research in rural Cambodia is presented. Thereafter, the results of the discrete choice experiment regarding microinsurance demand are presented. The presentation of all three—methodology, research design and results—follows the description of Fiala and Wende (2016).[29]

Application of Discrete Choice Modelling to Flood Insurance in Developing Countries

In recent years, discrete choice experiments became increasingly popular for economic valuations and are most commonly applied in health economic research in developed countries; however, only a small amount of examples can be found in developing countries or are related to climate change and flood risk (Mangham et al. 2009; Navrud and Magnussen 2013; Brouwer et al. 2013; Guo 2015). The discrete choice models allow for the analysis of insurance demand against disaster risk in developing countries by identifying the relationship between different attributes of the insurance scheme and the individual's willingness to pay (Brouwer and Akter 2010; Reynaud and Nguyen 2016). Although the insurance product is hypothetical, this model provides important insights into the households' demand for different types of disaster insurances under different provision conditions and contractual designs (Brouwer and Akter 2010).

[29]The methodology and results for the discrete choice experiment in rural Cambodia are published as a working paper: "The impact of trust, risk and disaster exposure on microinsurance demand: Results of a DCE analysis in Cambodia" (Fiala and Wende 2016). While the working paper focuses solely on the analysis of several demand-side effects, this thesis investigates microinsurance demand in a broader context as an instrument of disaster risk management, including an in-depth analysis of the effect of risk exposure and disaster experience.

Stated preference approaches in order to estimate households' willingness to pay (WTP) for flood insurance can often be found in the form of either contingent valuation methods or discrete choice experiments (Navrud and Magnussen 2013; Reynaud and Nguyen 2016). The former estimate the WTP using a bidding method in the survey and is applied in studies regarding disaster insurance against flood and droughts in Pakistan (Arshad et al. 2016) as well as in studies on crop index insurance in Sri Lanka (Heenkenda 2014) and Nepal (Guo 2015). Discrete choice modelling is used in order to estimate WTP for catastrophe insurance in Bangladesh (Brouwer and Akter 2010) as well as flood and health insurance in Vietnam (Nghiem and Duong 2012; Reynaud and Nguyen 2012; Brouwer et al. 2013). Jin et al. (2006) conclude that both choice modelling and the contingent valuation method can be applied to estimate WTP in this context and provide similar estimates. However, the following description focuses on discrete choice modelling.

Theoretical Framework of DCE

General Research Design The respondents in a discrete choice experiment are required to state their choice over sets of alternatives, whereby each hypothetical alternative is described by several attributes (characteristics). The responses are used in a regression analysis to estimate the value of each attribute and the willingness to trade one attribute for another. Therefore, the determinants of product choices including product attributes and individual characteristics can be identified. The method is based theoretically on random utility theory and relies on the assumptions of utility maximisation and economic rationality. The individual is assumed to choose the alternative which yields to its highest utility, based on their own assessment of risk attitudes and preferences. In comparison to other techniques, which ask respondents to rank alternatives, DCE more closely resembles real-world decisions (Mangham et al. 2009; Nghiem and Duong 2012).

Mangham et al. (2009) describe the main stages involved in the design of a DCE. Firstly, the various attributes and their levels are established. In general, there are no design restrictions on the number of attributes, however in practice, less than ten attributes are used in order to reduce cognitive difficulty; the respondents should be able to consider all attributes when making their choice. Secondly, the hypothetical alternatives are generated and combined into choice sets. A choice set usually consists of two or more alternatives, often with an additional 'opt-out' option (see below).

A full factorial design can be created, consisting of all possible combinations of the different attribute levels. To construct larger choice sets with several attributes and levels, a fractional factorial design can be used. Such a design must be both orthogonal and balanced. While the former guarantees that the estimated parameters in the linear model are uncorrelated (the attributes of the design are statistically independent), the latter ensures that each attribute level occurs equally often (Huber and Zwerina 1996; Mangham et al. 2009).

Willingness to Pay The DCE can be used to calculate the willingness to pay (WTP) for a unit change in each attribute, which provides more detailed information than standard techniques that calculate WTP for the product as a whole. The WTP corresponds to minus the marginal rate of substitutions between the considered attributes and the cost of the programme (Mangham et al. 2009; Reynaud and Nguyen 2016).

'Opt-out' Option An 'opt-out' or 'status quo' option is often available in the choice sets of a DCE, presenting the choice of the baseline alternatives without any insurance cover. The baseline alternative is usually not further specified due to its differences across communities and individual respondents (Brouwer et al. 2013). However, when such a 'opt-out' option is available, it may be selected repeatedly by a significant proportion of the respondents and can lead either to a 'true zero bid' or a 'false zero bid'; the former describes that households are indifferent to the product and therefore are not willing to pay, while in the latter, households have a positive valuation for the product, but are not able to afford it (Reynaud and Nguyen 2016).

Assumptions A significant assumption of discrete choice experiments is that respondents know their preferences and that these are stable and coherent. By presenting alternatives for an insurance product, the respondents are therefore expected to be capable to select the most preferred policy based on the presented characteristics. A lack of familiarity and experience with the product may undermine this assumption (Brown et al. 2008; Brouwer et al. 2013).

Furthermore, no observation of actual behaviour exists (referred to as 'revealed preferences'). As described above, DCE are surveys based on the responses given, referred to as 'stated preferences' (WHO 2012).

Methodology

The underlying model of random utility consists of a deterministic and a stochastic part. The deterministic part is expressed by indirect utility as a function of the attributes of alternatives and individual characteristics. The stochastic part represents a random component, which is an error term capturing factors that influence utility, but which are not observed by the research (Reynaud and Nguyen 2016).

The indirect utility function is often simply a linear function of all attributes and—if applicable—an 'opt-out' option. Individual characteristics are included as interactions with either attributes of the insurance product or with the 'opt-out' option (Reynaud and Nguyen 2012; Brouwer et al. 2013).

The analysis of a DCE typically involves regression models that have a dichotomous or polychotomous categorically dependent variable (Mangham et al. 2009). In the literature, conditional logit, mixed logit/random parameter logit and multinomial logit specifications are used to estimate the utility function (Mangham et al. 2009; Brouwer et al. 2013; Reynaud and Nguyen 2016).

Empirical Evidence

Only a limited number of articles have investigated the WTP for flood insurance in developing countries (Reynaud and Nguyen 2016). In the following, the relevant research using DCE and the main results are presented.

Brouwer and Akter (2010) conducted a rural household survey with households in Bangladesh which were severely affected by floods in 2004. Four main microinsurance schemes were offered (property damage, crop damage, illness, and loss of income due to temporary unemployment). Furthermore, the attributes of the conducted DCE comprised several coverage sums, premiums and microinsurance providers (private company, central government, local microfinance institution, and local user group cooperative). Although familiarity with the concept of insurance was limited, most households were interested in microinsurance. As expected, affordability played an important role, but the experience of disaster assistance did not affect the demand. Crop insurance was the most in demand and the central government was the most preferred insurance provider (Brouwer and Akter 2010).

Nghiem and Duong (2012) studied preferences for microinsurance products in Vietnam. They found that clients were willing to pay higher premiums in order to receive higher pay-out levels. In addition, clients expressed a particular interest in a simpler claim procedure (Nghiem and Duong 2012).

Reynaud and Nguyen (2012) investigated the demand for flood insurance in Vietnam. Different insurance types (health, agriculture, house), insurance providers (state-owned firms, privately-owned firms and non-governmental organisations) as well as several cover sums and premiums were offered. They found strong preferences for the status quo option (no insurance). However, almost a third of the respondents included flood insurance as one of their four preferred flood management policies. The costs of the insurance product had a generally negative effect on demand. In addition, the respondents were more interested in health insurance and preferred products provided by a state-owned firm (Reynaud and Nguyen 2012).

Brouwer et al. (2013) additionally investigated WTP for flood insurance in Vietnam, including attempts to estimate the value of a statistical life in relation to catastrophic flooding. In general, respondents had a substantial demand for flood insurance, although the demand had a ceiling. They preferred higher insurance cover with the government as the provider. After excluding households who were unable to afford insurance, no significant effect of the household income could be shown (Brouwer et al. 2013).

4.3.3 Research Design for Discrete Choice Experiment in Cambodia

In September 2014, an experiment was conducted in the Battambang province of rural Cambodia (see Sect. 3.3 for an overview of the study area). After the risk and trust game as well as the questionnaire, the discrete choice experiment was carried out. The following description of the specific research design follows Fiala and Wende (2016).

In the initial stage, several relevant attributes for insurance products were selected. Based on the available research presented above, the attributes covering sum, premium and provider were chosen (Brouwer and Akter 2010; Reynaud and Nguyen 2012; Brouwer et al. 2013; Arshad et al. 2016). Due to the fact that no crop microinsurance existed in Cambodia at the time of the experiment, assumptions for premium and cover sums had to be made based on available data from microinsurance demand studies in other countries in addition to data regarding economic performance in Cambodia (Brouwer and Akter 2010; Akter 2012; Cai et al. 2013; Cambodia National Institute of Statistics 2014; World Bank 2014). Due to missing information regarding specific levels of flood risk and the lack of any existing insurance products in the study area, affordability and the relation of premium to offered cover were chosen as premium characteristics, in order to adjust the price of the hypothetical product to existing schemes in other countries. The premium was between 1% and 5% of household income and therefore orientated itself around the analyses of Brouwer and Akter (2010) and Akter (2012). The attribute 'provider' had five levels: national as well as provincial government, private company, non-governmental organisation and village (the community itself). Following the discussion in Sect. 4.1, the attribute 'pay-out condition' examines preferences for indemnity-based or index-based insurance (Mechler et al. 2006; Skees 2008; Clarke and Grenham 2013). In addition, the literature discusses the combination of insurance products with credits in order to reduce adverse selection (Cohen and McCord 2003; Mechler et al. 2006; Clarke and Grenham 2013). Therefore, the preference for a bundle of credit and insurance or the insurance instrument on its own will be examined. Furthermore, to investigate the relationship between insurance demand and prevention (Mechler et al. 2006; Surminski and Oramas-Dorta 2014; Linnerooth-Bayer and Hochrainer-Stigler 2015), the requirement for prevention was added as an attribute. However, for both credit bundle and prevention effort, no specific costs or further information were given. Table 4.8 concludes the list of attributes and their levels. Finally, an 'opt-out' option was added to every choice set, giving the household the choice to choose the baseline alternative without any insurance cover (see above).

In the next stage, 24 choice sets were constructed, each consisting of three alternatives (flood insurance A, flood insurance B, no insurance). The attributes were chosen to be independent and equally distributed over the choice sets. Taking into account the cognitive capacity of respondents, the 24 choice sets have been grouped into four versions of the choice experiment (Reynaud and Nguyen 2012).

Table 4.8 Attributes and levels of discrete choice experiment

Attribute	Level
Cover for loss	200,000 Riel
	500,000 Riel
	1,000,000 Riel
Premium (per week)	800 Riel
	2,000 Riel
	4,000 Riel
Condition for pay-out	Pay-out after a visit of insurance employee (indemnity-based)
	Pay-out if measuring station has indicated a flood (index-based)
Credit	Combination of insurance with loan
	No combination of insurance and loan
Prevention	No prevention effort
	Insurance requires additional prevention effort
Provider	National government
	Provincial government
	Private company
	NGO
	Village

Table following Fiala and Wende (2016)

Each respondent in the experiment was presented one group containing six choice sets. A sample of a choice set is presented in the Appendix. The discrete choice experiment was accompanied by several questions.[30]

The six attributes presented above yield to 360 possible insurances. In order to create a fractional factorial design, the rotation design algorithm by Aizaki (2012) was applied. Using the catalogue-based approach by Johnson et al. (2007) and Chrzan and Orme (2000) on 36 blocks with three alternatives including the opt-out possibility, there are 48 unique alternatives representing all characteristics of the insurances.

The choice of one alternative in the choice set could be seen as a process of utility maximisation. Here it will be assumed that the utility of one alternative (j) given a choice set (k) consists of a deterministic part $V(X_{jk}|\beta)$ and a random part ϵ_{ijk}. Further, let ϵ be from a type I extreme value distribution and the individual utility for alternative (j) U_{ijk} given by

$$U_{ijk} = V\left(X_{ijk}|\beta\right) + \epsilon_{ijk} \tag{4.2}$$

[30]Questions were asked regarding the individuals' knowledge and experience with insurance. Furthermore, if the participant answered 'no insurance' at least four out of six times, he was asked for the reason (no interest, satisfaction with situation, affordability, responsibility of government). In addition, preferences for provider, in combination with credit and prevention were asked. The questionnaire ended by asking if the household was willing to increase production or try new crops if they were to have an insurance.

which leads to a conditional logit model in order to assess average individual preferences. This starts with a basic model where the utility of each alternative is given by an additive function of its attributes and a dummy variable represents the overall utility of the opt-out option:

$$V_j = Premium_j + Cover_j + Provider_j + Type_j + Prevention_i + Credit_j + Optout \tag{4.3}$$

The cover sum as well as the weekly premium are noted in Cambodian Riel. Regarding the condition of pay-out, the type of insurance is equal to one if it is index based. The attribute 'prevention' is equal to one if the insurance requires prevention effort. The dummy variable 'credit' is equal to one if the insurance is bundled together with a loan. Provider is a dummy variable which equals one on the following levels: non-governmental organisation, private company, provincial government and village.

4.3.4 The Demand for Microinsurance: Results of a Discrete Choice Experiment

Following the research design presented above, a conditional logit model was estimated to elicit the various preferences of the discrete choice experiment. Table 4.9 presents the results of the estimation, following Fiala and Wende (2016). In addition, the various effects will be discussed in detail and conclusions regarding the hypotheses will be presented.[31]

Attributes of Discrete Choice Experiment

The premium of the insurance product has a significant and negative impact on the demand for insurance, however this effect decreased slightly with increasing income. This observation follows both the standard theory and the empirical findings (Giné et al. 2008; Brouwer and Akter 2010; Viverita et al. 2010; Mobarak and Rosenzweig 2012; Cole et al. 2013; Karlan et al. 2014; Arshad et al. 2016). Therefore, economic factors play a significant role in determining demand for microinsurance and the hypothesis H6 can be rejected.

The combination of the insurance product with a credit has a positive impact on the demand. Therefore, a complementary relationship between credit and insurance can be concluded, as found by Giné et al. (2008), Akter et al. (2008) and Arshad et al. (2016). However, the combination of the insurance with a loan

[31]Note that the analysis is based on the hypothetical offer of insurance only, and that insurance is a relatively new and unfamiliar concept for many respondents (only one person had a life insurance policy, no other experience with insurance was evident).

Table 4.9 Results of discrete choice experiment

	Conditional Logit Model		
	(11)	(12)	(13)
Premium	−127.010*** (42.562)	−156.786*** (44.567)	−194.924*** (55.600)
Cover	0.082 (0.130)	0.116 (0.134)	0.184 (0.143)
Condition for pay-out (Index-based insurance)	0.115 (0.112)	0.105 (0.118)	0.237* (0.134)
Credit (Combination with loan)	0.184* (0.105)	0.187* (0.110)	0.537*** (0.175)
Prevention (Insurance requires additional prevention effort)	−0.137 (0.105)	−0.104 (0.110)	−1.541*** (0.527)
Provider (Provincial government)	0.133 (0.146)	0.193 (0.151)	0.156 (0.162)
Provider (Private company)	0.172 (0.150)	0.212 (0.156)	0.264 (0.172)
Provider (Non-governmental organisation)	0.379** (0.157)	0.404** (0.163)	0.296 (0.182)
Provider (Village)	0.106 (0.141)	0.144 (0.147)	0.147 (0.162)
No insurance	−0.373** (0.185)	−1.179*** (0.370)	−1.670** (0.778)
No insurance : Affected		0.659*** (0.184)	2.128*** (0.407)
No insurance : Share bet in risk game		−0.928** (0.384)	−1.624*** (0.543)
No insurance : Share sent in trust game		1.988*** (0.384)	1.957*** (0.550)
No insurance : Financial literacy		−0.466*** (0.069)	−0.388*** (0.095)
Premium : Total income per capita in US Dollars (2013)			0.216* (0.114)
Credit (Combination with loan) : Household without credit			−0.403* (0.210)
Prevention (Insurance requires effort) : Importance of prevention			0.328*** (0.115)
No insurance : Ability for prevention			0.244** (0.103)
No insurance : Consequences of flood			−0.730*** (0.108)
No insurance : Vulnerability of household			0.119 (0.175)
No insurance : Received money/goods from government			0.737** (0.288)
No insurance : Received money/goods from charities			0.211 (0.288)
No insurance : Agricultural land owned in ha			0.159* (0.086)
No insurance : Use of chemical fertiliser			1.021*** (0.320)
Number of observations	3309	3219	2949
Akaike information criterion (AIC)	1955	1775	1351
Adjusted McFadden R^2	0.025	0.090	0.253

Standard errors in parentheses, ***$p < 0.01$, **$p < 0.05$, *$p < 0.10$. Results following Fiala and Wende (2016) was specifically preferred by households which already have credit (in contrast, households without a current loan were less interested in such a bundle). Therefore, interlinking credit and insurance may not be the most suitable instrument in order to provide liquidity to households which are not able to afford insurances due to a lack of credit access (De Bock and Gelade 2012).[32] Furthermore, this result indicates that familiarity with financial instruments, or more generally financial literacy, impacts the demand for insurance products (see below).

Households which expect themselves to have a higher ability for prevention are less likely to demand insurance (the preference for the status quo increases). In contrast, flood insurance is especially needed by the households which are more vulnerable (less able to protect themselves) to the adverse effects of a disaster. Moreover, insurance requiring some additional hypothetical prevention efforts are less preferred than adequate products without such a condition, with a smaller effect for households which assess prevention as more important. However, for a more detailed consideration of the effect of prevention requirements in the insurance product, this analysis lacks specific prevention projects with associated costs.[33]

Furthermore, respondents preferred non-governmental organisations over the national government as the insurance provider (however, this effect is in regression (13) no longer significant). Other possible insurance providers were not significantly preferred in the discrete choice experiment.[34] Finally, regression (13) shows some significance for an index insurance contract in preference to an indemnity-based scheme.

Every choice set included an 'opt-out' option, representing the status quo. However, the attribute 'No insurance' is significant and negative, indicating that the insurance—and therefore change—is preferred to the status quo. A 'status quo bias'—the tendency of doing nothing in a decision-making process—cannot be found, which is in contrast to the finding of Reynaud and Nguyen (2012) investigating the demand for flood insurance in Vietnam.

The demand for insurance is even higher with increasing financial literacy of the respondents (the interaction term of 'No insurance' and 'Financial Literacy' is negative). This result supports previous studies, postulating that low financial literacy and therefore low understanding of the product is an important determinant

---

[32]In answer to a corresponding question in the questionnaire, 92.5% of respondents would be more interested in an insurance if it came bundled with a loan.

[33]In contrast to the result of the DCE, 91.8% of households answered in the questionnaire that they would increase their prevention efforts if required by the insurance.

[34]However, in the questionnaire asking households directly for their preferred insurance provider, the village community is preferred by 34.6% of respondents, followed by national government (28.3%) and non-governmental organisations (18.9%).

of low take-up rates of insurance (Giné et al. 2008; Patt et al. 2009; Akotey et al. 2011; Cai et al. 2011; Gaurav et al. 2011; Cole et al. 2013; Brata et al. 2014; Heenkenda 2014; Dercon et al. 2014). Therefore, the hypothesis H9 can be rejected.

No significance of attributes (regarding cover or other providers) used in the DCE analysis could be found. However, important implications can be obtained from interaction effects with disaster experience, risk behaviour and the individual level of trust.

Experience with Natural Disaster

The interaction effect between 'Affected' and 'No insurance' is positive, indicating that the experience of a natural disaster increases the preference for the status quo and therefore lowers the demand for microinsurance. However, households which expect more severe consequences of a future disaster are more likely to buy insurance. Therefore, the hypothesis H12 can be rejected.

The results regarding disaster experience are in contrast to several previous results of risk exposure (Akter et al. 2008; Arun and Bendig 2010; Brata et al. 2014; Turner et al. 2014; Liu et al. 2015), although there are references supporting these findings (Giesbert et al. 2011; Arun et al. 2012; Grislain-Letrémy 2015). Ultimately, the distinction of several factors explaining risk exposure is difficult, including update of information, development of adaptation strategies and external assistance (see Sect. 4.2.3). The strong negative impact of disaster experience on the demand for insurance indicates that update of information may be of particular importance. Hereby, the disaster experience provides information about existing coping strategies and the stability of informal risk-sharing instruments. Furthermore, the assessment of experienced losses as well as information about frequency and severity of floods may provide new insights into the individuals' resilience. In addition, if households anticipate severe consequences of future floods (potentially indicative of past experiences), the inefficiency of existing risk management options may become apparent, which increases the demand for insurance products. However, the observation may also be the result of household heuristics, underestimating autocorrelation and therefore underestimating the risk of future events after the experience of a severe adverse shock (Galarza and Carter 2011; De Bock and Gelade 2012).

Support received from the government reduces the demand for insurance significantly, indicating a substitutional relationship between external aid and insurance. The crowding-out of market-based risk-financing instruments by external assistance is referred to as charity hazard (Raschky and Schwindt 2011; Raschky et al. 2012; Kousky et al. 2013). This result confirms recent evidence found in developing countries (Turner et al. 2014; Grislain-Letrémy 2015; Liu et al. 2015). In conclusion, the hypothesis H11 can be rejected.

Although disaster risk insurance is specifically targeted at rural farmers, the experiment shows that households owning more agricultural land are less likely to demand insurance (more likely to choose the opt-out strategy). This result aligns with observations by Arshad et al. (2016) in Pakistan, finding that a high proportion of rural farm households dismissed the idea of insurance. Using the adaptation of chemical fertiliser as an indicator for more developed farmers (55.4% of the households), a higher preference for the opt-out option can be established. However, this may also be a sign that adaptation strategies have already been developed—particularly by individuals in an industry exposed to adverse weather conditions—in order to increase the individual resilience, ranging from physical coping mechanisms to psychological strategics which reduce the perception of the damage (Turner et al. 2014).

Risk Behaviour

Risk-averse behaviour has a negative impact on the demand for microinsurance. Although in contrast to the traditional insurance theory, this follows the overwhelming empirical evidence in the field of microinsurance (Giné et al. 2008; Giné and Yang 2009; Dercon et al. 2011; Giesbert et al. 2011; Cole et al. 2013). Prospect theory was introduced in Sect. 4.2.2 in order to explain these observations. Hwang (2016) shows theoretically that loss aversion is negatively correlated with insurance demand, given narrow framing and the status quo without insurance as reference point. In this case, insurance itself is seen as a risky instrument. Furthermore, ambiguity aversion may explain why more risk-averse individuals have a lower interest in insurance (Bryan 2010). As expected, the hypothesis H7 can therefore be rejected.[35]

Level of Trust

An individual's higher level of trust has a negative effect on interest in insurance, as indicated by a higher preference for status quo. Therefore, the hypothesis H8 cannot be rejected. However, this is in contrast to overwhelming empirical evidence showing a positive relation between trust and microinsurance demand (Giné et al. 2008; Cai et al. 2009; Dercon et al. 2011; De Bock and Gelade 2012; Cole et al. 2013; Liu et al. 2013; Eling et al. 2014).

Interpersonal trust, as measured by the trust game, is expected to work both as an indicator of trust towards others in general as well as of trust in information of trusted intermediaries (De Bock and Gelade 2012). However, due to the de facto non-existent experience with insurances (one single participant had life insurance), trust in previous experience or advanced information of trusted community members (peer effects) does not seem to explain the measured effect. Furthermore, due to the general positive attitude towards the offered insurance products, a positive effect of trust could be expected in this case. In addition, to interpret the result of

---

[35]The relatively high lump sum received as a pay-out in case of a disaster in combination with the observation of a positive relationship between risk-taking behaviour and insurance take-up, may lead to the view of insurance as a pure gamble to improve the individual's livelihood (e.g. migration into urban areas, etc.). However, no indicators for such changing behaviour due to the existence of microinsurance can be found in the literature. Furthermore, the hypothetical pay-out in this specific case was between USD 50 and USD 250, while the household income per year was measured as between USD 1193 (in a flood year) and USD 1945 (in a usual year).

trust measured in the experiment as an abstract level of trust towards others in general—and therefore also insurance providers, etc.—also does not seem adequate by comparison to the mostly positive relationship found in empirical studies. However, such a strong negative effect of trust on the demand for microinsurance can be explained if the measured level of trust in this context is seen solely as interpersonal trust within the community. Therefore, trust may indicate the efficiency of an informal, community-based risk-sharing instrument. In this case, informal risk-sharing instruments may operate in a substitutional relationship with insurance products (Arnott and Stiglitz 1991; De Bock and Gelade 2012; Brata et al. 2014). Although the presence of social capital and networks does not automatically imply the existence of informal insurance, access to social capital and networks is used as a proxy for informal risk-sharing instruments (Dercon 2002; Morsink 2012). Along with this interpretation of the level of trust, Jowett (2003) provides empirical evidence for lower interest in health insurance for individuals living in more cohesive communities as well as a higher reliance on informal financial arrangements (Jowett 2003).

Although other effects of informal risk-sharing instruments were analysed (the role of remittances, membership in an agricultural community, and household size), none have been found to be significant for insurance demand in the presented experiment. Due to the interpretation of trust, but also due to missing evidence regarding other effects, the hypothesis H10 cannot be rejected.

4.4 Conclusion

This chapter introduced microinsurance as a promising and rapidly growing instrument of disaster risk management in developing countries. Furthermore, a comprehensive overview about the individual determinants of microinsurance demand was presented. Economic, social, structural and personal factors can be distinguished. In preparation for the following empirical analysis, the relationship between disaster experience and the demand for microinsurance was identified by six demand determinants, which are directly or indirectly impacted by exposure to a natural disaster. These include wealth and income, risk aversion, non-performance risk, trust, the existence of informal risk-sharing instruments and direct risk exposure (including the experience with external aid after the adverse shock). Finally, several hypotheses were analysed in the empirical part by a simple Poisson regression, identifying factors which may explain the interest in insurance, and by a more complex conditional logit regression of a discrete choice experiment, investigating individual preferences for various insurance attributes.[36] Table 4.10 summarises the empirical results regarding the hypotheses H6 to H12.

[36]The methodology and results of the discrete choice experiment follows Fiala and Wende (2016).

Table 4.10 Result of analysis regarding hypotheses about demand for microinsurance

Hypotheses		Result of analysis
H6	Economic factors, such as price of the insurance and the individual's wealth and income, are not significant determinants in explaining microinsurance demand	Rejected
H7	Risk-taking behaviour (risk aversion) will have a negative (positive) impact on the demand for microinsurance	Rejected
H8	Individuals' higher levels of trust have a negative effect on the take-up rate of microinsurance	Not rejected
H9	Individuals' financial literacy has a negative impact on the demand for microinsurance	Rejected
H10	The availability of informal risk-sharing activities reduces the demand for formal insurance products due to their substitutive relationship	Not rejected
H11	Receiving external assistance following a previous disaster has no significant effect on the demand for microinsurance	Rejected
H12	The experience of natural disaster in general has no significant effect on the take-up rate of microinsurance against disaster risk	Rejected

Implications

Overall, a general preference towards change—and therefore insurance products—can be found in the empirical analysis presented above. A significantly negative relationship between disaster experience and individual demand was presented, which can be explained by the particular importance of updating information following a disaster. Hereby, the adverse shock provides information about existing coping strategies and individual resilience. In addition, it may show the particular role of heuristics in order to assess future risks towards the household. Furthermore, the experience may change individual risk attitudes (as discussed in detail in Chap. 3) and impact the personal choice of a reference point in light of the prospect theory.

Furthermore, the experiment finds the microinsurance-typical relation between risk-taking behaviour and positive insurance take-up, which can be explained by narrow framing in combination with loss aversion or by ambiguity aversion towards insurance products (Bryan 2010; Hwang 2016). Financial education may be one instrument which can reduce decision makers' narrow framing, by focusing on the hedging effect of insurance (Hwang 2016). This aligns with the empirical finding that individuals with a higher level of financial literacy are more likely to purchase insurance. If the effect of narrow framing cannot be reduced, the insurance can be framed in a different way by combining it with other financial products, such as savings (Hwang 2016). Although preferences for bundles of insurance and loans have been found in general, this effect is stronger for households which already have a credit. This effect could be prevalent due to the different ways in which insurance products are framed for individuals who are already familiar with financial services in general. Moreover, financial education can lead to a change of reference points, where the existence of insurances may be seen as the status quo

(Hwang 2016). Finally, Hwang (2016) suggests that subsidising insurances can also change the decision-making process under prospect theory.

In contrast to the findings of most previous studies, a significant negative effect of trust on insurance demand can be found. However, a high level of trust may indicate the efficiency of existing informal community-based risk-sharing mechanisms. In this case, demand for insurance is higher if the trust in the substitutive instrument is lower, thus a crowding-out between informal and formal risk-sharing approaches can be concluded.

Limitation of Research and Critical Appraisal

Although the results present valuable insights into microinsurance demand in general and the effect of disaster experience specifically, various limitations arise from this methodology and will be discussed briefly. Although it is one important instrument of disaster risk management, naturally microinsurance is not the only solution for addressing uncertainty due to natural disasters, and in some contexts, it may not be a feasible solution. In addition, the instrument cannot work efficiently on its own, but it relies on a broader disaster risk management scheme. Although this broader context cannot be simulated for the experiment, the findings of this analysis help to identify significant effects and interception points as well as possible conflicts and problems with such a complex risk management concept. However, the role of microinsurance as part of broader disaster risk management will be discussed in more detail in Chap. 5.

The discrete choice experiment is one approach to examine the impact of several factors on insurance demand; however, other instruments are needed to receive a broader picture. Qualitative information is particularly useful in order to create insurance products which will meet the needs and preconditions of potential clients. Furthermore, this research concentrates on demand-side effects; however, to create a sustainable product, supply-side effects must be investigated more in detail.

Stated preference methods (such as the DCE) are valuable because of their potential to reveal preferences where no actual behaviour is observable and therefore no revealed preferences can be considered (WHO 2012). However, they rely on the decision of respondents towards purely hypothetical choices. This is even more challenging for the research of demand-side factors, when no such instruments exist at all in the research area—as in the present research. Together with the non-existence of essential information regarding specific local flood risk and damages, this impacts the choice of hypothetical attributes and their associated levels. In addition, the collection of data and the conduction of experiments in developing countries provides specific challenges, described in more detail in Sect. 3.6.

Although the important critical remarks and limitations are presented above, this research presents valuable insights into the demand for microinsurance. Using a unique data set following an extensive survey, two behavioural experiments and a discrete choice experiment in rural Cambodia, significant household level evidence can be contributed to the current literature regarding the impact of disaster experience and the role of risk and trust on the demand for disaster microinsurance.

Chapter 5 will discuss selected findings of this research and their relevance for economic development.

References

Ahsan D (2014) Does natural disaster influence people's risk preference and trust? An experiment from cyclone prone coast of Bangladesh. Int J Disaster Risk Reduction 9:48–57
Aizaki H (2012) Basic functions for supporting an implementation of choice experiments in R. J Stat Softw 50:1–24
Akotey OJ, Osei KA, Gemegah A (2011) The demand for micro insurance in Ghana. J Risk Finance 12:182–194
Akter S (2012) The role of microinsurance as a safety net against environmental risks in Bangladesh. J Environ Dev 21:263–280
Akter S, Brouwer R, Chowdhury S, Aziz S (2008) Determinants of participation in a Catastrophe Insurance Programme: empirical evidence from a developing country. Canberra
Albarran P, Attanasio OP (2005) Do public transfers crowd out private transfers? Evidence from a randomized experiment in Mexico. In: Dercon S (ed) Insurance against poverty. UNU-WIDER Studies in Development Economics/Oxford University Press, Oxford, pp 281–304
Arnott R, Stiglitz JE (1991) Moral hazard and nonmarket institutions: dysfunctional crowding out or peer monitoring? Am Econ Rev 81:179–190
Arshad M, Amjath-Babu TS, Kächele H, Müller K (2016) What drives the willingness to pay for crop insurance against extreme weather events (flood and drought) in Pakistan? A hypothetical market approach. Clim Dev 8:234–244
Arun T, Bendig M (2010) Risk management among the poor: the case of microfinancial services. IZA discussion paper 5174, Bonn
Arun T, Bendig M, Arun S (2012) Bequest motives and determinants of micro life insurance in Sri Lanka. World Dev 40:1700–1711
Barberis N, Huang M, Thaler RH (2006) Individual preferences, monetary gambles, and stock market participation: a case for narrow framing. Am Econ Rev 96:1069–1090
Barnett BJ, Barrett CB, Skees JR (2008) Poverty traps and index-based risk transfer products. World Dev 36:1766–1785
Benson C, Clay EJ (2004) Understanding the economic and financial impacts of natural disasters. The World Bank, Washington, DC
Berg J, Dickhaut J, McCabe K (1995) Trust, reciprocity, and social history. Games Econ Behav 10:122–142
Biener C, Eling M (2012) Insurability in microinsurance markets: an analysis of problems and potential solutions. Geneva Pap Risk Insur Iss Pract 37:77–107
Binswanger HP (1981) Attitudes toward risk: theoretical implications of an experiment in rural India. Econ J 91:867–890
Botzen WJW, van den Bergh JCJM, Bouwer LM (2009) Climate change and increased risk for the insurance sector: a global perspective and an assessment for the Netherlands. Nat Hazards 52:577–598
Brata AG, Rietveld P, de Groot HLF, et al (2014) Living with the Merapi Volcano: risks and disaster microinsurance. ANU working papers in trade and development 13, Canberra
Brouwer R, Akter S (2010) Informing micro insurance contract design to mitigate climate change catastrophe risks using choice experiments. Environ Hazards 9:74–88
Brouwer R, Tinh BD, Tuan TH et al (2013) Modeling demand for catastrophic flood risk insurance in coastal zones in Vietnam using choice experiments. Environ Dev Econ 19:228–249
Brown W, Churchill C (2000) Insurance provision in low-income communities—Part II: Initial lessons from micro-insurance experiments for the poor. Microenterprise Best Practices, Bethesda

Brown TC, Kingsley D, Peterson GL et al (2008) Reliability of individual valuations of public and private goods: choice consistency, response time, and preference refinement. J Public Econ 92:1595–1606

Bryan G (2010) Ambiguity and insurance. Yale University, New Haven

Cai H, Chen Y, Fang H, Zhou L-A (2009) Microinsurance, trust and economic development: evidence from a randomized natural field experiment. NBER working paper series 15396, Cambridge MA

Cai J, De Janvry A , Sadoulet E (2011) Social networks and insurance take-up: evidence from a randomized experiment in China. Geneva: Microinsurance innovation facility research paper 8

Cai H, Chen Y, Fang H, Zhou L-A (2013) The effect of microinsurance on economic activities: evidence from a randomized field experiment. University of Pennsylvania, Philadelphia

Cambodia National Institute of Statistics (2014) Cambodia socio-economic survey 2013. Kingdom of Cambodia, Ministry of Planning, Phnom Penh

Cameron L, Shah M (2015) Risk-taking behavior in the wake of natural disasters. Hum Resour 50:484–515

Carter MR (2012) Designed for development impact: next-generation index insurance for smallholder farms. In: Churchill C, Matul M (eds) Protecting the poor—a microinsurance compendium, vol II. Munich, Geneva, pp 238–257

Carter M, De Janvry A, Sadoulet E, Sarris A (2014) Index-based weather insurance for developing countries: a review of evidence and a set of propositions for up-scaling. FERDI, AFD, Paris

Cassar A, Healy A, von Kessler C (2012) Trust, risk, and time preferences after a natural disaster: experimental evidence from Thailand. University of San Francisco, San Francisco

Castillo M, Carter M (2011) Behavioral responses to natural disasters. GMU Interdisciplinary Center for Economic Science, Arlington

Chhibber A, Laajaj R (2013) The interlinkages between natural disasters and economic development. In: Guha-Sapir D, Santos I (eds) The economic impacts of natural disasters. Oxford University Press, New York, pp 28–56

Chrzan K, Orme B (2000) An overview and comparison of design strategies for choice-based conjoint analysis. In: Proceedings of the Sawtooth Software Conference. Sawtooth Software Conference Proceedings, Sequim, WA, pp 161–178

Churchill C (2006a) What is insurance for the poor? In: Churchill C (ed) Protecting the poor—a microinsurance compendium. Munich, Geneva, pp 12–24

Churchill C (ed) (2006b) Protecting the poor—a microinsurance compendium. Munich, Geneva

Churchill C (2007) Insuring the low-income market: challenges and solutions for commercial insurers. Geneva Pap Risk Insur Iss Pract 32:401–412

Churchill C, Matul M (eds) (2012) Protecting the poor—a microinsurance compendium, vol II. Munich, Geneva

Churchill C, McCord MJ (2012) Current trends in microinsurance. In: Churchill C, Matul M (eds) Protecting the poor—a microinsurance compendium, vol II. Munich, Geneva, pp 8–39

Clarke DJ (2011) A theory of rational demand for index insurance. University of Oxford, Oxford

Clarke D, Dercon S (2009) Insurance, credit and safety nets for the poor in a world of risk. UN/DESA working paper 81, New York

Clarke DJ, Grenham D (2013) Microinsurance and natural disasters: challenges and options. Environ Sci Policy 27:S89–S98

Clarke D, Kalani G (2012) Microinsurance decisions: evidence from Ethiopia. Microinsurance innovation facility research paper 19, Geneva

Clarke D, Das N, de Nicola F, et al (2012) The value of customized insurance for farmers in rural Bangladesh. IFPRI discussion paper 1202, Washington, DC

Cohen M, McCord MJ (2003) Financial risk management tools for the poor. In: Microinsurance Cent. Brief. Note #6. http://www.microsave.net/files/pdf/MIC_BN_6.pdf. Accessed 26 Nov 2015

Cohen M, Sebstad J (2005) Reducing vulnerability: the demand for microinsurance. J Int Dev 17:397–474

Cole S, Tobacman J, Topalova P (2007) Weather insurance: Managing risk through an innovative retail derivative. Havard Business School; Oxford University, IMF, Cambridge MA; Oxford & Washington, DC

Cole S, Bastian GG, Vyas S et al (2012) The effectiveness of index-based micro-insurance in helping smallholders manage weather-related risks. EPPI-Centre, Social Science Research Unit, Institute of Education, University of London, London

Cole S, Giné X, Tobacman J et al (2013) Barriers to household risk management: evidence from India. Am Econ J Appl Econ 5:104–135

Crayen D, Hainz C, de Martínez CS (2013) Remittances, banking status and the usage of insurance schemes. J Dev Stud 49:861–875

Dang DA (2012) On the sources of risk preferences in rural Vietnam. MPRA paper 38058, Munich

De Bock O, Gelade W (2012) The demand for microinsurance: a literature review. Microinsurance innovation facility research paper 26, Geneva

de Weerdt J (2005) Risk-sharing and endogenous network formation. In: Dercon S (ed) Insurance against poverty. UNU-WIDER Studies in Development Economics/Oxford University Press, Oxford, pp 197–216

Deblon Y, Loewe M (2012) The potential of microinsurance for social protection. In: Churchill C, Matul M (eds) Protecting the poor—a microinsurance compendium, vol II. Munich, Geneva, pp 40–58

Dercon S (2002) Income risk, coping strategies, and safety nets. World Bank Res Obs 17:141–166

Dercon S (2005) Risk, insurance, and poverty: a review. In: Dercon S (ed) Insurance against poverty. UNU-WIDER Studies in Development Economics / Oxford University Press, Oxford, pp 9–37

Dercon S, Gunning J, Zeitlin A (2011) The demand for insurance under limited trust: evidence from a field experiment in Kenya. University of Wisconsin, Agriculture & Applied Economics, Madison

Dercon S, Gunning JW, Zeitlin A, Lombardini S (2012) The impact of a health insurance programme: evidence from a randomized controlled trial in Kenya. Microinsurance innovation facility research paper 24, Geneva

Dercon S, Hill RV, Clarke D et al (2014) Offering rainfall insurance to informal insurance groups: evidence from a field experiment in Ethiopia. J Dev Econ 106:132–143

Dror DM, Piesse D (2014) What is microinsurance? In: Radermacher R, Roth K (eds) A practical guide to impact assessments in microinsurance. Microinsurance Network and Micro Insurance Academy, Luxembourg, pp 23–39

Eckel CC, Grossman PJ (2008) Forecasting risk attitudes: an experimental study using actual and forecast gamble choices. J Econ Behav Organ 68:1–17

Eckel CC, El-Gamal MA, Wilson RK (2009) Risk loving after the storm: a Bayesian-network study of Hurricane Katrina evacuees. J Econ Behav Organ 69:110–124

Ehrlich I, Becker G (1972) Market insurance, self-insurance, and self-protection. J Polit Econ 80:623–648

Elbers C, Gunning JW, Kinsey B (2007) Growth and risk: methodology and micro evidence. World Bank Econ Rev 21:1–20

Eling M, Pradhan S, Schmit JT (2014) The determinants of microinsurance demand. Geneva Pap Risk Insur Issues Pract 39:224–263

Fiala O, Wende D (2016) The impact of trust, risk and disaster exposure on microinsurance demand: results of a DCE analysis in Cambodia. Dresden Contributions to Economics, Dresden

Fleming DA, Chong A, Bejarano HD (2014) Trust and reciprocity in the aftermath of natural disasters. J Dev Stud 50:1482–1493

Fonteneau B, Galland B (2006) The community-based model: mutual health organizations in Africa. In: Churchill C (ed) Protecting the poor—a microinsurance compendium. Munich, Geneva, pp 378–400

Galarza FB, Carter MR (2011) Risk preferences and demand for index insurance in Peru: a field experiment. Universidad del Pacífico, Documento de Discusión DD/11/08, Lima

Gaurav S, Cole S, Tobacman J (2011) Marketing complex financial products in emerging markets: evidence from rainfall insurance in India. J Market Res 48:S150–S162
Gehrke E (2014) The insurability framework applied to agricultural microinsurance: what do we know, what can we learn? Geneva Pap Risk Insur Iss Pract 39:264–279
Gheyssens J, Günther I (2011) Risk experiments in gains and losses: do rural villagers want micro-insurance? ETH discussion paper, Zurich
Giesbert L, Steiner S, Bendig M (2011) Participation in micro life insurance and the use of other financial services in Ghana. J Risk Insur 78:7–35
Giné X, Yang D (2009) Insurance, credit, and technology adoption: field experimental evidence from Malawi. J Dev Econ 89:1–11
Giné X, Townsend R, Vickery J (2008) Patterns of rainfall insurance participation in rural India. World Bank Econ Rev 22:539–566
Goes A, Skees JR (2003) Financing natural disaster risk using charity contributions and ex ante index insurance. American Agricultural Economics Association Annual Meeting 2003, Montreal
Grislain-Letrémy C (2015) Natural disasters: exposure and underinsurance. CREST, Paris-Dauphine University, Paris
Guo W (2015) Farmers' perception of climate change and willingness to pay for weather-index insurance in Bahunepati, Nepal
Hanaoka C, Shigeoka H, Watanabe Y (2015) Do risk preferences change? Evidence from panel data before and after The Great East Japan Earthquake. NBER working paper series 21400, Cambridge, MA
Hazell P, Anderson J, Balzer N et al (2010) The potential for scale and sustainability in weather index insurance for agriculture and rural livelihoods. World Food Programme, Rome
Heenkenda S (2014) Prospective demand for an index-based microinsurance in Sri Lanka. MPRA paper 54420, Munich
Hellmuth ME, Osgood DE, Hess U et al (2009) Index insurance and climate risk: prospects for development and disaster management, Climate and society, vol 2. International Research Institute for Climate and Society (IRI), Columbia University, New York
Hochrainer-Stigler S, Sharma RB, Mechler R (2012) Disaster microinsurance for pro-poor risk management: evidence from South Asia. J Integr Disaster Risk Manag 2:70–88
Holt CA, Laury SK (2002) Risk aversion and incentive effects. Am Econ Rev 92:1644–1655
Hong KK (2013) The assessing of perspective on the micro insurance market in Cambodia. Bundelkhand University, Jhansi
Huber J, Zwerina K (1996) The importance of utility balance in efficient choice designs. J Market Res 23:307–317
Hussels S, Ward D, Zurbruegg R (2005) Stimulating the demand for insurance. Risk Manag Insur Rev 8:257–278
Hwang ID (2016) Prospect theory and insurance demand. University of Illinois, Urbana
Ingwersen N (2014) Impact of a natural disaster on observed risk aversion. Duke University, Durham
IPCC (2012) Managing the risks of extreme events and disasters to advance climate change adaptation. A special report of working groups I and II of the intergovernmental panel on climate change. Cambridge University Press, Cambridge, UK, New York
Jacquier C, Ramm G, Marcadent P, Schmitt-Diabate V (2006) The social protection perspective on microinsurance. In: Churchill C (ed) Protecting the poor—a microinsurance compendium. Munich, Geneva, pp 45–64
Janzen SA, Carter MR (2013) The impact of microinsurance on asset accumulation and human capital investments: evidence from a drought in Kenya. Agricultural & Applied Economics Association Annual Meeting 2013, Washington DC
Jin J, Wang Z, Ran S (2006) Comparison of contingent valuation and choice experiment in solid waste management programs in Macao. Ecol Econ 57:430–441

Johnson FR, Kanninen B, Bingham M, Özdemir S (2007) Valuing environmental amenities using stated choice studies. In: Kanninen BJ (ed) Valuing environmental amenities using stated choice studies. Springer, Netherlands, Dordrecht, pp 159–202
Jowett M (2003) Do informal risk sharing networks crowd out public voluntary health insurance? Evidence from Vietnam. Appl Econ 35:1153–1161
Kahneman D, Lovallo D (1993) Timid choices and bold forecasts: a cognitive perspective on risk taking. Manage Sci 39:17–31
Kahneman D, Tversky A (1979) Prospect theory: an analysis of decision under risk. Econometrica 47:263–292
Karim A, Noy I (2016) Poverty and natural disasters – a qualitative survey of the empirical literature. Singap Econ Rev 61:1640001
Karlan D, Osei R, Osei-Akoto I, Udry C (2014) Agricultural decisions after relaxing credit and risk constraints. Q J Econ 129:597–652
Kouame EBH, Kouam E (2012) Risk preferences and demand for insurance under price uncertainty: an experimental approach for cocoa farmers in Côte D'Ivoire risk preferences and demand. Microinsurance innovation facility research paper 13, Geneva
Kousky C, Michel-Kerjan EO, Raschky P A (2013) Does federal disaster assistance crowd out private demand for insurance. University of Pennsylvania, Working Paper 2013–10, Philadelphia
Kunreuther H (1996) Mitigating disaster losses through insurance. J Risk Uncertain 12:171–187
Kunreuther H, Pauly M (2004) Neglecting disaster: why don't people insure against large losses? J Risk Uncertain 28:5–21
Lashley JG, Warner K (2015) Evidence of demand for microinsurance for coping and adaptation to weather extremes in the Caribbean. Clim Change 133:101–112
Leblois A, Quirion P (2013) Agricultural insurances based on meteorological indices: realizations, methods and research challenges. Meteorol Appl 20:1–9
Leblois A, Quirion P, Alhassane A, Traoré S (2013) Weather index drought insurance: an ex ante evaluation for millet growers in Niger. Environ Resource Econ 57:527–551
Levine R, Loayza N, Beck T (2000) Financial intermediation and growth : causality and causes. J Monet Econ 16:31–77
Levy JS (1992) An introduction to prospect theory. Polit Psychol 13:171–186
Li J-Z, Li S, Wang W-Z et al (2011) Are people always more risk averse after disasters? Surveys after a heavy snow-hit and a major earthquake in China in 2008. Appl Cogn Psychol 25:104–111
Linnerooth-Bayer J, Hochrainer-Stigler S (2015) Financial instruments for disaster risk management and climate change adaptation. Clim Change 133:85–100
Linnerooth-Bayer J, Mechler R (2006) Insurance for assisting adaptation to climate change in developing countries: a proposed strategy. Clim Policy 6:621–636
Linnerooth-Bayer J, Mechler R, Hochrainer-Stigler S (2011) Insurance against losses from natural disasters in developing countries. Evidence, gaps and the way forward. J Integr Disaster Risk Manag 1:59–81
Liu Y, Chen KZ, Hill RV, Xiao C (2013) Borrowing from the insurer: an empirical analysis of demand and impact of insurance in China. Microinsurance innovation facility research paper 34, Geneva
Liu X, Tang Y, Miranda MJ (2015) Does past experience in natural disasters affect willingness-to-pay for weather index insurance? Evidence from China. Agricultural & Applied Economics Association annual meeting 2015, San Francisco
Lloyd's & Microinsurance Centre (2009) Insurance in developing countries: exploring opportunities in microinsurance, London
Mahul O, Skees J (2007) Managing agricultural risk at the country level: the case of index-based livestock insurance in Mongolia. The World Bank policy research working paper 4325, Washington, DC
Mangham LJ, Hanson K, McPake B (2009) How to do (or not to do)...Designing a discrete choice experiment for application in a low-income country. Health Policy Plan 24:151–158

Matul M, Dalal A, De Bock O, Gelade W (2013) Microinsurance why people do not buy microinsurance and what can we do about it. Microinsurance innovation facility microinsurance paper 20, Geneva

McCord MJ (2006) The partner-agent model: challenges and opportunities. In: Churchill C (ed) Protecting the poor—a microinsurance compendium. International Labour Office, Geneva, Munich, pp 357–377

Mechler R, Linnerooth-Bayer J, Peppiatt D (2006) Disaster insurance for the poor? A review of microinsurance. ProVention, IIASA, Geneva, Vienna

Mobarak AM, Rosenzweig M (2012) Selling formal insurance to the informally insured. Economic growth center discussion paper 1007, New Haven

Morduch J (2006) Micro-insurance: the next revolution? In: Banerjee A, Benabou R, Mookherjee D (eds) Understanding poverty. Oxford University Press, New York, pp 337–356

Morsink K (2012) Weathering the storm: the demand for and impact of microinsurance in Africa. University of Twente

Mosley P (2009) Assessing the success of microinsurance programmes in meeting the insurance needs of the poor. UN/DESA working paper 84, New York

Munich Re Foundation (2013) The landscape of microinsurance in Asia and Oceania 2013. Munich

Navrud S, Magnussen K (2013) Valuing the impacts of natural disasters and the economic benefits of preventing them. In: Guha-Sapir D, Santos I (eds) The economic impacts of natural disasters. Oxford University Press, New York, pp 57–79

Nghiem SH, Duong AH (2012) Preferences of micro-insurance products: evidence from the mutual assistance fund in Vietnam. J Agric Econ Dev 1:106–114

Nguyen M-H, Reynaud A, Thomas A, Thanh ND (2012) Do natural disasters modify individual preferences: evidences from a field experiment in Vietnam. School of Economics, Toulouse

Outreville JF (2013) The relationship between insurance and economic development: 85 empirical papers for a review of the literature. Risk Manag Insur Rev 16:71–122

Oviedo AM, Moroz H (2014) A review of the ex post and ex ante impacts of risk. Washington, DC: The World Bank, Background paper for the world development report 2014

Page L, Savage DA, Torgler B (2014) Variation in risk seeking behaviour following large losses: a natural experiment. Eur Econ Rev 71:121–131

Patt A, Peterson N, Carter M et al (2009) Making index insurance attractive to farmers. Mitig Adapt Strat Glob Chang 14:737–753

Qin T, Gu X, Tian Z et al (2016) An empirical analysis of the factors influencing farmer demand for forest insurance: based on surveys from Lin'an County in Zhejiang Province of China. J For Econ 24:37–51

Raschky PA, Schwindt M (2011) Aid, catastrophes and the Samaritan's dilemma. Monash University, Melbourne

Raschky PA, Schwarze R, Schwindt M, Zahn F (2012) Uncertainty of governmental relief and the crowding out of flood insurance. Environ Resource Econ 54:179–200

Reinhard D, Qureshi Z (2013) How to provide sustainable insurance for low-income. I-VW-HSG Trendmonitor, 13–16

Reynaud A, Nguyen M-H (2012) Monetary valuation of flood insurance in Vietnam. Vietnam Center of Research in Economics, Management and Environment 01-2012, Hanoi, Ho Chi Minh City

Reynaud A, Nguyen M-H (2016) Valuing flood risk reductions. Environ Model Assess:1–47

Roth J, McCord MJ, Liber D (2007) The landscape of microinsurance in the World's 100 poorest countries. The MicroInsurance Centre, LLC, Appleton

Said F, Afzal U, Turner G (2015) Risk taking and risk learning after a rare event: evidence from a field experiment in Pakistan. J Econ Behav Organ 118:167–183

Schechter L (2007) Traditional trust measurement and the risk confound: an experiment in rural Paraguay. J Econ Behav Organ 62:272–292

Schmidt U (2016) Insurance demand under prospect theory: a graphical analysis. J Risk Insur 83:77–89

Schmidt U, Starmer C, Sugden R (2008) Third-generation prospect theory. J Risk Uncertain 36:203–223

Schwarze R, Wagner GG (2007) The political economy of natural disaster insurance: lessons from the failure of a proposed compulsory insurance scheme in Germany. Eur Environ, 403–415

Skees JR (2008) Innovations in index insurance for the poor in lower income countries. Agric Resour Econ Rev 1:1–15

Skees J, Varangis P, Larson DF, Spiegel P (2005) Can financial markets be tapped to help poor people cope with weather risks? In: Dercon S (ed) Insurance against poverty. UNU-WIDER Studies in Development Economics/Oxford University Press, Oxford, pp 422–438

Skees JR, Murphy A, Collier B et al (2007) Scaling up index based insurance: what is needed for the next big step forward? Microinsurance Centre, LCC, Geneva

Surminski S, Oramas-Dorta D (2011) Building effective and sustainable risk transfer initiatives in low- and middle-income economies: what can we learn from existing insurance schemes? Centre for Climate Change Economics and Policy, Grantham Research Institute on Climate Change and the Environment, London

Surminski S, Oramas-Dorta D (2014) Flood insurance schemes and climate adaptation in developing countries. Int J Disaster Risk Reduct 7:154–164

Thornton RL, Hatt LE, Field EM et al (2010) Social security health insurance for the informal sector in Nicaragua: a randomized evaluation. Health Econ 19:181–206

Tower C, McGuinness E (2011) A friend indeed: evaluation of an insurance education radio campain in Kenya. Microfinance Opportunities, Washington, DC

Turner G, Said F, Afzal U (2014) Microinsurance demand after a rare flood event: evidence from a field experiment in Pakistan. Geneva Pap Risk Insur Iss Pract 39:201–223

Tversky A, Kahneman D (1974) Judgment under uncertainty: heuristics and biases. Science 185 (80):1124–1131

UNDP (2013) Microinsurance study: the understanding and needs of low-income populations regarding microinsurance. United Nations Development Programme, Phnom Penh

van den Berg M, Fort R, Burger K (2009) Natural hazards and risk aversion: experimental evidence from Latin America. International association of agricultural economists conference 2009, Beijing

Viverita R, Setiati R, Abdurrahman IAAF (2010) A study on demand for micro insurance for low-income households in disaster-prone areas of Indonesia. Universitas Indonesia, Depok

Voors M, Nillesen E, Verwimp P, et al (2010) Does conflict affect preferences? Results from field experiments in Burundi. MICROCON research working paper 21, Brighton

WHO (2012) How to conduct a discrete choice experiment for health workforce recruitment and retention in remote and rural areas: a user guide with case studies, Geneva

World Bank (2005) Managing agricultural production risk—innovations in developing countries. The World Bank, Washington, DC

World Bank (2007) Disasters, climate change, and economic development in Sub-Saharan Africa—lessons and future directions. Washington, DC

World Bank (2013) World development report 2014: risk and opportunity—managing risk for development. Washington, DC

World Bank (2014) World development indicators. In: World Dev. Indic. http://databank.worldbank.org/. Accessed 15 Aug 2014

Yeboah AK, Obeng CK (2016) Effect of financial literacy on willingness to pay for microinsurance by commercial market business operators in Ghana. MPRA paper 70135, Munich

Zelizer V (1979) Morals and markets: the development of life insurance in the United States. Transaction Publishers, New York

Chapter 5
Going Forward: Building Resilience with Microinsurance

This study investigates the impact of disaster experience on individual behaviour as well as the demand for microinsurance within the complex contexts of natural disasters, economic development and disaster risk management. The following chapter will highlight and discuss important results and conclusions, such as the role of individual behaviour, substitutes to microinsurance and the possible benefits of insurance for prevention and productivity.

As discussed at length in Chap. 2, natural disasters affect millions of people every year and have devastating social and economic effects with possible and significant long-term consequences to human, social and physical capital—a trend likely to increase in the future due to a higher frequency and intensity of extreme weather events caused by climate change. Developing countries are particularly exposed to natural hazards due to their location in tropical regions as well as high urbanisation rates in exposed river and coastal regions. Furthermore, people in developing economies are often more vulnerable to the adverse effects of shocks due to limited accessibility and affordability of effective coping mechanisms (IPCC 2012; Kousky 2012; World Bank 2013; Oviedo and Moroz 2014; Hallegatte et al. 2016).

Risk is an essential part of everyday life in developing countries and is intimately linked to poverty. Hereby, the relationship between natural disasters and levels of development is highly complex and significant causalities can be found in both directions. Firstly, less developed economies are more vulnerable to natural disasters and their consequences and are less able to reduce exposure, with higher losses in relative terms compared to more developed economies. Secondly, natural disasters and their various impacts on household income, human capital, social infrastructure, individual behaviour, etc. significantly affect a country's level of development and can increase poverty. The close interconnection between risk and poverty has led to proposals to define poverty as a combination of income categorisation, lack of access to social protection and the inability to cope with hazards (Cohen and Sebstad 2005; van den Berg et al. 2009; Summer 2013; World Bank 2013; Oviedo and Moroz 2014; Hallegatte et al. 2016).

O. Fiala, *Natural Disasters and Individual Behaviour in Developing Countries*, Contributions to Economics, DOI 10.1007/978-3-319-53904-1_5

Due to their combination of higher vulnerability and exposure, developing countries in general, and the poor in particular, are less resilient to the various and complex effects of natural disasters. Comprehensive and innovative risk management strategies are needed to develop social protection and make development processes more resilient. Hereby, building resilience not only protects people and assets from hazards, but empowers individuals and communities to develop despite the risk of disaster (Mosley 2009; Hallegatte 2012; The Royal Society 2014; Gehrke 2014).

In order to deal with these risks, individuals and communities must be able to access both ex ante and ex post strategies. While the latter are necessary to cope efficiently with the consequences of disasters, ex ante approaches can reduce risks before the impacts are realised. A framework for disaster risk management was proposed, comprised of the components knowledge, protection, insurance and coping (see Sect. 2.3). One possible instrument is insurance used as a risk-financing strategy, which can—if appropriated designed—work both as ex ante and ex post approach to build sustainable resilience. It can offer opportunities to manage the long-term and complex effects of disaster risk such as investment in low-risk, low-return strategies and long-lasting disaster impacts on human and social capital, which may otherwise result in persistent poverty otherwise (Dercon 2005a; World Bank 2013).

Recent literature highlights the importance of expectations and perceptions in the assessment of risks and disaster outcomes. Behavioural choices and expectations play a significant role in explaining subjective exposure to disasters and therefore the choice of risk management strategies as well as the relationship between development and disaster impacts. This thesis finds empirical significance for both the impact of disaster experience on decision-making processes and the impact of individual behaviour and perceptions on the demand of microinsurance (Kellenberg and Mobarak 2008; Karim and Noy 2016).

The role of individual behaviour will be highlighted in Sect. 5.1, and the substitutes to microinsurance will be discussed in Sect. 5.2. Section 5.3 will discuss the specific benefits of microinsurance for prevention and long-term productivity. The chapter will close with an outlook on the future of microinsurance in Sect. 5.4 and a commentary on disaster risk management in Sect. 5.5.

5.1 The Role of Individual Behaviour in Decision-Making Processes

The presented analysis in Cambodia and recent literature highlight the importance of expectations and perceptions, particularly for decision-making under risk and uncertainty. Highlighting the main outcomes of the presented research, the following section will discuss various approaches. Overall, the significance of individual expectations and perceptions in the assessment of both risks and disaster outcomes will be emphasised (IPCC 2014; Karim and Noy 2016).

As discussed in depth in Chap. 3, both risk and trust are important determinants in most economic decision-making processes. Furthermore, they are of particular interest in decisions regarding disaster risk management strategies due to the high level of uncertainty.

The presented empirical analysis displays a significant positive impact of disaster experience on the individual's risk-taking propensity, which does not align with the expected economic effect resulting from a loss of wealth. However, in a world of imperfect information, the experience of a natural disaster may provide new information and therefore change the individual's perceptions about the probabilities and consequences of adverse shocks. Furthermore, psychological factors may change individual risk perceptions and the observed result can be explained by the theory of the Gambler's Fallacy, the under-estimation of the probability for a similar event shortly after its occurrence. In addition, the prospect theory also comprises the idea of gains and losses (relative to a reference point, to be determined) and loss aversion. Finally, risk-taking behaviour following a disaster can be explained by the role of emotions in the decision-making process. Therefore, both the theoretical and empirical analysis highlight the role of expectations, perceptions and psychological factors in the determination of risk behaviour (Kahneman and Tversky 1979; Loewenstein et al. 2001; Pat-Horenczyk et al. 2007; Eckel et al. 2009; Nguyen et al. 2012; Ingwersen 2014; Page et al. 2014; Said et al. 2014; Cameron and Shah 2015).

It was found that the individual's level of trust was reduced following the experience of a natural disaster in rural Cambodia. This observation can be explained by social rivalry in the aftermath situation and altering compositions of communities and networks due to migration. Furthermore, the experience of a disaster and the asymmetric information received about its individual damages may excuse the breaking of economic and social contracts. This is of particular importance as pre-existing social capital in general, and levels of trust and networks in particular, are found to help with recovery from disaster and building resilience. This can be attributed to the fact that they function as informal insurances, promoting collective actions and mobilising communities. However, the impacts of disasters on social capital and trust can have persisting effects in the long run (Cassar et al. 2012; Fleming et al. 2014).

Chapter 4 discusses microinsurance as an instrument of disaster risk management and presents trust and risk as important factors for the viability of disaster insurance. Thereby, in the literature, trust is mostly discussed as trust in the insurance company to provide timely payments and remain solvent. Figure 4.2 presented a framework in order to investigate the impact of natural disaster on the demand for microinsurance, focussing on wealth and income, risk aversion, non-performance risk, trust, informal risk-sharing, and risk exposure. The empirical analysis found a significantly negative impact of disaster experience on the hypothetical demand for microinsurance. The experience of an adverse shock can hereby change subjective probabilities and damage assessments or inform about the stability of informal risk management strategies (update of information). Furthermore, previous shocks may have encouraged households to adopt physical, psychological and other strategies to cope with the negative effects, which function in some ways as a substitute to formal insurance products. Finally, psychological factors may impact perceptions and expectations of both severity and frequency of future floods (Mechler et al. 2006; De Bock and Gelade 2012; Cole et al. 2013; Eling et al. 2014; Turner et al. 2014; Liu et al. 2015).

The analysis of disaster experience on both risk behaviour and microinsurance demand highlights the importance of perceptions, expectations, heuristics and psychological factors in decision-making processes. Therefore, when assessing long-term post-disaster outcomes, the adjustment in expectations towards future events may be more important than the level of destruction or the degree of preparedness. This is of particular importance as changes in the subjective level of disaster risk depend partly on socio-economic backgrounds, with significant effects for the role of poverty traps. Although more research is certainly needed for a better understanding of risk perceptions and their impacts, policies can be designed more effectively by considering expectations and behavioural biases, for instance with participatory, reflexive and iterative communication approaches (Weber and Johnson 2012; IPCC 2014; Karim and Noy 2016).

5.2 Substitutes to Microinsurance

Both the theoretical and empirical discussions in this thesis include other instruments of disaster risk management, which can be in a complementary or substitutional relationship to insurance products. Hereby substitutes (complements) between two factors are understood in the way that an increase in one factor will decrease (increase) the marginal utility of another (Dercon et al. 2014). In the following section, the role of informal risk-sharing networks and external assistance will be discussed.

The Role of Informal Risk-Sharing Networks The presence of social capital—represented by a high level of trust—does not automatically imply that informal insurances or networks exist; however it is often used as a proxy for informal risk-sharing instruments (Dercon 2002; Morsink 2012). If this is transferred to the empirical analysis for rural Cambodia, a high level of trust towards other members of the immediate community—and therefore a high level of social capital—may indicate the existence of informal and community-based risk-sharing and coping mechanisms. Furthermore, the negative relationship between trust and insurance demand found in the present study suggests a crowding-out effect of formal insurance by informal risk management approaches. Similar empirical evidence is presented by Jowett (2003) for health insurance in Vietnam and by Brata et al. (2014) for disaster insurance in Indonesia.

In general, informal risk-sharing instruments often depend on trust, kin and reciprocity. Their advantage lies in the reduction of typical insurance problems, such as asymmetric information and moral hazard, due to frequent personal communication and monitoring. However, while these instruments generally work well for idiosyncratic and small systemic events, they are problematic for large systemic events, where the entire risk-sharing community is affected. Furthermore, due to uncertainty about the actual protection in the case of a shock, such instruments often cannot prevent inefficient investment strategies in low-risk, low-return crops. In addition, within the household, such instruments benefit participants differently based on their gender and the relationship between the spouses. Finally, informal arrangements relying on social ties and shared norms often exclude minorities, are not necessarily stable in the case of in-migration and show a general inability to handle change (Dercon 2002, 2005a; Cohen and Sebstad 2005; de Weerdt 2005; Goldstein et al. 2005; Mobarak and Rosenzweig 2012; World Bank 2013).

To conclude, existing informal risk-sharing and risk-coping approaches may contain important lessons for the organisation and implementation of social protection. Furthermore, public action may crowd out informal mechanisms—or are crowded out by them as indicated in rural Cambodia—and therefore the interdependencies of these instruments should be better understood. However, by creating a favourable legal environment and increasing government capacities, the role of informal risk-sharing networks can be strengthened, improving their role in the risk management framework. Finally, linking both formal and informal insurance systems can help to overcome the shortcomings of both instruments. One approach towards how this could be developed is the existence of group insurances against disaster risk offered to a community, who in return take responsibility for distribution within (Albarran and Attanasio 2005; de Weerdt 2005; Dercon 2005b; World Bank 2013).

The Impact of External Assistance Another crowding-out effect can be found in the role that external assistance plays for insurance demand. Support received from the government following a disaster significantly reduces the demand for insurance in rural Cambodia. Evidence for so-called 'charity hazard'—the substitution of formal insurance by government or charity transfers—has also been found in other developing countries (Turner et al. 2014; Grislain-Letrémy 2015; Liu et al. 2015).

Furthermore, previous studies in this context also discuss the impact of external assistance on risk behaviour. Whilst this research in rural Cambodia cannot show any empirically significant correlations between external assistance and risk behaviour, other references show a significant impact of governmental support on risk aversion. Although assistance from government or charities relaxes liquidity and increases wealth, ambiguous impacts on risk aversion can be found. Finally, the expectation of external assistance following a natural disaster in the future can be an important factor in the perception of financial constraints (Ingwersen 2014; Said et al. 2014; Cameron and Shah 2015).

Although there is often some form of short-term humanitarian relief in the aftermath of a disaster, the long-term impacts of post-disaster assistance—that aims to provide lasting and positive consequences—is less understood. The results of this study for rural Cambodia suggest a higher risk-taking behaviour of disaster-affected households. Therefore, it may be effective to provide incentives for long-term investments which are consistent with the individuals' risk attitudes. Business capital and job training, in addition to cash-for-work programmes, may be possible approaches. However, public and private external assistance must be designed with attention to existing informal and formal insurance systems which may be in place. Despite the pressure on governments and non-governmental organisations to act following an adverse shock, the role of insurance markets and their possible long-term effects on development and poverty alleviation should be considered and public disaster policy should follow a cohesive and comprehensive disaster risk management strategy, which takes into account all potential assistance providers (Albarran and Attanasio 2005; Skees 2008; Ingwersen 2014; Cameron and Shah 2015).

5.3 The Benefits of Microinsurance for Prevention and Productivity

Microinsurance—like every type of insurance—focuses most notably on the minimisation of financial losses and the provision of security from risks. However, microinsurance products have been widely recognised as instruments for risk reduction and prevention against extreme weather events, and therefore they are mechanisms of both mitigation and adaptation. Furthermore, these financial products can set incentives for higher productivity and long-term growth by reducing the individuals' level of vulnerability towards natural disasters and helping them to overcome poverty traps (Hochrainer-Stigler et al. 2012; Arshad et al. 2016).

Risk Reduction and Prevention Most environmental risks faced by individuals are endogenous to some degree and actions can be undertaken either to reduce the likelihood of the event (self-protection) or to reduce the costs once the event occurs (self-insurance). If correctly designed and implemented, microinsurance can be used to provide incentives for risk reduction and investments in preventive measures, leading to an overall reduction of individual disaster risks. In return for investments in disaster prevention, insurers can offer lower premiums to reward the desired behaviour (Mechler et al. 2006; Brouwer et al. 2013; Surminski and Oramas-Dorta 2014).

In studying the demand for hypothetical microinsurance in rural Cambodia, it is evident that respondents had a significantly lower preference for products requiring their own prevention efforts as compared to products without such conditions. However, almost 92% of the sample answered in the questionnaire that they would be willing to increase their prevention efforts if insurance would then become cheaper. A more detailed analysis of the relationship between microinsurance and prevention is needed, facing real cost-benefit-decisions of the households.

Overall, a positive impact of weather and livestock microinsurance on protection can be found, although the contribution towards the long-term reduction of losses and levels of vulnerability is mixed. Finally, improved protection drives economic development towards riskier behaviours and can therefore increase exposure. Although protection reduces the pure probability of disaster impacts on the individual, the effects on risk are more complex, transferring risk from frequent and low-cost events to rare and high-cost events (Mechler et al. 2006; Hallegatte 2012; De Bock and Ontiveros 2013).

The Impact of Microinsurance on Productivity and Growth In addition to substantial impacts once a disaster has occurred, there are also significant ex ante impacts such as households' engagement in low-risk, low-return strategies to decrease income variability and reduce risks (see Chap. 2 for a detailed description of ex ante disaster impacts). This follows the idea that income smoothing strategies, aimed at reducing the risk faced by the household, raises opportunity costs. These can include lower future income opportunities due to lower investments in new technologies or low-return crops. In the long run, vulnerability and exposure to disasters leads to more negative disaster consequences, which harm development and contribute again to higher vulnerability and exposure, an effect introduced in Chap. 2 as the 'poverty trap'. Microinsurance can play a role in providing both security from risks and incentives for sustainable, long-term productivity and income growth[1] (Chhibber and Laajaj 2013; Oviedo and Moroz 2014; Hallegatte et al. 2016).

Insured households become more creditworthy, independent of a disaster occurrence, and are provided with access to post-disaster liquidity, cushioning the burdens from floods and other extreme weather events by securing livelihoods and providing financial resources for reconstruction. In this context, an insurance contract is often seen as more dignified and more reliable than dependency on possible external ad hoc assistance following disasters. Furthermore, microinsurance can be bundled with microfinance loans, providing additional liquidity to poor households. Previous studies also found positive effects of weather and livestock insurance on investment. Households provided with rainfall insurance show increasing farm expenditures and investments, overcoming erroneously conceived liquidity constraints. The significant effect of enhanced risk-taking behaviour can be found in the use of chemical fertilisers and increased overall productivity (Mechler et al. 2006; Linnerooth-Bayer et al. 2011; De Bock and Ontiveros 2013; Awel and Azomahou 2014; Karlan et al. 2014).

[1]Almost three quarters (74.2%) of respondents in rural Cambodia stated that they would increase their production or try new crops with higher returns if they would have insurance against flood damage. However, during the survey the questions were asked with no further information provided regarding the insurance design and cannot be validated in a real-world situation.

Furthermore, the above discussed effects of risk reduction and prevention can motivate farmers and households towards high-risk, high-return activities by transforming uncertain and large losses into small and certain regular premiums. Similar effects can be found for households with loans: memberships of microfinance institutions reduce the probability of becoming poor. Furthermore, insurance products have attracted interest in combination with the provision of loans by reducing the borrowers' vulnerability and increasing the stability of the microfinance institution through improved repayment rates. Finally, microinsurance can contribute to economic growth beyond promoting financial stability by encouraging new capital accumulation and more efficient allocations (Sadoulet 2005; Linnerooth-Bayer et al. 2011; Outreville 2013; Lensink et al. 2015).

Conclusion Beyond humanitarian reasons for providing microinsurance products to the poor, there are significant and positive economic effects of this instrument. By providing better social protection, there are indications that correctly designed and implemented insurance schemes may improve prevention, facilitate growth and support poverty reduction. However, the overall empirical evidence for the long-term effects of microinsurance products is still limited and research must be increased in this area (Dercon 2005b; Radermacher et al. 2012).

5.4 Microinsurance Outlook

Creating a sustainable microinsurance scheme is challenging given the trade-off between three objectives: coverage focusing on the needs of low-income households, transaction and operating costs for the insurer, and affordability in price and transaction costs for the clients. Strategies used to achieve sustainability include the limiting of benefits, the focus on efficiency and the diversification of income sources. Various challenges at different levels (clients, providers, regulators, environment) limit the expansion of microinsurance. These include lack of client education and insurance culture, ineffective business models and delivery channels, unsupportive regulation, unstable financial markets and missing key data. The following section discusses some of many innovative approaches to create sustainable and efficient microinsurance products, particularly in the light of climate change (Botero et al. 2006; Churchill and Garand 2006).

Role of Governments and Innovative Microinsurance Products In the context of microinsurance and social protection against disaster risk, governments can play three roles. Firstly, governments can provide social protection, such as healthcare, pensions, flood protection, etc (Jacquier et al. 2006; Clarke and Dercon 2009; Deblon and Loewe 2012). However, the fiscal resources needed to provide basic social safety nets are often constrained, particularly in developing countries (Trommershäuser et al. 2006). Secondly, governments are responsible for overall framework conditions, hence the supervision and regulation of the insurance industry; these include the protection of policy holders as well as the development of insurance markets, for under-served segments of the society in particular (Trommershäuser et al. 2006; Wiedmaier-Pfister and Chatterjee 2006). Thirdly, governments can take the role of facilitators for insurances, helping to overcome market imperfections by promoting microinsurance; this is particularly important if the insurance product is seen as an instrument of social protection (Trommershäuser et al. 2006). The latter can include the creation of a legal framework, risk prevention policies and mitigation of risks, social marketing, research and information, as well as the provision of financial assistance (Trommershäuser et al. 2006; Hazell et al. 2010; Cole et al. 2013; Carter et al. 2014; Dao and Van Tai 2014).

One promising way of increasing coverage and making microinsurance schemes more sustainable is seen in private-public partnerships. The private insurer could provide products for less severe, idiosyncratic and localised risks, using for instance community-based schemes with their advantage of avoiding information asymmetries; in contrast, the government, or more broadly the public sector, can insure covariant and systemic risks—such as disaster risks—due to their capability for pooling risks over a larger group (Linnerooth-Bayer et al. 2011; Reinhard and Qureshi 2013; Gehrke 2014; Swain 2015). India, the worldwide leader in microinsurance volume and innovation, enhanced the provision of such insurance products successfully by public investments in safety nets, private-public partnerships, incentivising products through subsidies, and favourable regulation (Chatterjee 2012; Ruchismita and Churchill 2012). Furthermore, some aspects of agricultural insurance, such as data collection for reliable indices, are natural monopolies (Reinhard and Qureshi 2013).

Government or donor-sponsored microinsurance schemes often have a market development role. However, in order to scale-up microinsurance schemes, growth of insurances and coverages have to be market-driven. Insurance providers have found that microinsurance can be profitable if the operation is kept simple and efficient and reaches large numbers of poor households. Therefore, insurance supervisors and regulatory institutions should motivate existing insurers to adapt and innovate their schemes as well as encourage new microinsurance providers. Furthermore, such institutions can motivate take-up on the demand side and help to formalise informal insurance networks in order to make them more resilient and sustainable. In addition, developed reinsurance systems must be in place—either market-based or offered publicly—in order to provide capital backup, particularly for large, catastrophic shocks (Lloyd's and Microinsurance Centre 2009; World Bank 2013; Linnerooth-Bayer and Hochrainer-Stigler 2015).

Hochrainer-Stigler et al. (2012) see awareness and information as keys to increasing the diffusion of disaster microinsurance, finding high recommendation rates of clients towards friends as well as an increase in demand after non-insured individuals were given information about the relevance and prices of insurance. However, although microinsurance products are aimed at low-income households, existing programmes are often not available or accessible to the most vulnerable households. Subsidies or the connection of insurances with savings and loans are seen as possible ways to focus the provided services, especially on the poor. As discussed in Chap. 4, microfinance institutions often have an existing reputation that can be built on for the provision of microinsurance (Dercon 2005a; Sadoulet 2005; Mosley 2009; Hochrainer-Stigler et al. 2012).

The Role of Climate Change Climate change, and its local impacts as discussed in Chap. 2, are future challenges to the provision of resilient disaster microinsurance. While awareness of climate change may contribute to people's willingness to pay for disaster or agricultural insurance, additional stress and risks will be imposed on insurance schemes against weather-related shocks. This requires higher investments in disaster-related infrastructure, technical assistance to optimise product design as well as awareness about the role of disaster insurance as an instrument to manage climate risks (Linnerooth-Bayer et al. 2011; Loster and Reinhard 2012; Clarke and Grenham 2013; Guo 2015).

Microinsurance in Cambodia As discussed in greater depth in Chap. 2, Cambodia's special hydrological regime and low development of water control infrastructure partially explains its level of vulnerability towards natural disasters. As the nation has experienced several devastating floods in recent years, the government's main focus was laying on ex post actions (emergency measures and relief) rather than on ex ante instruments of social protection (including financial instruments such as microinsurance).[2] Although risk reduction activities gained more attention as part of disaster risk management, they are only seen as feasible instruments for the long-term. This includes the allocation of special funds for mitigation and preparedness, the increase of emergency funds and the product development of risk transfer instruments including crop or disaster insurance (National Committee for Disaster Management 2008; Vathana et al. 2013; Mochizuki et al. 2015).

However, the insurance industry in Cambodia is still in the early stages of its development. General awareness and understanding of insurances is still relatively low, although there has been a significant increase in recent years. However, local expertise is still limited and the judicial system is often weak. Furthermore, there is a lack of historical, meteorological and climatological data for efficient risk assessment as well as a lack of flood hazard maps. Despite these shortcomings, microinsurance providers have strong interests to engage in this market, and various research projects—including the present one—have demonstrated the interest of the majority of low-income households in such products. A high potential demand is seen, particularly for crop insurance (floods and droughts) as well as for health insurance. However, the provision of agricultural insurance is especially complex and requires very specific organisational and technical competencies. Currently,

---

[2]The response-orientated view of disaster risk management is reflected in international disaster aid allocation (Mochizuki et al. 2015). From 1990 to 2010, Cambodia received in total USD785.4 million, whereof 54.9% was used for emergency response and 34.8% for reconstruction and rehabilitation; only 10.2% of international disaster aid was used for disaster preparedness and prevention (AidData 2016).

such microinsurance is not perceived to be financially feasible from the commercial perspective. Besides the potential of long-term financial stability, microfinance institutions as possible providers see the mistrust of farmers towards formal insurance as a central issue. Opportunities for agricultural insurance against weather risks should be analysed in more detail through pilot projects on the ground, combining research with good practice experiences (UNDP 2013; World Bank et al. 2013; Van Wingerden and Brouwer 2014).

Conclusion Microinsurance should be seen as one important instrument of risk management that increases social protection, particularly for low-income households. However, the resilience and sustainability of such instruments depends crucially on the specific context and framework conditions. Furthermore, more research is certainly needed, particularly to understand wealth dynamics for the poor in the long-term and to determine which role microinsurance can play in this context. This is of particular importance due to the multi-risk environment in developing countries, where disaster risk is only one amongst many. Finally, microinsurance should be analysed in the context of a comprehensive disaster risk management strategy, including the various levels of risk management. The following section concludes this discussion by casting a glance at this broader approach.

5.5 Going Forward in the Context of Disaster Risk Management

Climate change could pull up to 100 million people into poverty by 2030, a number which can be significantly reduced by climate-informed development and effective disaster risk management (Hallegatte et al. 2016). A comprehensive risk management approach can prevent a substantial, negative impact of climate change on poverty. As discussed in Chap. 2, disaster risk management includes four components: knowledge, protection, insurance and coping. When respondents in Cambodia were asked about their needs for better protection against extreme floods, their answers reflected the various components of preparation (Fig. 5.1). As the present study has focused on households and communities, the following policy recommendations for risk management also concentrate on these sectors.

The Role of Social Protection The provision of social protection—also often described as social safety nets such as conditional and unconditional cash transfers—is seen as an efficient tool to reduce the impact of natural disasters and economic shocks on poverty. Correctly designed, it can support a long-term transformation to more resilient societies, if they maintain incentives to invest in adaptation. Safety nets can help vulnerable people in particular to accumulate assets and human capital and to take more risks in productive activities. To allow the poor to cope with disaster shocks or other fundamental changes, these social

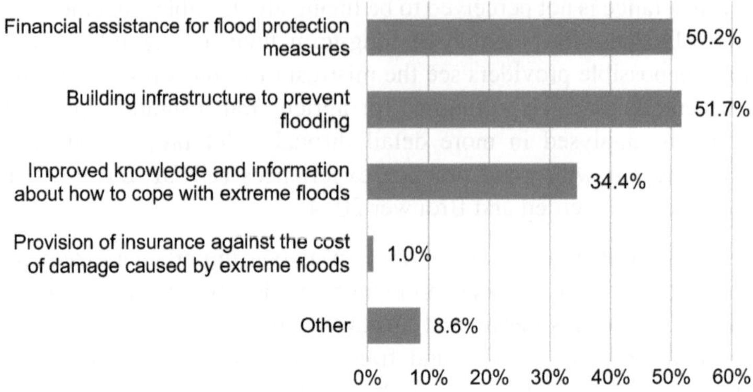

Fig. 5.1 Participants' needs for better preparations against extreme floods

protection programmes must be designed for scalability and flexibility. However, the right social protection instrument is highly context specific. The conditions of safety nets depend on clear and pre-announced terms, even in the case of a large covariate shock. They therefore require a commitment of resources and substantial planning (Dercon 2005a; Jalan and Ravallion 2005; World Bank 2013; Hallegatte et al. 2016).

Financial Tools as Instruments of Disaster Risk Management In a broader risk management framework, it is important to view microinsurance—with its goal to reduce vulnerability and poverty through insurance against risks—within existing social protection policies. However, microinsurance is only one instrument among others and its role of providing efficient protection against disaster risks is context-specific and depends on other existing social protection approaches. Furthermore, microinsurance products are perceived as more effective if combined with other complementary instruments such as social insurance or cash transfers (Deblon and Loewe 2012; De Bock and Ontiveros 2013).

Besides the role of microinsurance as an instrument of social protection, the provision of insurance products is often discussed in the context of financial inclusion for the poor in developing countries. Financial products are seen as crucial components of risk management strategies, however poor households in particular often lack access to formal financial services such as savings, credits or insurances due to cost, distance and time constraints. Therefore, investments in financial infrastructure are necessary in order to reduce costs and increase trust in financial institutions and their products (World Bank 2013; Hallegatte et al. 2016).

Integration of Risk Management into Economic, Fiscal and Environmental Policy The direct and indirect effects of natural disasters significantly affect the public finance of an exposed country. Mochizuki et al. (2015) assess disaster risk in Cambodia, finding a high probability of a fiscal resource gap (50% in the next 5 years, 90% in the next 10 years). However, investments of USD100 million annually would reduce the probability of a fiscal resource gap to 36%. Although awareness of fiscal issues related to disaster expenditures is found at the national level, it has not been translated into specific risk management approaches (Mochizuki et al. 2015).

In order to build resilience in the context of poverty and climate change, disaster risk management should be integrated into economic and fiscal policy with the overall goal of reducing vulnerability and exposure—and therefore risks—over time. Although ex ante reduction of risks in most cases outweigh the costs, developing and financially vulnerable countries are often unlikely to implement effective risk financing instruments themselves. However, governments in these countries should increase poverty reduction efforts and design social safety nets to reduce vulnerabilities towards weather-related events before climate change impacts become larger. Until recently, Cambodia has followed a reactive disaster management approach; however, a paradigm shift towards investments in proactive risk management approaches has started.[3] Finally, in order to reduce the significant and persistent short- and long-term effects of natural disasters on the poor, social protection for the most vulnerable must be increased and a focus must be given to emission-reduction policies in order to reduce the long-term effects of climate change (Mechler et al. 2010; General Directorate of Agriculture 2013; Mitchell et al. 2014; Mochizuki et al. 2015; Hallegatte et al. 2016).

References

AidData (2016) Disaster aid tracking. http://gfdrr.aiddata.org/. Accessed 22 Mar 2016

Albarran P, Attanasio OP (2005) Do public transfers crowd out private transfers? Evidence from a randomized experiment in Mexico. In: Dercon S (ed) Insurance against poverty. UNU-WIDER Studies in Development Economics/Oxford University Press, Oxford, pp 281–304

Arshad M, Amjath-Babu TS, Kächele H, Müller K (2016) What drives the willingness to pay for crop insurance against extreme weather events (flood and drought) in Pakistan? A hypothetical market approach. Clim Dev 8:234–244.

Awel YM, Azomahou TT (2014) Productivity and welfare effects of weather index insurance: quasi-experimental evidence. Maastricht

Botero F, Churchill C, McCord MJ, Qureshi Z (2006) The future of microinsurance. In: Churchill C (ed) Protecting the poor—a microinsurance compendium. Munich, Geneva, pp 583–623

Brata AG, Rietveld P, de Groot HLF et al (2014) Living with the Merapi Volcano: risks and disaster microinsurance. ANU Working Papers in Trade and Development 13, Canberra

Brouwer R, Tinh BD, Tuan TH et al (2013) Modeling demand for catastrophic flood risk insurance in coastal zones in Vietnam using choice experiments. Environ Dev Econ 19:228–249

Cameron L, Shah M (2015) Risk-taking behavior in the wake of natural disasters. Hum Resour 50:484–515

[3]In this context, Mochizuki et al. (2015) discuss an iterative risk management approach which promotes risk-sensitive investment decisions, development strategies and an adjustment of these policies in the light of new data and information, despite remaining uncertainty about future disaster occurrences and impacts. Efforts must be made to remove cognitive, economic and institutional barriers in Cambodia (Mochizuki et al. 2015).

Carter M, De Janvry A, Sadoulet E, Sarris A (2014) Index-based weather insurance for developing countries: a review of evidence and a set of propositions for up-scaling. FERDI, AFD, Paris
Cassar A, Healy A, von Kessler C (2012) Trust, risk, and time preferences after a natural disaster: experimental evidence from Thailand. University of San Francisco, San Francisco
Chatterjee A (2012) Access to insurance and financial-sector regulation. In: Churchill C, Matul M (eds) Protecting the poor—a microinsurance compendium, vol II. Munich, Geneva, pp 548–572
Chhibber A, Laajaj R (2013) The interlinkages between natural disasters and economic development. In: Guha-Sapir D, Santos I (eds) The economic impacts of natural disasters. Oxford University Press, New York, pp 28–56
Churchill C, Garand D (2006) Strategies for sustainability. In: Churchill C (ed) Protecting the poor—a microinsurance compendium. Munich, Geneva, pp 564–582
Clarke D, Dercon S (2009) Insurance, credit and safety nets for the poor in a world of risk. UN/DESA Working Paper 81, New York
Clarke DJ, Grenham D (2013) Microinsurance and natural disasters: challenges and options. Environ Sci Policy 27:S89–S98
Cohen M, Sebstad J (2005) Reducing vulnerability: the demand for microinsurance. J Int Dev 17:397–474
Cole S, Giné X, Tobacman J et al (2013) Barriers to household risk management: evidence from India. Am Econ J Appl Econ 5:104–135
Dao HTT, Van Tai L (2014) Agriculture insurance market development—the role of Vietnam government. Int J Econ Commer Manag II:1–12
De Bock O, Gelade W (2012) The demand for microinsurance: a literature review. Microinsurance Innovation Facility Research Paper 26, Geneva
De Bock O, Ontiveros DU (2013) Literature review on the impact of microinsurance. Microinsurance Innovation Facility Research Paper 35, Geneva
de Weerdt J (2005) Risk-sharing and endogenous network formation. In: Dercon S (ed) Insurance against poverty. UNU-WIDER Studies in Development Economics/Oxford University Press, Oxford, pp 197–216
Deblon Y, Loewe M (2012) The potential of microinsurance for social protection. In: Churchill C, Matul M (eds) Protecting the poor—a microinsurance compendium, vol II. Munich, Geneva, pp 40–58
Dercon S (2002) Income risk, coping strategies, and safety nets. World Bank Res Obs 17:141–166
Dercon S (2005a) Risk, poverty, and public action. In: Dercon S (ed) Insurance against poverty. UNU-WIDER Studies in Development Economics/Oxford University Press, Oxford, pp 439–450
Dercon S (2005b) Overview. In: Dercon S (ed) Insurance against poverty. UNU-WIDER Studies in Development Economics/Oxford University Press, Oxford, pp 1–8
Dercon S, Hill RV, Clarke D et al (2014) Offering rainfall insurance to informal insurance groups: evidence from a field experiment in Ethiopia. J Dev Econ 106:132–143
Eckel CC, El-Gamal MA, Wilson RK (2009) Risk loving after the storm: a Bayesian-network study of Hurricane Katrina evacuees. J Econ Behav Organ 69:110–124
Eling M, Pradhan S, Schmit JT (2014) The determinants of microinsurance demand. Geneva Pap Risk Insur Issues Pract 39:224–263
Fleming DA, Chong A, Bejarano HD (2014) Trust and reciprocity in the aftermath of natural disasters. J Dev Stud 50:1482–1493
Gehrke E (2014) The insurability framework applied to agricultural microinsurance: what do we know, what can we learn? Geneva Pap Risk Insur Issues Pract 39:264–279.
General Directorate of Agriculture (2013) Plan of action for disaster risk reduction in agriculture 2014-2018. Kingdom of Cambodia, Ministry of Agriculture, Forestry, and Fisheries, Phnom Penh
Goldstein M, de Janvry A, Sadoulet E (2005) Is a friend in need a friend indeed? Inclusions and exclusion in mutual insurance networks in Southern Ghana. In: Dercon S (ed) Insurance

against poverty. UNU-WIDER Studies in Development Economics/Oxford University Press, Oxford, pp 217–246

Grislain-Letrémy C (2015) Natural disasters: exposure and underinsurance. CREST, Paris-Dauphine University, Paris

Guo W (2015) Farmers' perception of climate change and willingness to pay for weather—Index Insurance in Bahunepati, Nepal

Hallegatte S (2012) An exploration of the link between development, economic growth, and natural risk. The World Bank Policy Research Working Paper 6216, Washington, DC

Hallegatte S, Bangalore M, Bonzanigo L et al (2016) Shock waves: managing the impacts of climate change on poverty. The World Bank, Washington, DC

Hazell P, Anderson J, Balzer N et al (2010) The potential for scale and sustainability in weather index insurance for agriculture and rural livelihoods. World Food Programme, Rome

Hochrainer-Stigler S, Sharma RB, Mechler R (2012) Disaster microinsurance for pro-poor risk management: evidence from South Asia. J Integr Disaster Risk Manag 2:70–88

Ingwersen N (2014) Impact of a natural disaster on observed risk aversion. Duke University, Durham

IPCC (2012) Managing the risks of extreme events and disasters to advance climate change adaptation. In: A special report of working groups I and II of the Intergovernmental Panel on Climate Change. Cambridge University Press, Cambridge, New York

IPCC (2014) Climate change 2014: impacts, adaptation, and vulnerability. Part A: global and sectoral aspects. In: Contribution of working group II to the Fifth Assessment Report of the Intergovernmental Panel on Climate Change. Cambridge University Press, Cambridge, New York

Jacquier C, Ramm G, Marcadent P, Schmitt-Diabate V (2006) The social protection perspective on microinsurance. In: Churchill C (ed) Protecting the poor—a microinsurance compendium. Munich, Geneva, pp 45–64

Jalan J, Ravallion M (2005) Household income dynamics in Rural China. In: Dercon S (ed) Insurance against poverty. UNU-WIDER Studies in Development Economics/Oxford University Press, Oxford, pp 107–123

Jowett M (2003) Do informal risk sharing networks crowd out public voluntary health insurance? Evidence from Vietnam. Appl Econ 35:1153–1161

Kahneman D, Tversky A (1979) Prospect theory: an analysis of decision under risk. Econometrica 47:263–292

Karim A, Noy I (2016) Poverty and natural disasters – a qualitative survey of the empirical literature. Singapore Econ Rev 61:1640001

Karlan D, Osei R, Osei-Akoto I, Udry C (2014) Agricultural decisions after relaxing credit and risk constraints. Q J Econ 129:597–652

Kellenberg DK, Mobarak AM (2008) Does rising income increase or decrease damage risk from natural disasters? J Urban Econ 63:788–802

Kousky C (2012) Informing climate adaptation: a review of the economic costs of natural disasters, their determinants, and risk reduction options. Resources for the Future Discussion Paper, Washington, DC, pp 12–28

Lensink R, Servin R, van den Berg M (2015) Do savings and credit institutions reduce vulnerability? New evidence from Mexico

Linnerooth-Bayer J, Hochrainer-Stigler S (2015) Financial instruments for disaster risk management and climate change adaptation. Clim Change 133:85–100

Linnerooth-Bayer J, Mechler R, Hochrainer-Stigler S (2011) Insurance against losses from natural disasters in developing countries. Evidence, gaps and the way forward. J Integr Disaster Risk Manag 1:59–81

Liu X, Tang Y, Miranda MJ (2015) Does past experience in natural disasters affect willingness-to-pay for weather Index Insurance? Evidence from China. In: Agricultural and Applied Economics Association annual meeting 2015, San Francisco

Lloyd's and Microinsurance Centre (2009) Insurance in developing countries: exploring opportunities in microinsurance. Lloyd's and Microinsurance Centre, London

Loewenstein GF, Weber EU, Hsee CK, Welch N (2001) Risk as feelings. Psychol Bull 127:267–286

Loster T, Reinhard D (2012) Microinsurance and climate change. In: Churchill C, Matul M (eds) Protecting the poor—a microinsurance compendium, vol II. Munich, Geneva, pp 83–111

Mechler R, Linnerooth-Bayer J, Peppiatt D (2006) Disaster insurance for the poor? A review of microinsurance. ProVention, IIASA, Geneva, Vienna

Mechler R, Hochrainer S, Pflug G, et al (2010) Assessing the financial vulnerability to climate-related natural hazards. The World Bank Policy Research Working Paper 5232, Washington, DC

Mitchell T, Mechler R, Peters K (2014) Disaster risk management and adaptation to extreme events. In: Markandya A, Galarraga I, de Murieta ES (eds) Routledge handbook of the economics of climate change adaptation. Routledge, London, pp 417–436

Mobarak AM, Rosenzweig M (2012) Selling formal insurance to the informally insured. Economic Growth Center Discussion Paper 1007, New Haven

Mochizuki J, Vitoontus S, Wickramarachchi B et al (2015) Operationalizing iterative risk management under limited information: fiscal and economic risks due to natural disasters in Cambodia. Int J Disaster Risk Sci 6:321–334

Morsink K (2012) Weathering the storm: the demand for and impact of microinsurance in Africa. University of Twente

Mosley P (2009) Assessing the success of microinsurance programmes in meeting the insurance needs of the poor. UN/DESA Working Paper 84, New York

National Committee for Disaster Management (2008) Strategic national action plan for disaster risk reduction 2008-2013. Kingdom of Cambodia, Ministry of Planning, Phnom Penh

Nguyen M-H, Reynaud A, Thomas A, Thanh ND (2012) Do natural disasters modify individual preferences: evidences from a field experiment in Vietnam. School of Economics, Toulouse

Outreville JF (2013) The relationship between insurance and economic development: 85 empirical papers for a review of the literature. Risk Manag Insur Rev 16:71–122

Oviedo AM, Moroz H (2014) A review of the ex post and ex ante impacts of risk. Background Paper for the World Development report, The World Bank, Washington, DC

Page L, Savage DA, Torgler B (2014) Variation in risk seeking behaviour following large losses: a natural experiment. Eurasian Econ Rev 71:121–131

Pat-Horenczyk R, Peled O, Miron T et al (2007) Risk-taking behaviors among Israeli adolescents exposed to recurrent terrorism: provoking danger under continuous threat? Am J Psychiatry 164:66–72

Radermacher R, McGowan H, Dercon S (2012) What is the impact of microinsurance? In: Churchill C, Matul M (eds) Protecting the poor—a microinsurance compendium, vol II. Munich, Geneva, pp 59–82

Reinhard D, Qureshi Z (2013) How to provide sustainable insurance for low-income. I-VW-HSG Trendmonitor, pp 13–16

Ruchismita R, Churchill C (2012) State and market synergies: insights from India's microinsurance success. In: Churchill C, Matul M (eds) Protecting the poor—a microinsurance compendium, vol II. Munich, Geneva, pp 427–463

Sadoulet L (2005) Learning from visa? Incoporating insurance provision in microfinance contracts. In: Dercon S (ed) Insurance against poverty. UNU-WIDER Studies in Development Economics/Oxford University Press, Oxford, pp 387–421

Said F, Afzal U, Turner G (2014) Attitudes towards risk in the wake of a rare event: evidence from Pakistan. CREB Working Paper 02-14, Lahore

Skees JR (2008) Innovations in Index Insurance for the poor in lower income countries. Agric Resour Econ Rev 1:1–15

Summer A (2013) Disaster resilience in a poverty reduction goal. In: Mitchell T, Jones L, Comba E, Lovell E (eds) Disaster risk management in post-2015 development goals. Overseas Development Institute, London, pp 57–70

Surminski S, Oramas-Dorta D (2014) Flood insurance schemes and climate adaptation in developing countries. Int J Disaster Risk Reduct 7:154–164

Swain M (2015) Performance of crop yield and rainfall insurance schemes in Odisha: some empirical findings. Agric Econ Res Rev 28:201

The Royal Society (2014) Resilience to extreme weather. The Royal Society, London

Trommershäuser S, Lindenthal R, Krech R (2006) The promotional role of governments. In: Churchill C (ed) Protecting the poor—a microinsurance compendium. Munich, Geneva, pp 508–523

Turner G, Said F, Afzal U (2014) Microinsurance demand after a rare flood event: evidence from a field experiment in Pakistan. Geneva Pap Risk Insur Issues Pract 39:201–223

UNDP (2013) Microinsurance study: the understanding and needs of low-income populations regarding microinsurance. United Nations Development Programme, Phnom Penh

van den Berg M, Fort R, Burger K (2009) Natural hazards and risk aversion: experimental evidence from Latin America. In: International Association of Agricultural Economists conference, Beijing

Van Wingerden LA, Brouwer JH (2014) Is the time right for agricultural micro insurance in Cambodia? A scoping study for Achmea. Wageningen, Centre for Development Innovation

Vathana S, Oum S, Kan P, Chervier C (2013) Impact of disasters and role of social protection in natural disaster risk management in Cambodia. ERIA Discussion Paper 2013-10, Jakarta

Weber EU, Johnson EJ (2012) Psychology and behavioral economics lessons for the design of a green growth strategy. The World Bank Policy Research Working Paper 6240, Washington, DC

Wiedmaier-Pfister M, Chatterjee A (2006) An enabling regulatory environment for microinsurance. In: Churchill C (ed) Protecting the poor—a microinsurance compendium. Munich, Geneva, pp 488–507

World Bank (2013) World development report 2014: risk and opportunity—managing risk for development. World Bank, Washington, DC

World Bank, United Nations Office for Disaster Risk Reduction, National Hydrological and Meteorological Services, et al (2013) Country assessment report for Cambodia—strengthening of hydrometeorological services in Southeast Asia. Washington, DC

Chapter 6
Conclusion

This study has investigated the complex link between natural disasters, individual behaviour—in the form of an individual's risk-taking propensity and level of trust—and the demand for microinsurance, using a unique data set for rural Cambodia based on a survey, experimental games and a discrete choice experiment.

Firstly, the presented empirical analysis shows a significant positive impact of disaster experience on the individual's risk-taking propensity, a result which suggests that in a world of imperfect information, perceptions of risks, emotional states and psychological factors seem to hold importance in explaining risk behaviour after the experience of a natural disaster. Furthermore, a significant and negative effect of disaster experience on the individual's level of trust are found. Lower levels of trust may arise from rivalry within the community to receive scarce recovery resources in the aftermath of a disaster. Moreover, natural disasters have a considerable impact on internal and external migration, changing the social structure of a community.

Secondly, this study investigates the impact of individual behaviour, as well as other social, structural, economic and personal factors, on the demand for microinsurance. The empirical analysis shows a significant preference for change and openness towards insurance products. However, disaster experience has a negative impact on the hypothetical demand for microinsurance, which can be explained by the importance of updating information or the use of heuristics. External assistance from government and charities in the aftermath of disasters may lead to a crowding-out effect for insurance demand. Furthermore, the microinsurance-typical relationship between risk-taking behaviour and positive insurance take-up are found, indicating that insurance instruments themselves are seen as risky investments for low-income households. Higher levels of trust have a significant negative effect on microinsurance demand, which may indicate the efficiency of existing informal risk-sharing instruments in communities with a high level of social capital.

Moreover, these results highlight the importance of perceptions, expectations, heuristics and psychological factors in decision-making processes with substantial

O. Fiala, *Natural Disasters and Individual Behaviour in Developing Countries*,
Contributions to Economics, DOI 10.1007/978-3-319-53904-1_6

consequences for long-term economic perspectives and poverty alleviation. Therefore, when assessing long-term post-disaster outcomes, the adjustment in expectations towards future events may be more important than the level of destruction or the degree of preparedness. A better understanding as to how disasters may change individual behaviour as well as social ties within communities is also important for the effective design of aftermath policies.

Finally, correctly designed and implemented, microinsurance products—which set incentives for risk reduction and have positive effects on investments in productive activities—can be powerful and efficient tools of social protection against disaster risks. However, in order to effectively reduce vulnerability and increase resilience, microinsurance must be set within a comprehensive and systematic risk management framework.

Appendix A: Procedure of the Experiment

Introduction

At the beginning of the experiments the participants were welcomed and the research team introduced themselves. A short description of the experiment was given—two games and a questionnaire—but no details were provided about the content or the purpose. The participants were told that the games are common in this research sector and are played in a similar manner in different countries across the world. They were also informed that they would play with money provided by the University of Dresden for research purposes. Anyone was free to leave at any point before or during the experiment.

The participants were instructed that they were not allowed to talk about the games at any point during the experiment, otherwise they would have to be disqualified. They were free to talk about other topics and one research assistant remained with the participants at all times, ensuring that this rule was followed. We also assured all participants that the result of the study would be used for research purposes only and that any personal information would be kept strictly confidential.

Everyone drew a number out of a bag, which allowed for a random order of participants in the games. At the end of the introduction, the 'show-up' fee of 4000 Cambodian Riel (USD1) was distributed to each participant.

Risk Game

The first game began with a description of rules. To address issues of low literacy, the procedures were explained to all participants with the use of graphs. Additionally, the local members of the research team enacted various game situations in front of the participants. The examples were defined and oriented towards the examples provided by Schechter (2007). The players were informed that questions

O. Fiala, *Natural Disasters and Individual Behaviour in Developing Countries*, Contributions to Economics, DOI 10.1007/978-3-319-53904-1

were not allowed in the group setting, but could be asked of the researchers in private. At the beginning of the game, every player was asked if she understood the game. If they did not, the research team would explain the rules again in private and answer any questions. The participants were called by the number they had drawn from the bag. To decrease the length of time needed for the game, it was necessary to play it simultaneously at two different stations. Both stations were occupied by two research assistants at all times. As in many experiments in rural areas, to ensure that participants understood the games, neither the risk nor the trust game was double blind (Barr 2003; Karlan 2005; Schechter 2007).

The participants were told that everyone would receive 6000 Riel (USD1.50) in yellow-coloured play money. These looked similar to the real notes, so that the participants could make the connection to the actual money. They were told that the play money would be exchanged at the end of the experiment, one-to-one, into real money. Each player received six 1000 Riel notes for use in the game.

The players were told that they had the opportunity to bet any share of this money, which included the choice not to bet at all. After the player decided the amount they wanted to bet, they rolled an unbiased six-sided die. The following distribution of possible outcomes was given, which is based on previous studies by Schechter (2007) and Ahsan (2014). If the die landed on one, the player would lose the money she bet. If the die landed on two, the player would lose half of the money. If the die showed three, the player would keep the amount she bet. If the die landed on 4/5/6, the player would receive 1.5/2.0/2.5 times her bet, respectively. Thus, a roll of one or two would have a negative result, a roll of three would have a neutral result, and rolls of four, five or six would have positive results. Participants were reminded that they could finish the game with more or less than the original amount of 6000 Riel.

After one round, the game was over. The game was played only once with each participant. Each participant could take away the share she did not bet, plus the money she won through rolling the die (if any). The total money from the game was paid out in play money at the end of the round.

Figure A.1 summarises the procedure of the game. A translated version of this figure was also used by the research team to explain the game.

Trust Game

After the risk game the participants were gathered as one large group again for an explanation of the second game. The success of the trust game largely depends on the participants' understanding of the rules (Ahsan 2014). As in the first game, the procedures were explained aloud in front of all participants, with the support of graphs. As before, the local members of the research team enacted various (previously defined) situations and demonstrated the procedures of the game. The participants were not allowed to discuss the game amongst themselves, but they were told that any questions could be asked to the researchers in private. The explanation of the trust game was more time-consuming than that of the risk game.

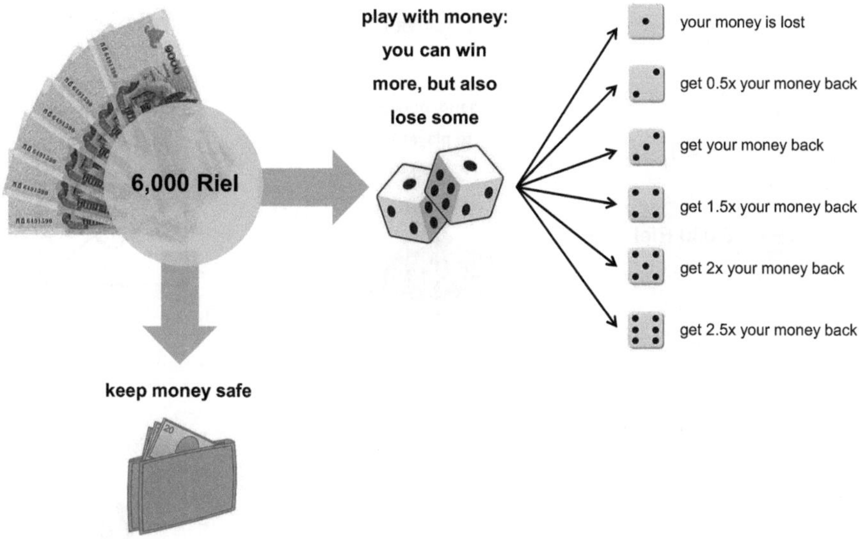

Fig. A.1 Procedure of risk game

The game is played by pairs of individuals: player 1 and player 2. Each participant played the role of player 1 in the first round and the role of player 2 in the second round. The players were told that they would always play with other people from their village, but each time with a different person. Participants were notified that nobody would know exactly with whom they were playing.

The participants were called again by their number. As in the risk game, the game was played at two different stations simultaneously, and both stations were occupied by two research assistants each.

In the first round of the game, each participant was given 6000 Riel (USD1.50) in red play money, in the form of six 1000 Riel notes. This different colour was used to prevent confusion and crossover of play money between the two games.

Player 1 then had the opportunity to send a share of their 6000 Riel to an anonymous player 2. Whatever amount player 1 sent was tripled by the researcher before it was put in an envelope in front of the participants. Each envelope was marked with a different letter combination. If no money was sent by player 1, the envelope remained empty. After every participant played their role as player 1, the envelopes were shuffled in front of the whole group.

In the next phase, all participants were called again by their number to play their role as player 2. On the way to the station they took an envelope from the top of the stack. The players were told that they should not receive their own envelope. If they had drawn their own, they should return it and pick the next one. The participants opened the envelopes in front of the research assistants and saw how much (if any) money was sent from player 1. Then they decided how much money they wanted to keep and how much they wanted to return to player 1.

Therefore, the participants finished the game with whatever they kept as player 1 (from the original 6000 Riel), plus whatever they kept from the tripled amount in

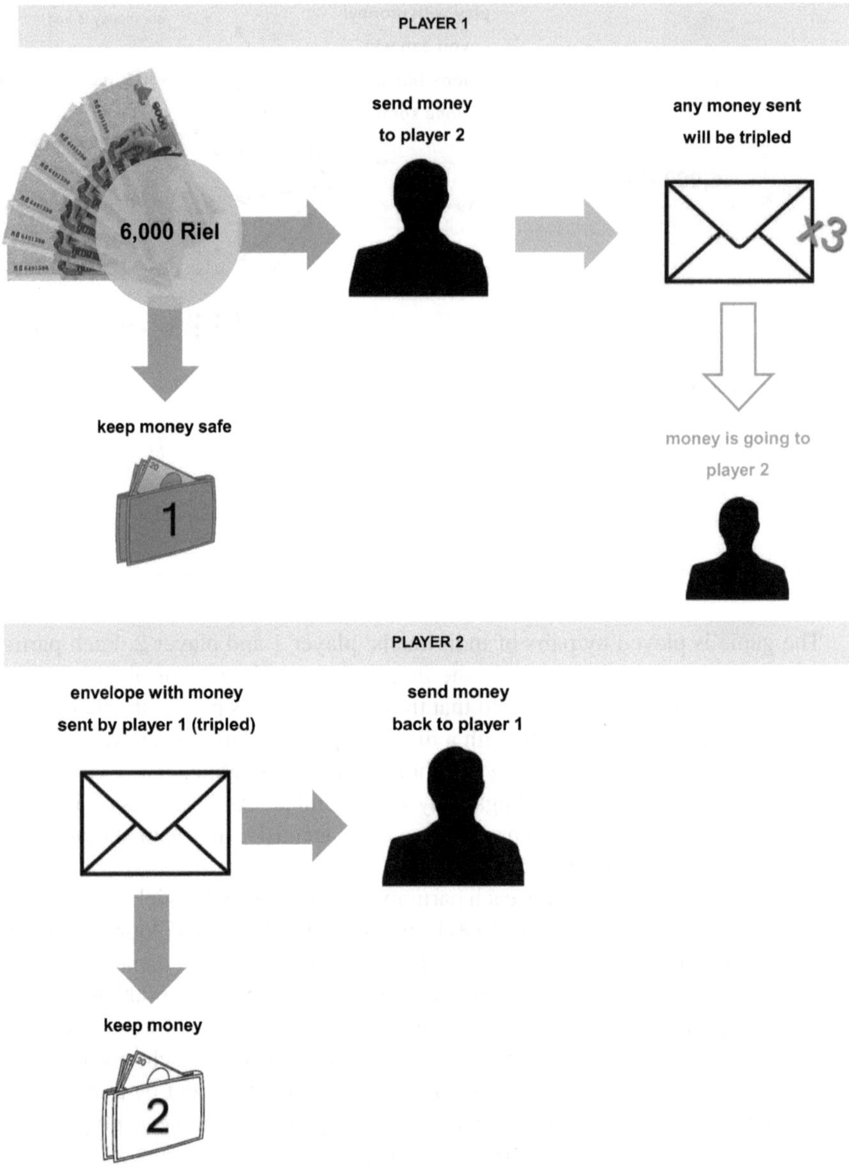

Fig. A.2 Procedure of trust game for player 1 and 2

their role as player 2, plus whatever they found in their original envelope as player 1 (which was returned by another player 2). Each player was informed that they could finish with more or <6000 Riel as a result of the game.

Figure A.2 summarises the procedure of the game. A translated version of this figure was also used by the research team to explain the game.

Questionnaire

After both games the participants were called by their number to one of the six research assistants, and were asked the questions from the set questionnaire. The research team asked all questions in person and no questionnaires were distributed to the participants. The questionnaire took place at the end of the experiment, so that questions had no influence on the behaviour during the games. They also received their original envelope from the trust game (as player 1), with the money (if any) sent back by player 2. After the questionnaires, the participants approached the author to immediately exchange their play money for real money. The questionnaire contained the sections household information, experiences with natural disasters, disaster risk management activities, prevention and preparedness, and demand for insurance.

Discrete Choice Experiment

The discrete choice experiment comprises 48 alternatives, presented in 24 choice sets, each consisting of three alternatives (flood insurance A, flood insurance B, no insurance). A sample of one choice set in English is presented in Fig. A.3.

	Insurance A	Insurance B	No Insurance
Cover for loss	1,000,000 Riel	500,000 Riel	–
Weekly premium	2,000 Riel	2,000 Riel	–
Condition for pay-out	Pay-out after a visit of insurance employee	Pay-out if measuring station has shown flood	–
Credit	without loan	without loan	–
Prevention	No prevention	Prevention effort	–
Provider	Village	National government	–

Fig. A.3 Sample of choice set

References

Ahsan D (2014) Does natural disaster influence people's risk preference and trust? An experiment from cyclone prone coast of Bangladesh. Int J Disaster Risk Reduct 9:48–57.

Barr A (2003) Trust and expected trustworthiness: experimental evidence from Zimbabwean villages. Econ J 113:614–630.

Karlan DS (2005) Using experimental economics to measure social capital and predict financial decisions. Am Econ Rev 95:1688–1699.

Schechter L (2007) Traditional trust measurement and the risk confound: an experiment in rural Paraguay. J Econ Behav Organ 62:272–292.

Appendix B: Descriptive Statistics: Livelihoods and Coping with Natural Disasters in Rural Cambodia

Household Information

Table B.1 summarises the most significant results of the individual statistics. In total, 209 persons from 5 villages participated.[1]

37.5% of the participants were male, 62.5% were female (n = 208). Whilst the average age was 50.9, the youngest participant was 19 and the oldest was 95. 97.6% of the participants were married (n = 207) and Buddhism was the dominant religion (96.2%); the rest were Christians (n = 209). Two thirds of the respondents were female.

Figure B.1 shows the level of education of the participants (n = 209). While 37.8% of the participants had no formal education at all, only 57.9% had completed primary or secondary school, although strong differences between the male and female participants can be observed.

59.6% of participants described themselves as literate (n = 203). The results also differ significantly between genders (Fig. B.2). While 83.3% of the men described themselves as literate, only 44.4% of women did so. To measure financial literacy, Clarke and Kalani (2012) asked their participants short mathematical questions and used the number of correct answers as a proxy for financial literacy. For this analysis, the same method with the given questions was used.[2] 22.4% gave no correct answers, another 22.4% gave one correct answer, 24.9% two correct answers, 21.5% three correct answers and 8.8% were able to answer all questions correctly (n = 205).

[1]Three participants, who were under the age of 18 and did not disclose this fact at the beginning, were deleted from the sample. Another five participants in one village came to participate, but finished the experiment too early or did not start at all. They were also deleted from the sample.

The number of answers for each question varies; therefore the actual number of observations is provided for each question.

[2]The mathematical questions were the following: $5 + 3 = ?$, $3 \times 7 = ?$, 1/10th of $300 = ?$, 5% of $200 = ?$

O. Fiala, *Natural Disasters and Individual Behaviour in Developing Countries*, Contributions to Economics, DOI 10.1007/978-3-319-53904-1

Table B.1 Individual statistics summary

Characteristics	Mean	Min	Max
Male (%)	37.5%		
Age	50.9	19	95
Married (%)	97.6%		
Buddhist (%)	96.2%		
No education (%)	37.8%		
Literate (%)	59.6%		
Financially literate	1.7	0	4
Household size	5.6	1	17
Head of household (%)	67.9%		
Living in village <15 years (%)	9.7%		
Households with credit (%)	48.1%		
Land owned (%)	59.3%		
Land owned (ha)	2.87	0.08	15
Growing rice (%)	55.8%		
Households with livestock (%)	23.9%		
Total livestock units, usual year (2012)	0.24	0	6.5
Total livestock units, last year (2013)	0.34	0	6.5
Per-capita income, usual year (US Dollars)	379	0	16,676
Per-capita income, last year (US Dollars)	257	0	5000
No. of observations	209		

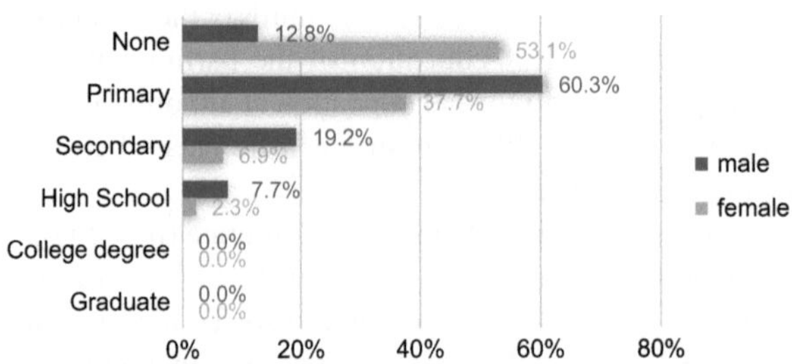

Fig. B.1 Level of education completed

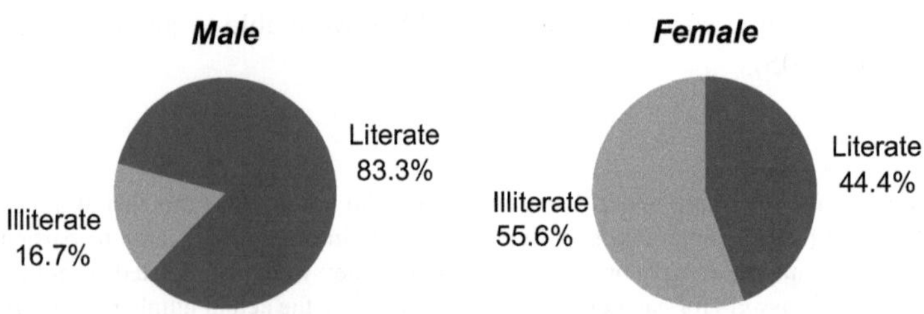

Fig. B.2 Literacy

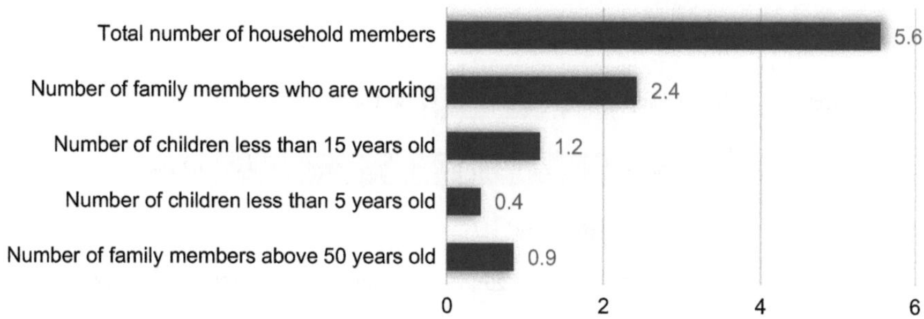

Fig. B.3 Number of household members

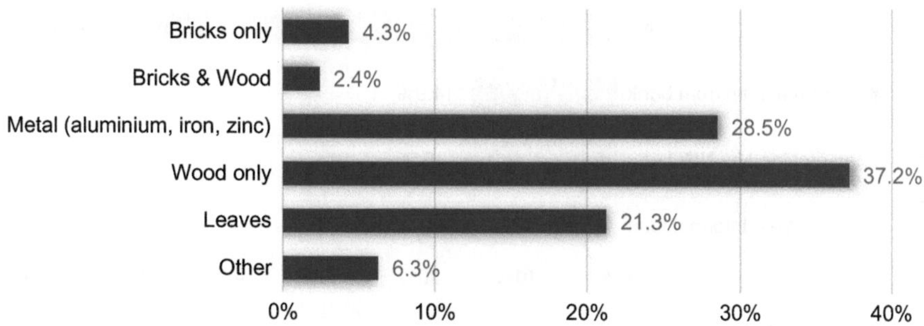

Fig. B.4 Materials used to construct house walls

67.9% of participants answered that they are the head of their households (n = 209). Figure B.3 shows the average number of household members. The average size of the total number of household members was 5.6, whilst the smallest household was formed of 1, and the largest made up of 17 persons (n = 209).

Almost two thirds of the participants had lived in their village for their entire lives (61.5%). 80 participants moved to their villages later in life, on average 23.9 years ago (min 1, max 40 years). Only 9.6% of the participants had lived in their village for <15 years (n = 207).

The next questions reveal the living conditions of the participants. Figure B.4 shows the material used to build the walls of participants' houses. While 28.5% used different kind of metals, 58.5% had walls of wood or leaves (n = 207). The majority of the participants (95.2%) used a different kind of metal for their roofs (n = 208).

Figure B.5 shows the participants' sources of water for daily use. 62.2% of the sample obtained their water from river and ponds, followed by 30.1% who had a well or hand pump. 'Other' (7.7%) includes those who purchased water for daily use (n = 209). 86.1% of participants had access to electricity (n = 208).

Figure B.6 shows the proportion of participants who had applied for various types of credit. 51.9% had not borrowed any money. Of those who had borrowed money, the majority received it from informal sources: family, friends or

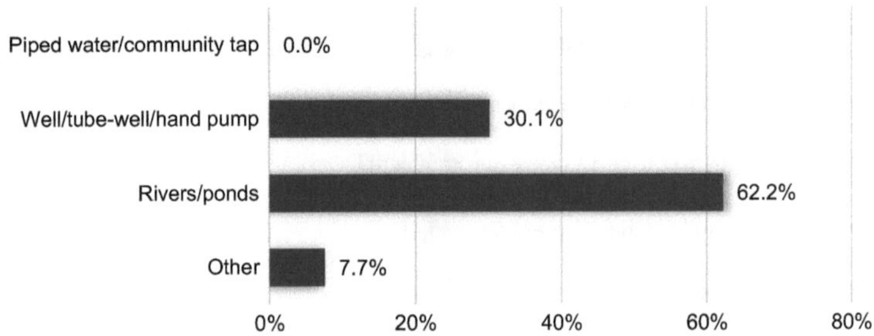

Fig. B.5 Source of water for daily use

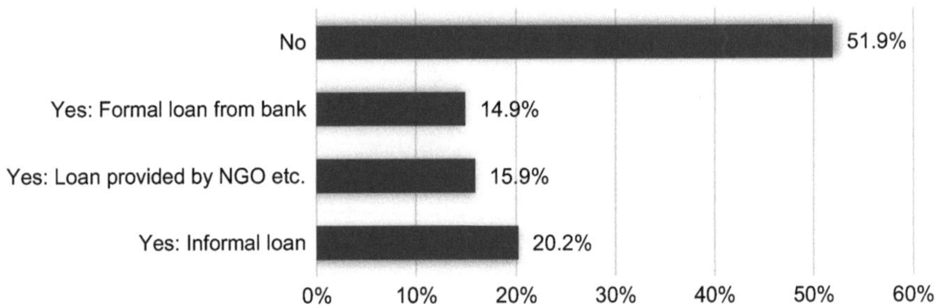

Fig. B.6 Households with credit/loans

neighbours (20.2%). Less common were formal loans from banks (14.9%) or NGOs (15.9%). Only 7.2% had deposited money in an account and therefore had contact with formal banks (multiple answers were possible; n = 208).

59.3% of households owned agricultural land. The average size of the land was 2.87 ha (min 0.08, max 15 ha). The questionnaire also asked about household livestock ownership. In the literature, a method of 'tropical livestock units' (TLU) is described, which allows the calculation of wealth based on the ownership of livestock and allows for comparison between households (Dercon 2004; Chilonda and Otte 2006; Clarke and Kalani 2012). The following calculation is based on the livestock unit coefficients for East and Southeast Asia of Chilonda and Otte (2006).[3] 23.9% of the households owned livestock, the average TLU account for 0.24 in a usual/average year and 0.34 in the last/extreme year.[4,5]

[3]Cattle 0.65, pigs 0.25, chicken 0.01. Due to a lack of a coefficient for ducks, in comparison with Njuki et al. (2011), the coefficient 0.03 was assumed.

[4]The questionnaire distinguished between a 'usual year' (without extreme floods), whereby the interviewers asked for information about the year 2012, and 'last year' (2013) when extreme flooding occurred in October.

[5]Number of animals is based on answers of participants. If only one amount was provided, it was assumed that this amount referred to last year (2013). In cases such as these, the figure for a usual year was calculated based on the quantification of damages, otherwise it was recorded as a missing value.

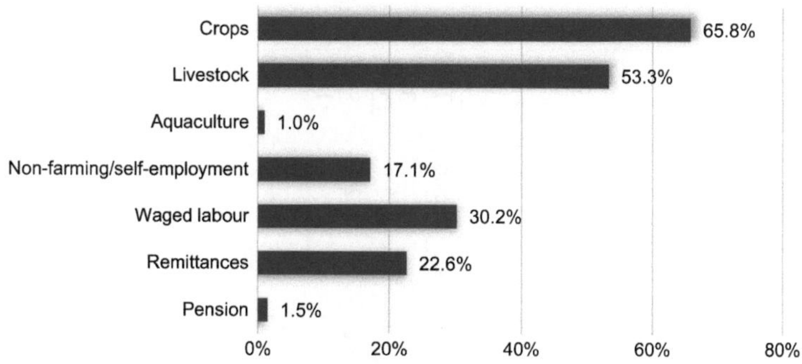

Fig. B.7 Percentage of participants earning from various sources of income

The questionnaire asked about different sources of income,[6] including income from:

- Growing crops[7]
- Raising livestock
- Aquaculture[8]
- Non-farming/self-employment
- Waged labour
- Remittances
- Pension

Figure B.7 shows the proportion of the various income sources per household. 65.8% of all participants gained income from growing crops, followed by raising livestock (53.3%) and waged labour (30.2%). Another important source of income was remittances (22.6%) and income from self-employment (17.1%). Aquaculture and pensions can be neglected (n = 199).

Table B.2 shows the income from various sources from 199 participants in a usual year (2012) and last year (2013).[9] In 2012 the average income per capita was

[6]The questionnaire asked for annual income. However, many participants are not aware of their income per year but were able to provide information per month or per day. In the latter case, an average of 27 working days per month was assumed. The relevant exchange rates are 32.33 Thai Baht for USD1 and 4000 Cambodian Riel for USD1.

[7]If no income information was provided, the annual household income was calculated on the basis of the amount of crops produced. If the sales price for 1 t of rice was given in the interview, this was used for the income calculation. Otherwise the average sales price was calculated and assumed for the other households in the same village. Because of different types of rice crops and different sales markets, a generally accessible price cannot be assumed. When crops were mentioned 'for consumption' no amount was attributed and no income was calculated. One household produced cassava—based on Reuy (2013), 1 t of cassava has the value of USD160.

[8]One household mentioned only the amount of fish sold, but not income. Based on information from Yady et al. (2012), 1 kg of fish has the value of USD0.44.

[9]All income information was originally recorded per household and transferred to per-capita based on household sizes. For the various sources of income (except the total income), the conditional average income was calculated (based on the number of participants who earned money from the various sources).

Table B.2 Average income per capita from various sources, in US Dollars

	Crops	Live-stock	Aqua-culture	Self-employment	Waged labour	Remittances	Pensions	Total
Income usual year (2012)	272	6	8	133	169	122	39	369
Income last year (2013)	113	7	88	176	171	224	56	247
Percentage change	−58.7%	17.1%	1027%	32.0%	1.2%	82.6%	44.2%	−33.1%
Number of observations (2013)	131	106	2	34	60	45	3	199

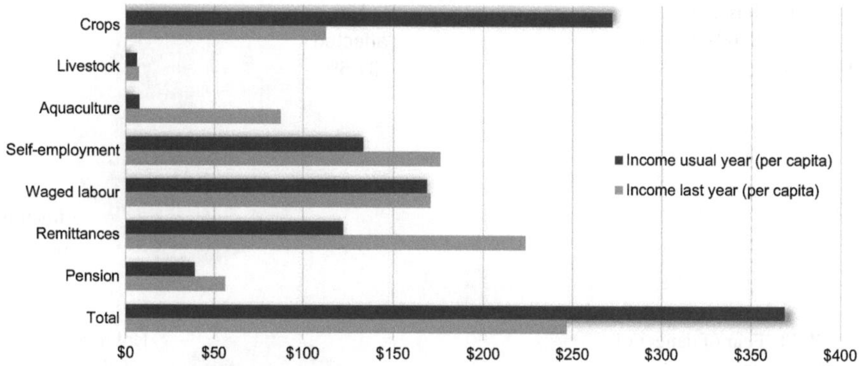

Fig. B.8 Average income from various sources and total average income per capita

Table B.3 Summary of participants' experiences with natural disasters

Characteristics	Mean (%)
Experienced flooding in the last 5 years	68.4
Observed flooding	97.9
Strong fear of danger of damages through floods	67.7
Faced severe consequences of flooding	73.0
Believes that extreme floods are becoming more frequent	74.6
Damage to household property due to extreme flood in 2013	26.4
Damage to household production due to extreme flood in 2013	88.7

USD369, which shrank by 33.1% to USD247 in 2013. The average income from growing crops per capita, livestock income and pensions also decreased. In contrast, the average income from other sources increased, particularly average remittances.

Figure B.8 presents the numbers from the table above and highlights the differences of the income sources over the 2 years (2012 and 2013). In 2012, growing crops was the dominant source of income, followed by waged labour, self-employment and remittances; this picture changed in 2013.

Experiences with Natural Disasters

Part II of the questionnaire was intended to investigate participants' experiences with natural disasters. Different questions about experiences, assessments of flood risks and actual damages were asked. Table B.3 provides a short summary of the key results.

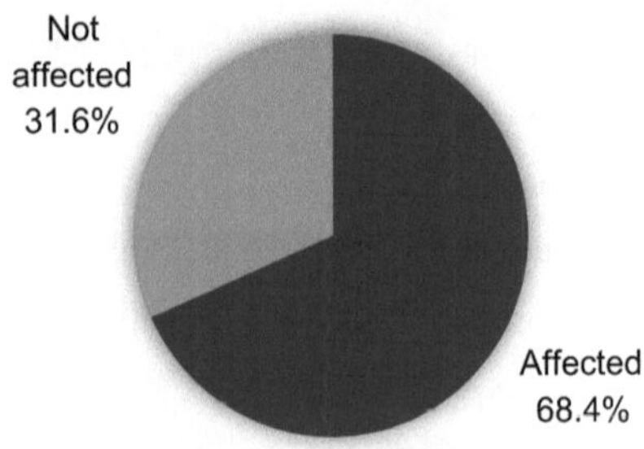

Fig. B.9 Households affected by floods within the last 5 years

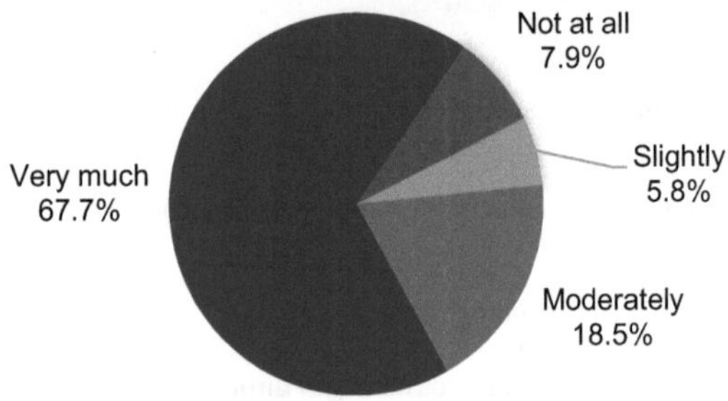

Fig. B.10 Fear of danger of flood damage

As illustrated in Fig. B.9, 68.4% of households answered that their house was flooded in the last 5 years, while 31.6% had no such experience (n = 209).[10] However, almost everyone (97.9%) had observed the effects of floods, e.g. on relatives, neighbours or friends (n = 189).

Two thirds of the participants had a fear of flood damage, another 18.5% were moderately fearful and 5.8% slightly fearful of flood damage (Fig. B.10). Only 7.9% answered that they do not fear flood damage at all (n = 189).

The participants were asked to compare their own vulnerability to other households within the same village. Relatively similar proportions assessed their own vulnerability as less than (36.0%), equal to (32.8%) and more than (31.2%) other households (n = 189).

Figure B.11 shows the expected severity of consequences if participants' houses were flooded. 73.0% of the households expected severe or extremely severe consequences, in contrast to 19.0% who expected small consequences or no consequences at all (n = 189).

Almost three quarters (74.6%) of participants believed that the frequency of extreme floods (of similar severity to October 2013 flood) had increased. 19.0% said the frequency had decreased and 5.8% answered that extreme flooding had 'stayed the same'. One participant stated that they did not know (n = 189).

[10]Six households answered that their houses were not flooded but reported, in a latter part of the interview, damages and knee-high water in the house, etc. These households were therefore valued as affected.

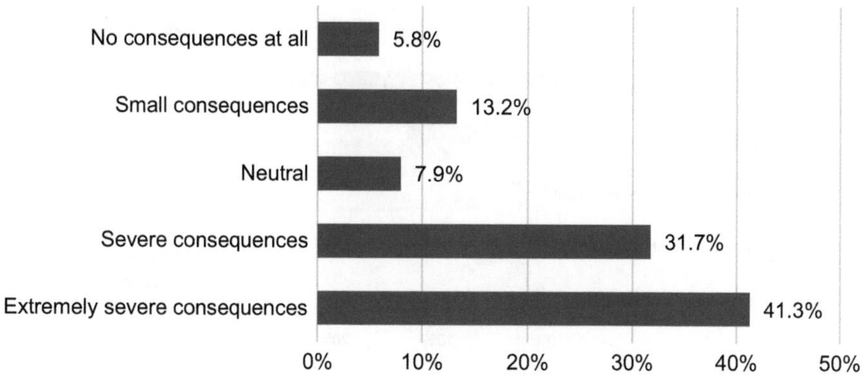

Fig. B.11 Participants' expectation of severity of consequences if house floods

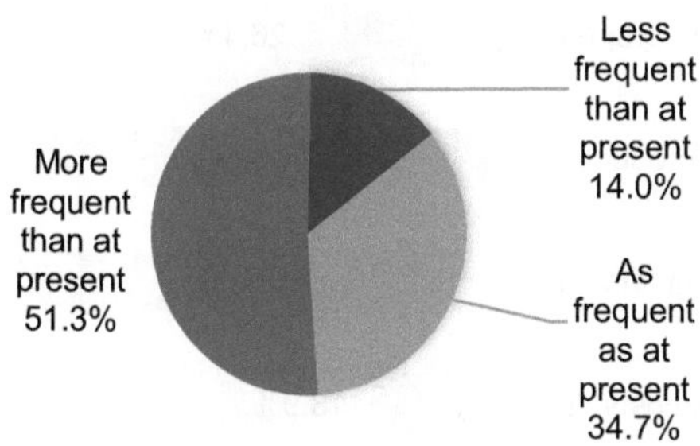

Fig. B.12 Participants' belief in the frequency of future household flooding

Looking to the future, 51.3% of participants believed that their house would be flooded more frequently than at present (Fig. B.12). 34.7% believed it would flood the same amount as at present and 14.0% believed it would happen less frequently (n = 150).[11]

52% of flood-affected households are flooded, to some extent, during the rainy season every year (n = 150). Figure B.13 shows the maximum height of floodwater reached during annual floods compared to the height of water during the extreme floods of 2013. The figure shows the height of water during the annual floods and the October 2013 flood (n = 91 for annual floods, n = 149 for flood in 2013).

For 2.7% of participants, during the flood in October 2013, the area in and around the house was flooded for 1 week only, for 17.8% the floodwater remained for 1 to 2 weeks, for 21.9% between 2 and 4 weeks and for the majority (48.6%), it took between 1 and 2 months for the floodwater to subside. For 8.9% the flood lasted for more than 2 months (n = 146).

The last question in part II of the questionnaire focused on the experienced damages of the 2013 flood. Figure B.14 shows the share of households who suffered

[11]This and the following questions in this section of the questionnaire were asked only to those who were flood-affected. Therefore, the number of observations is smaller.

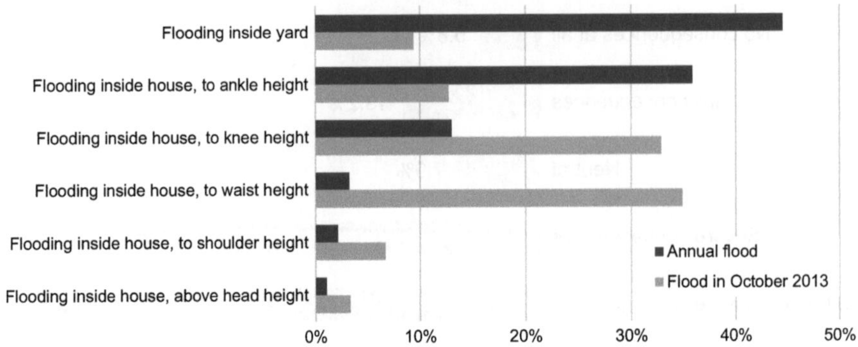

Fig. B.13 Maximum height of water during annual floods and the extreme flood in 2013

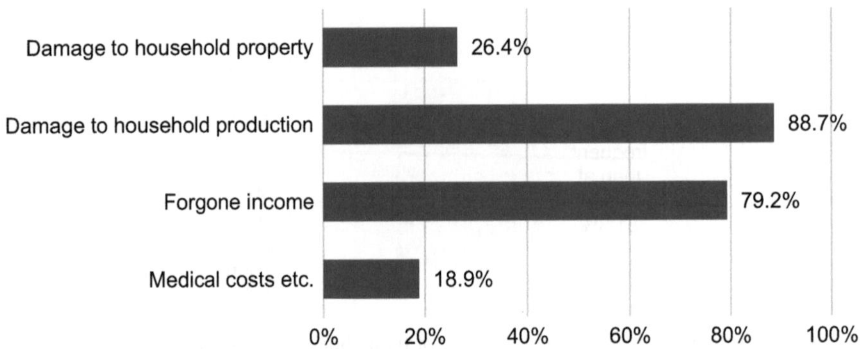

Fig. B.14 Household damage by extreme flooding in October 2013

from this disaster. 106 households reported damages, 88.7% of these to household production, e.g. their crops or livestock, 26.4% to household property. 12.3% reported forgone income (opportunity costs), an average of USD73.[12] Another 18.9% mentioned medical costs as an additional loss of income due to the flood (the average cost for medical care was USD179).

Disaster Risk Management Activities

Part III of the questionnaire focused on existing disaster risk management activities. To assess the degree of organisation of the participants, the initial questions asked about membership in local organisations and groups. Only 7.2% were members of a local organisation, only 8.2% were part of a local savings group and 11.1%

[12]If amount of forgone income was not provided, the amount was calculated by multiplying the level of flood duration by regular income (only wages/self-employment were considered).

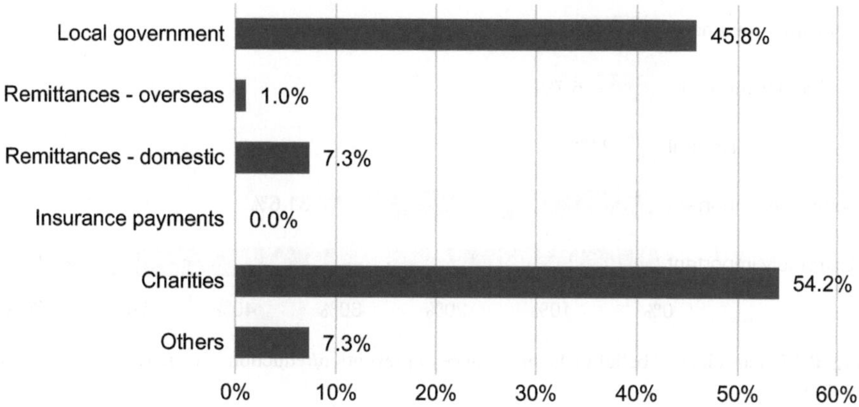

Fig. B.15 Households who received aid from various sources

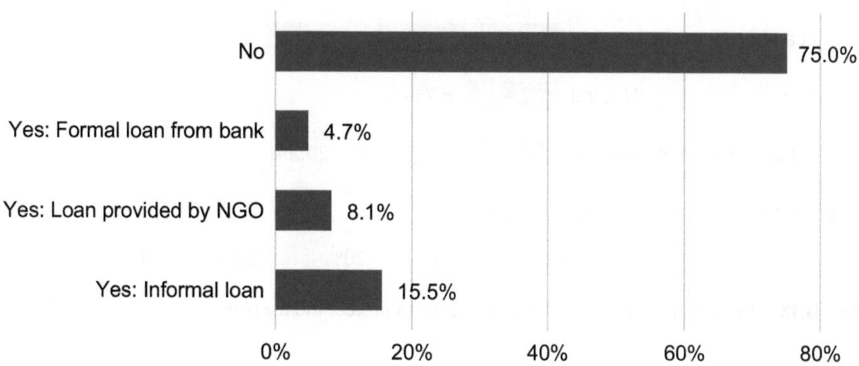

Fig. B.16 Households borrowing money after flood damage

belonged to an agricultural community (n = 207). Flood information was exchanged regularly between neighbours by 86.9% of the participants.

96 participants (45.9% of the sample) reported that they received money or goods from various sources as one-off support after the flood of 2013. Figure B.15 shows the different sources of this aid. The two biggest donors were the government and charity organisations.[13] 45.8% of households who received support, received this from the local government; 54.2% received help from charities.

The majority of the households did not borrow money to aid recovery from regular or extreme floods (Fig. B.16). If households borrowed money, this was

[13]A common misunderstanding when answering the questionnaire was that the help of charity organisations (rice, food etc.) was often noted under 'overseas remittances from friends/neighbours'. This was clarified with the local research team and the packages of rice, food, etc. were ascribed to charities.

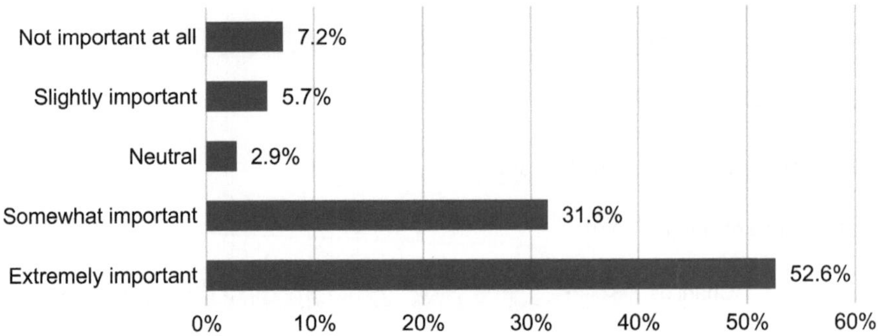

Fig. B.17 Participants' belief in the importance of prevention/reduction of negative consequences of floods

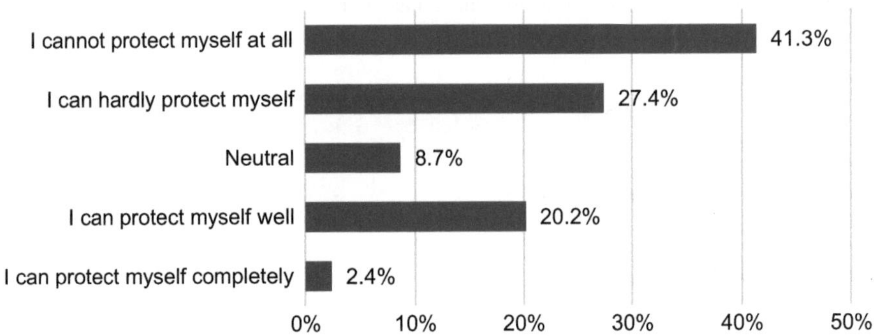

Fig. B.18 Participants' judgement of own ability to protect themselves

mostly done on an informal basis from relatives, friends or neighbours (multiple answers were possible; n = 161).

The two final questions examined the sale of production assets or valuable items as a source of income after the floods. 10.8% of households sold production assets after the 2013 flood including machines, tools, animals or land; only 3.4% sold valuable items such as jewellery or gold (n = 148).

Prevention and Preparedness

Part IV of the questionnaire focused on household assessments of prevention against flood events. For 84.2% of the participants it was somewhat or extremely important to prevent or reduce the negative consequences of floods (Fig. B.17). 12.9% answered that prevention has only little importance or is not important at all (n = 209).

Figure B.18 shows the judgement of the participants of their own ability to protect themselves from the negative consequences of floods. 68.8% of the

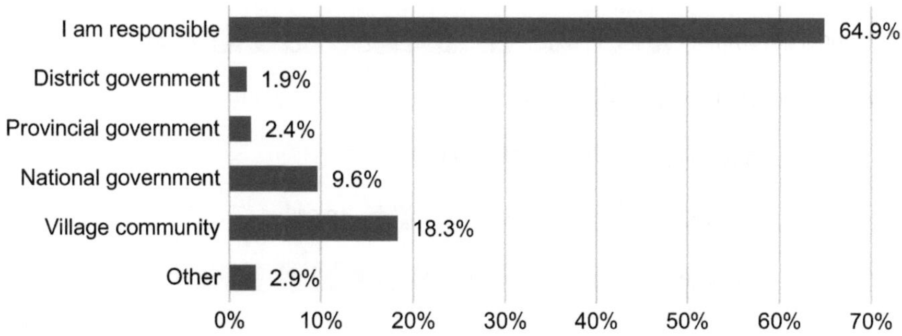

Fig. B.19 Participants' belief in who is responsible to provide flood protection

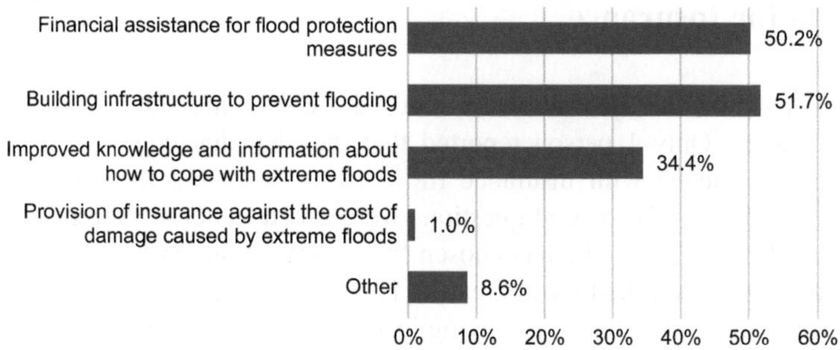

Fig. B.20 Participants' needs for better preparations against extreme floods

households answered that they could not protect themselves at all or could hardly protect themselves. In contrast, 22.6% said they could protect themselves well or completely (n = 208). 43.5% of the households were satisfied with their current level of protection against extreme flood events, while 56.5% answered that they were dissatisfied in this regard (n = 209).

Figure B.19 shows who participants believe was mainly responsible for providing flood protection. 66.8% of the participants stated that it is their own responsibility, followed by the village community (18.8%) and national government (10%) (n = 202).

47.1% of households modified the timing of crop planting so that the harvest would precede the expected arrival of floods (n = 206) and 55.4% of households used chemical fertiliser (n = 204). The last question was focused on the participants' needs for better preparation against extreme flood events like the one in October 2013 (multiple answers were possible)—Fig. B.20 displays the answers. Building infrastructure to prevent floods and financial assistance for flood protection measures were the most popular responses (51.7 and 50.2% of the participants mentioned these respectively). Improved knowledge of and information about coping mechanisms for extreme flooding were emphasised by 34.4%.

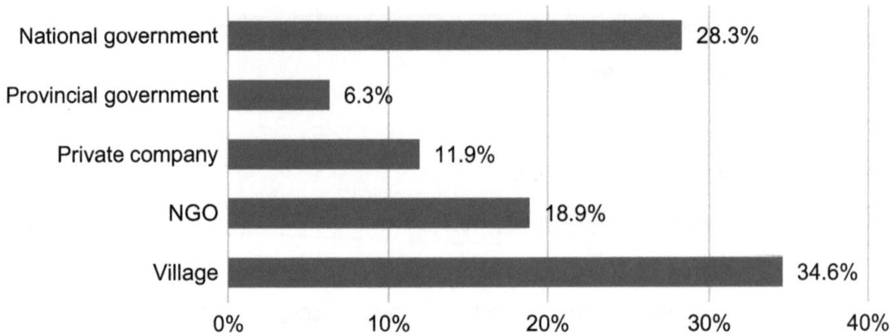

Fig. B.21 Participants' preference for insurance provider

Demand for Insurance

The last part of the questionnaire focused on the individuals' demand for microinsurance. Only 1 person reported that they had insurance (n = 120) and 4.9% knew someone with insurance (n = 163). Following the discrete choice analysis (see Sect. 4.3), several questions were asked to control the results of the estimation. Respondents who had chosen 'no insurance' at least four times (out of six choice sets) were asked for the reason. Hereby, 19 respondents agreed with the statement "I am not interested in buying insurance", while another 19 participants gave missing affordability as reason. The preferred provider was the village community, followed by national government and non-governmental organisations (n=159). The choice of a preferred provider is illustrated in Fig. B.21.

A overwhelming majority of respondents (92.5%) would be more interested in insurance if it was paired with a loan; 91.8% would increase their prevention efforts if the insurance would consequently become cheaper (n = 159). Finally, the individuals were asked if they would increase their production or try new crops with higher returns in the case that they would have insurance against flood damage. Although the truth of the answer cannot be validated in a real world situation, 74.2% of respondents would increase their productive activities (n = 159).

References

Chilonda P, Otte J (2006) Indicators to monitor trends in livestock production at national, regional and international levels.

Clarke D, Kalani G (2012) Microinsurance decisions: evidence from Ethiopia. Microinsurance Innovation Facility Research Paper 19, Geneva.

Dercon S (2004) Growth and shocks: evidence from rural Ethiopia. J Dev Econ 74:309–329.

Njuki J, Poole J, Johnson N et al (2011) Gender, livestock and livelihood indicators. International Livestock Research Institute (ILRI), Nairobi.

Reuy R (2013) Cassava production dropped in 2012. Phnom Penh Post. http://www.phnompenhpost.com/business/cassava-production-dropped-2012. Accessed 11 Nov 2014.

Yady M, Rajabova R, Long Y, Burja K (2012) Cambodia food price and wage bulletin. World Food Programme, Cambodia Agricultural Marketing Office, Phnom Penh.

Appendix C: Robustness Checks

The Impact of Natural Disasters on Individuals' Risk-Taking Propensity in Rural Cambodia

Section 3.4 presents empirical evidence for the impact of natural disasters on individuals' risk-taking propensity. In addition to the regressions (1) to (4) presented in Table 3.7 other control variables have been entered and removed, however no significant impact on the efficiency of the regression model could be found. The tested control variables include: education, religion, observation of floods, income distribution within village (Gini coefficient), mean income in village, amount of time a participant lived in the village, satisfaction with protection, fear of future floods, flood level in rainy season, post-disaster support by government or charity, and flood damages to household property or production assets. Tests for heteroskedasticity and a robust regression also confirmed the results of the presented regression. Finally, repeating the regressions without respondents who had not bet anything confirms the main findings, especially regarding disaster experience.

Identifying income as the core variable, which is significantly different between the affected and non-affected group, a propensity score matching of the sample regarding income was conducted. Regression (14) in Table C.1 using this propensity score matching dataset confirmed the direction and scale of the results presented in Sect. 3.4.

O. Fiala, *Natural Disasters and Individual Behaviour in Developing Countries*, Contributions to Economics, DOI 10.1007/978-3-319-53904-1

Table C.1 Regression for risk game based on propensity score matching sample

	Share bet in risk game
	(14)
(Constant)	0.079 (0.229)
Affected	0.202*** (0.051)
Age	0.018* (0.009)
Age squared	−0.017** (0.008)
Gender	−0.009 (0.050)
Married state	−0.320** (0.124)
Financial literacy	0.078*** (0.023)
Number of people living in the household	−0.033*** (0.011)
Number of children under 15 years in the household	0.047*** (0.017)
Total income per capita in US Dollars (2013)	−0.000 (0.000)
Number of observations	59

Standard errors in parentheses
***p < 0.01, **p < 0.05, *p < 0.10

Table C.2 Including wealth in Poisson regression for interest in insurance

	(9)	(10)
Wealth (TLU) per capita (2014)	−0.070 (0.221)	−0.125 (0.224)
Number of observations	126	126

Each column represents the regressions (9) to (10) for interest in insurance. Control variables included as in 4.7. Standard errors in parentheses

The Interest in Microinsurance: First Results from a Poisson Regression

Section 4.3.1 presents the results from a Poisson regression, investigating the impact of several social-economic variables on the interest in insurance (expressed by the amount a respondent chose any insurance contract). No significant effect of wealth per capita (calculated in 'tropical livestock units') can be found in the regressions (9) and (10), when substituting income per capita by wealth. The effects of other variables used in Table 4.7 stay consistent in direction of effect and significance (Table C.2).

Appendix D: Research Designs of Selected Empirical Studies

Section 4.2 analyses the role of 12 determinants for microinsurance demand, whereof risk aversion, trust and risk exposure are of particular interest for the empirical analysis of microinsurance demand in Cambodia (Sect. 4.3). Table D.1 combines the references regarding microinsurance demand and risk aversion (4.2), trust (4.3) and risk exposure (Table 4.4), and provides a short overview of the various research designs.

Table D.1 Research designs of selected empirical studies

Reference	Relevant determinants[a]	Research design
Akter et al. (2008)	Risk exposure	Household survey in six different districts in Bangladesh facing various levels of exposure to environmental risk. Discrete choice logit regression model investigates demand for hypothetical catastrophe insurance product Households in areas less exposed to environmental risks are less likely to buy catastrophe insurance
Giné et al. (2008)	Risk aversion, Trust	Household survey investigates determinants for demand for rainfall insurance products among smallholder farmers in India. Probit regression is used in order to explain decision for insurance purchase Uncertainty about the product leads to lower demand of risk-averse households and those with less trust in insurance provider
Cai et al. (2009)	Trust	Randomised field experiment in China, investigating take-up of insurance for sows and the impact on farmers' production decisions (OLS regression) Lack of trust in government-subsidised microinsurance is significant barrier for insurance take-up

(continued)

O. Fiala, *Natural Disasters and Individual Behaviour in Developing Countries*, Contributions to Economics, DOI 10.1007/978-3-319-53904-1

Table D.1 (continued)

Reference	Relevant determinants[a]	Research design
Giné and Yang (2009)	Risk aversion	Randomised field experiment in Malawi to investigate if provision of insurance against production risk animates credit demand to adopt new crop technology (OLS regression) Take-up of an uninsured loan is negatively associated with farmers' self-reported risk aversion
Arun and Bendig (2010)	Risk exposure	Household survey data from Sri Lanka, investigating the usage of financial services such as loans, insurance and savings (probit and logit regressions) Households with higher perceptions of risk exposure are more likely to use financial instruments, including insurances
Akotey et al. (2011)	Trust	Randomly sampled data from informal sector workers in Ghana in order to identify the factors influencing demand for microinsurance products against various economic risks (probit regression model) Improvement in the perception of insurers (trust) increases demand for microinsurance
Cai et al. (2011)	Trust	Randomised experiment in rural China, investigating the role of information for insurance take-up, offered both directly through financial education and indirectly through social networks (OLS/instrumental variables regression) Results emphasise the importance of social networks in insurance take-up (peer effects)
Dercon et al. (2011)	Risk aversion, Trust	Randomised and controlled trial of policies affecting demand for health insurance product in Kenya, in order to test theoretical model of demand for indemnity insurance under limited credibility. Combination of data from field experiment with laboratory-type experiments to measure risk preferences and level of trust. Probit model of purchase decision Demand for insurance (under limited trust) is negatively correlated with measures of risk aversion Significant impact of insurers' creditability on purchase decision for insurance
Giesbert et al. (2011)	Risk aversion, risk exposure	Analysis of households' determinants to take up life insurance, based on household survey data and multivariate probit model in Ghana. Risk-averse households are less likely to participate in microinsurance Individuals with higher risk exposure show less interest in life insurance

(continued)

Table D.1 (continued)

Reference	Relevant determinants[a]	Research design
Arun et al. (2012)	Risk exposure	Analysis of determinants for life insurance based on a household survey in Sri Lanka. Probit regressions for insurance take-up and premium Households with higher perception of risk exposure are less likely to purchase life insurance
Reynaud and Nguyen (2012)	Risk aversion, Trust	Calculation of willingness to pay for various flood insurance products in Vietnam, using a discrete choice experiment Risk-averse respondents value high level of insurance cover Trust and confidence in institution plays important role in insurance adoption and increases willingness to pay
Cole et al. (2013)	Risk aversion, trust	Randomised field experiments in rural India to test price and non-price factors as determinants for rainfall insurance products (OLS regression) Measured household risk aversion is negatively correlated with insurance demand Significantly higher demand for insurance if individuals trust insurance educator
Liu et al. (2013)	Trust	Randomised control trial in rural China, offering selected households new payment scheme for livestock insurance (double difference model) Significant insurance take-up if option is given to pay premium at the end of the insurance period
Brata et al. (2014)	Risk exposure	Analysis of how perception of disaster risk impacts hypothetical demand for disaster microinsurance in Java, Indonesia (logit model) Individuals with higher perception of disaster risk have higher probability to participate in insurance programme
Karlan et al. (2014)	Trust	Investigating credit market constraints and incomplete insurance and their effects on investment decisions. Experiments in Ghana with randomly assigned cash grants and opportunities to purchase rainfall index insurance (OLS/instrumental variables regression) Demand for microinsurance increases with observation of pay-out within social network (peer effects)
Turner et al. (2014)	Risk exposure	Analysis of flood experience on insurance demand, using village-level flood propensity scores based on pre-flood survey data and the comparison of affected and non-affected villages in Pakistan (OLS and probit models) Flood-affected households have higher demand for microinsurance in experimental insurance game

(continued)

Table D.1 (continued)

Reference	Relevant determinants[a]	Research design
Grislain-Letrémy (2015)	Trust, Risk exposure	Investigating determinants of demand for insurance coverage, using household-level data on insured and uninsured households in French overseas departments in Latin America and the Caribbean. Estimation of theoretical insurance supply and demand model. Take-up rate in the neighbourhood directly increases the individual probability of purchasing insurance (peer effects) The probability of purchasing insurance decreases with the number of past disasters that have occurred
Liu et al. (2015)	Risk exposure	Analysis of willingness to pay for a hypothetical rainfall index insurance in China (logit and tobit model) Significantly higher demand for rainfall index insurance by flood-affected households
Yeboah and Obeng (2016)	Trust	Analysis of financial literacy and other factors and their effects on willingness to pay for microinsurance among informal business operators in Ghana, using cross-sectional survey data (OLS regression) Negative impact of respondents' confidence in the contract on insurance demand; positive peer effects

[a]Relevant determinants for microinsurance demand; one or more of risk aversion, trust and risk exposure

References

Akotey OJ, Osei KA, Gemegah A (2011) The demand for micro insurance in Ghana. J Risk Financ 12:182–194.

Akter S, Brouwer R, Chowdhury S, Aziz S (2008) Determinants of participation in a Catastrophe Insurance Programme: empirical evidence from a developing country. Canberra.

Arun T, Bendig M (2010) Risk management among the poor: the case of microfinancial services. IZA Discussion Paper 5174, Bonn.

Arun T, Bendig M, Arun S (2012) Bequest motives and determinants of micro life insurance in Sri Lanka. World Dev 40:1700–1711

Brata AG, Rietveld P, de Groot HLF et al (2014) Living with the Merapi Volcano: risks and disaster microinsurance. ANU Working Papers in Trade and Development 13, Canberra.

Cai H, Chen Y, Fang H, Zhou L-A (2009) Microinsurance, trust and economic development: evidence from a randomized natural field experiment. NBER Working Paper Series 15396, Cambridge, MA.

Cai J, De Janvry A, Sadoulet E (2011) Social networks and insurance take-up: evidence from a randomized experiment in China. Microinsurance Innovation Facility Research Paper 8, Geneva.

Cole S, Giné X, Tobacman J et al (2013) Barriers to household risk management: evidence from India. Am Econ J Appl Econ 5:104–135.

Dercon S, Gunning J, Zeitlin A (2011) The demand for Insurance Under Limited Trust: evidence from a field experiment in Kenya. University of Wisconsin, Agriculture and Applied Economics, Madison.

Giesbert L, Steiner S, Bendig M (2011) Participation in micro life insurance and the use of other financial services in Ghana. J Risk Insur 78:7–35.

Giné X, Townsend R, Vickery J (2008) Patterns of rainfall insurance participation in rural India. World Bank Econ Rev 22:539–566.

Giné X, Yang D (2009) Insurance, credit, and technology adoption: field experimental evidence from Malawi. J Dev Econ 89:1–11.

Grislain-Letrémy C (2015) Natural disasters: exposure and underinsurance. CREST, Paris-Dauphine University, Paris.

Karlan D, Osei R, Osei-Akoto I, Udry C (2014) Agricultural Decisions after relaxing credit and risk constraints. Q J Econ 129:597–652.

Liu X, Tang Y, Miranda MJ (2015) Does past experience in natural disasters affect willingness-to-pay for Weather Index Insurance? Evidence from China. In: Agricultural and Applied Economics Association Annual Meeting 2015, San Francisco.

Liu Y, Chen KZ, Hill RV, Xiao C (2013) Borrowing from the insurer: an empirical analysis of demand and impact of insurance in China. Microinsurance Innovation Facility Research Paper 34, Geneva.

Reynaud A, Nguyen M-H (2012) Monetary valuation of flood insurance in Vietnam. Vietnam Center of Research in Economics, Management and Environment 01-2012, Hanoi, Ho Chi Minh City.

Turner G, Said F, Afzal U (2014) Microinsurance demand after a rare flood event: evidence from a field experiment in Pakistan. Geneva Pap Risk Insur Issues Pract 39:201–223.

Yeboah AK, Obeng CK (2016) Effect of financial literacy on willingness to pay for micro-insurance by commercial market business operators in Ghana. MPRA Paper 70135, Munich.

MIX
Papier aus verantwortungsvollen Quellen
Paper from responsible sources
FSC® C105338

If you have any concerns about our products,
you can contact us on
ProductSafety@springernature.com

In case Publisher is established outside the EU,
the EU authorized representative is:
Springer Nature Customer Service Center GmbH
Europaplatz 3, 69115 Heidelberg, Germany

Printed by Libri Plureos GmbH
in Hamburg, Germany